ALLISON-MAYERS FAMILY HISTORY

Portrait of an American Family

Robert A. Mayers

HERITAGE BOOKS

2011

HERITAGE BOOKS

AN IMPRINT OF HERITAGE BOOKS, INC.

Books, CDs, and more—Worldwide

For our listing of thousands of titles see our website
at
www.HeritageBooks.com

Published 2011 by
HERITAGE BOOKS, INC.
Publishing Division
100 Railroad Ave. #104
Westminster, Maryland 21157

Direct Descendants and Research Contributors:
Harriet Mills Chesi
Ted Jones
Alan Arthur Wickham

Cover: Stamford, Connecticut—Spring of 1642

Settlers Observe the Sabbath

This mural depicts the first Congregational meetinghouse to be built in Stamford. It was there when the Lawrence Ellison family passed through the town on their way to Hempstead, Long Island. It was surrounded by a stockade. It was the fort of the plantation and served as protection against Indian uprisings. A guard was on constant watch and the people were called to church on Sundays by a drummer. The slight man in ministerial garb is the Reverend Richard Denton who led the Ellisons and other families on their migration from Massachusetts to Hempstead, Long Island. Courtesy of Stamford Historical Society.

International Standard Book Numbers
Paperbound: 978-0-7884-5194-2
Clothbound: 978-0-7884-8730-9

DEDICATION

Since the dawn of history, people throughout the world have revered storytellers, shamans, scribes and archivists who recorded genealogy in chants, totems, hieroglyphics and finally, written script. They were esteemed people who were called upon by voices of the past. Only occasionally will someone pass on the history of a family.

This work is dedicated to those who accept the challenge to continue this work and other family histories for future generations. If you do, I promise you the most fascinating adventure of your life.

Robert A. Mayers

CONTENTS

Numbering used is the **Register Numbering Format**. The progenitor is given the number 1. Each child is numbered in birth order with lower case Roman numerals (i, ii, iii, iv, etc). Those lines that are carried on are also given consecutive Arabic numbers. For instance, if No. 1. had four children but only i and ii had descendants, they would also be given the Arabic numerals 2. and 3. (2.i and 3.i). Their children in turn are numbered from i upward and those having descendants are given in addition the Arabic numerals 4. 5. etc. The Register format is used in the New England Historic Genealogical Society Register.

In the text, direct line ancestors are in CAPS to make it easier for future generations to follow the direct line.

ACKNOWLEDGEMENTS

I owe a tremendous debt of gratitude to family members who shared my passion in tracing our ancestry and made enormous contributions to this work. My father, Robert E. Mayers related the few facts to me that had been passed down through oral tradition in our family. Listening to oft-repeated tales about ancestors was tedious for a young person and for many years I avoided his persistent efforts to tell me about our origins, but listening to him in later years inspired this search for my roots. It has proven to be a fascinating and obsessive adventure.

Harriet Mills Chesi, of Kerrville Texas, traces her ancestry to John Allison, our family's Revolutionary War soldier, through his daughter Sarah Brooks. She contributed the most valued type of information- oral history. Information passed down in her family was that John married a Sarah Noyell. This seemed to be an obvious variation of DeNoyelles, a family with large landholdings on Grassy Point, Haverstraw, adjacent to the Allison properties. This was vital evidence that the Allison Family in Monroe came from Haverstraw. I was delighted to meet this enthusiastic and accomplished genealogist who was working on the same lines of our ancestry as I was. Harriet grew up in Orange County and traces her ancestry to several families in the area. She has special expertise in accessing local data sources. At one time she lived close to Washington, D.C., where she could tap into the vast collection of the National Archives. She has proven to be a tireless researcher undaunted by the difficult research that can only be done on site.

My first cousin, Alan A. Wickham, shares these roots through his mother Margaret Mayers Wickham. His persistence in toughing it out through many weeks of searching land and probate records, and his willingness to travel nationally to important sources of information provided many of the pivotal clues that linked generations. Our field trips together included a trip to Yorkshire, England in 2004. While on opposite coasts of the country, our frequent chats and visits as well as his friendship over the years made this work a pleasant experience. Al Wickham's remarkable insight and hard work not only have enhanced the quality of these findings but also have inspired me to work through many frustrating dead ends. Coincidentally, he also traces his Wickham ancestry to Orange County, New York. The Wickhams settled in Ridgebury, only a few miles from the Allisons. His valuable contribution on early "Wickham Genealogy in England and America" was published in the *New England Historical and Genealogical Register* in 1996.

Ted Jones, another cousin, also traces his ancestry to Sarah Allison Brooks. What is truly astonishing is that Ted's branch of the family still lives in Woodbury, New York near the site of the Allison home over 200 years ago. Ted's knowledge of the area enabled us to find the exact location of the place.

John Eyre, a professional genealogist who specialized in the County of Cheshire, England, did all the laborious on site searching that extended the Mayers line in England back to the mid 1600s. I met him in Macclesfield, in 1978, and over a pint and a plowman's lunch I learned of the many challenges he met while tracing the Mayers Family in Cheshire. His meticulous research required examining parchment church records, in Latin, that dated from the 1500s.

Over the past two centuries, others have done much work tracking the genealogy of the Allison and Mayers families. Leonard Allison Morrison and Jonathan Barlow histories are invaluable and provide a common reference point for anyone tracing Allison ancestry. Work on the 15th and 16th century, the generations before Lawrence Ellison, the Puritan, is the collective effort of many researchers in the past. This data can be found on Allison and Ellison Websites, message boards and such worldwide databases as familysearch.org and gencircles.com.

Membership and the use of library resources of historical societies proved to be another extraordinary source of locally focused information. Original family history, periodicals, city directories, cemetery and church records were found here. Many are staffed by volunteers who are descendants of early area families. These multi-generational, bloodline caretakers have a wealth of local knowledge and collect and preserve original documents. The most valuable benefit of these groups is the opportunity to interface with other members. The historical and genealogical Societies of Orange County and Rockland County in New York and Passaic County in New Jersey, were especially valuable resources.

I am grateful to the professional staffs of research institutions and world-class archive collections. Among the most extensively used were the Central Library of York and the Archive and Record Service at Beverly, Yorkshire, England, The National Archives, The New York State Archives, Albany, N.Y. The New York Genealogical and Biographical Society, Budke Collection at the New York City Library, N.Y., The Newberry Library, Chicago, The Archibald S. Alexander at Rutgers University, Family History Archives, Salt Lake City, and the New City Library of Rockland County, N.Y. My hometown library in Watchung, New Jersey procured rare books for me from around the country through their interlibrary loan service.

The "Watchung Writers" is an eclectic group of skillful authors in my town. Led by Gordon McLenithan, they are dedicated to stimulating quality writing. Most of these creative people write fiction and juvenile books. Their infinite patience while critiquing my heavy doses of genealogy was appreciated. My heartfelt thanks go to all of them for their endurance and helpful suggestions. Finally, I wish to thank my wife, Norma, referred to by many as "that poor woman," for the years she endured long hours in libraries, trudging over historic sites, visiting graveyards, and even abandonment while I researched. Without her understanding and support, all of this would not have been possible.

PREFACE

This family history covers nineteen generations beginning around the year 1400. The earliest ancestors we can identify, and from whom we are directly descended, were born in Yorkshire, England.

My interest in exploring the past to discover family ancestry started in the bicentennial year of 1976. During the patriotic fervor of that time my father, Robert E. Mayers, passed on to me the few facts about our family history that have come down through oral tradition. At that time his generation could recall very little and nothing earlier than a hundred years ago

He knew that my great-grandmother, Sarah Ann Allison's family came from Haverstraw New York, and that she had "relatives that fought in the American Revolution". He knew that her husband James Mayers came from Macclesfield, England sometime in the 19th century. Nothing, beyond these few vague bits of information and two disintegrating portraits of Sarah Ann and James came down to us from the past. James Mayers and his wife Sarah Ann Allison, now have about a hundred living descendants.

This is the third edition of this family history. It has been updated and professionally published for worldwide distribution. It includes much new information, expands the historic background of each generation, updates current family trees and corrects previous inconsistencies. An index has been added for greater ease of use. The title has been changed to place the Allison name first. I have found that there are vast numbers of Allisons and Ellisons in America. Many researchers of that family had difficulty finding the work in reference libraries, since it appeared under Mayers not Allison and often was not cross-referenced.

Research began in 1976, when I prepared a manuscript from genealogy data sources then available. It was based largely on census and parish records and oral family history. The study was presented to family members, the following year, at the 50th wedding anniversary of my parents. In 1980, this work was enhanced by data from my efforts to link the Allison and Mayers families to earlier generations in America and England.

Over the years, I have researched the history of this family in virtually every possible source of genealogical information. During this period of my life I was preoccupied with raising a family and managing a very demanding business career in corporate America. For many years, little progress was made due to time constraints. With retirement I have accelerated my efforts to expand the study. As with all history, not having a written record can lead to all of these scattered bits of information being lost.

Over the years, several missing links were found, sites visited and a plethora of new information was discovered. Some of the conclusions reached in my earlier studies were found to be inaccurate. In 2005, a second edition was prepared to commemorate my own 50th wedding anniversary. Over fifty copies of this work were distributed to family members, historic societies and reference libraries in places where the families lived. This work included essential research contributions by two other descendants of the families, Harriet Mills Chesi and Alan Wickham. This self-published book was favorably reviewed by the New York Genealogical and Biographical Society Record and accepted for the collection of the Family History Library in Salt Lake City. "The Voyage of the Marion," the account of the trip of James Mayers to America in 1838, was featured in *Cheshire Magazine* in the United Kingdom.

This account encouraged me to write a full biography of Corporal John Allison, 1754-1828, whose life is summarized in this edition. For several years I traveled to battlefields and historic sites to follow in his footsteps. Accounts of these visits were combined with the discovery of original documents and oral history to provide a detailed account of the life of a soldier during the eight years of the American Revolution. John Allison's life, before and after the war, is equally fascinating. *The War Man* was published by Westholme Publishing in 2009, and offered to the public through bookstores, historic societies and at national and state parks shops as well as on line. I continue to be a frequent speaker at many historic and genealogical societies and contribute to their publications.

My motivation in all of these activities has been an intense curiosity to find my ancestors and to share my discoveries and research processes with others. I also knew that with the passing of my generation, all history of these families might be lost forever without a written record.

Who were those now forgotten people who came before us whose blood we share? How and when did they live and die? Beginning this search with just a few clues, it has proven to be one of the most challenging, fascinating and, at times, passionate experiences of my life. I sense that I have become closely acquainted with those who came before us. I have shared their hardships, understood what may have motivated them, and how they contributed to who we are today.

INTRODUCTION

SEARCHING for the ALLISON- MAYERS ANCESTRY

What has amazed me is that many of our direct ancestors were truly exceptional people who were driven with unusual courage to go beyond the norms of their time in history. Strong economic, patriotic and religious motivation caused them to venture into the unknown, travel to new lands and start new lives. They personally participated in some of the most significant events in American history.

As you read this family history you will get to know many of these fascinating people as well as I have. Going back over 600 years, the lives of our family members span pivotal periods in western history. Remember, these are not people who simply share our family surnames but as far as can be authenticated, we are their direct linear descendents.

Lawrence Ellison and his wife Mary Riston were Puritans who must have had unusually strong faith to leave their home in England. This courageous family sailed to America with the Winthrop Fleet in 1630 with their seven small children. Dissention in the church caused them to migrate from Massachusetts to what is now Hempstead, Long Island. This land was owned by the Dutch and inhabited by hostile Indian tribes.

In 1719, John Allison, the grandson of Lawrence, left Hempstead, Long Island where the family had lived for two generations. With his wife, whose name has been lost to history, and an infant son, he moved westward to the banks of the Hudson River. At that time this was the frontier of America. He purchased large tracts of land, which extended two miles along the Hudson River and encompassed the present town of Haverstraw, New York. Often controversial, and politically incorrect, at times his entrepreneurial activities, as a merchant, were unethical.

His son Joseph Allison was born in Haverstraw in 1721. Joseph was a captain in the Orange County, N.Y. militia during the French and Indian War and served as a minuteman with his two sons and three sons-in-law during the Revolutionary War. He was left with ten children when his wife Elizabeth Benson died in 1767. Two years later, he married eighteen-year-old Elsie Parsells. Together, they had more children. With the division of his large landholdings, Elsie and the children from both marriages were all amply provided for in Joseph's will.

Joseph's son, John Allison enlisted in the Continental Army in 1775, several months before the Declaration of Independence was signed. He marched north on the ill-fated campaign to capture Canada. He was one of a small unit that first engaged a main British force before the tragic American defeat at Fort Montgomery, New York. He survived six more years of active combat service to fight in the final victory at Yorktown, Virginia, and was finally discharged by General Washington in 1783.

William Allison, John's son, is one of the most obscure of our direct line ancestors. In 1826, he was trying to support a family of seven children in Monroe, New York, on a three-acre farm with one cow and two hogs. He chose to migrate thirty miles south for greater economic opportunity, to Paterson, New Jersey. This city, conceived by Alexander Hamilton, was emerging as America's first great manufacturing center.

On the trek south to Paterson, William and his young second wife, whose name we have not yet proven, brought their three-year-old daughter, Sarah Ann Allison. She was my great-grandmother.

Sarah Ann, also called Sally, married James Mayers, a young English immigrant, in about 1841. This joining of the Mayers and Allison Families created the lines of ancestry that are the focus of this entire historical and genealogical review.

James Mayers had left his family in Macclesfield, Cheshire, England, in 1839, at the age of twenty. After a winter voyage that took fifty days, he arrived in New York with a young friend, John Ryle. Within three years, in Paterson,

NJ, they started the first successful silk manufacturing business in America. This beginning spawned one of our country's largest nineteenth century industries.

The youngest son of James and Sarah Ann, John Mayers, was a skilled silk weaver. In 1913, at the Doherty Silk Mill in Paterson, he tore down his loom and went on strike to protest abysmal working conditions. He was promptly arrested. After that he joined thousands of militant, anti-capitalist Industrial Workers of the World, known as the Wobblies, in one of the most significant events in American labor history. Violence continued for ten months before the strike failed. The hardship and poverty endured by his wife, Margaret Bertram, and family during this time were often recounted to me by their youngest son, my father Robert E. Mayers. John was blacklisted for his union activism and forced to move from Paterson to find a job. On a visit to Moscow I found the graves of Wobbly leaders buried in the Kremlin.

Oral tradition in the family was that our Allisons were from Haverstraw, New York. Extensive research there in the Rockland County area, over several years, failed to turn up any link to them, though family stories are regarded as an especially valuable source of genealogical information. When I finally discovered the family, in the early 1800s, in Monroe, N. Y. in the adjacent County of Orange and not Haverstraw, I reluctantly began to doubt the accuracy of this oral tradition.

For several years this perplexing dilemma was a brick wall that blocked any further tracing of the Allison ancestry. An obscure 1820 land sale record, found in courthouse archives in Orange County, New York, showed two Allison names together. This single piece of evidence was the missing link that finally verified the family tradition. They had moved from Haverstraw, to Monroe, to Paterson over two generations. Suddenly, it was possible to extend the Allison line back another 400 years.

Why did James, the progenitor of our Mayers family, leave Macclesfield, England in the eighteenth century to come to America? A simple request to the National Archives in Washington, D.C. provided a wealth of information- a complete copy of the passenger list of the ship that brought him here in 1838. It provides the age, occupation and country of origin for all seventy-six passengers. It shows the name of the ship, its date of departure from Liverpool and its arrival in New York. It was easy to pick out the two young silk weavers- James Mayers and John Ryle. The list provided the pivotal data needed to trace his early years in this country and to trace the Mayers line back another 150 years in Cheshire, England.

There was a magic moment at the Drew University Archives while I was researching 18th century church records. Eight full boxes were wheeled to me on a gurney. After six days of sifting through this faded, and often illegible, material, I was rewarded. A small, fragmented tablet showed the name of Sarah Allison. Here was my great-grandmother, age four, in 1827, in Sunday school. This evidence verified the time frame of the family's migration to Paterson from New York.

This work would not be complete without visiting many of the actual sites where this history actually happened. My travels to towns, battlefields, cemeteries, churches, libraries, former home sites, historical societies, museums and public archives both here and in England have provided many stimulating adventures.

One evening, in Macclesfield, the sonorous pealing of bells was heard coming from the tower of the town's medieval cathedral. This ringing required investigation. Entering the darkened chapel, we passed a baptismal font used for at least ten generations of the family and then the supine effigy of a knight who rested there since 1442. Climbing a series of rickety ladders which were connected by trapdoors at each level, we finally reached the top of the tower. My wife Norma and I were amazed to find a group of bell ringers, each tugging on ropes to produce the perfectly synchronized clarion. They were obviously delighted to be visited by a native son returning after 150 years. I was assigned to a rope and encouraged to join the activities. Afterward, adjourning to a local pub, I was regaled by their stories of the old town's history.

The proximity of my home in Watchung, New Jersey to Paterson has provided many opportunities for nostalgic trips to explore sites where the families lived from 1826 to the 1920s. Little remains from our past. The ancestral, 18th century Mayers home at number five Mill Street, was razed in 1974 to make way for a highway which was never built. A shard of china, picturing children playing was found on the site by urban archeologists,. The dish must have belonged to Sarah Allison, my great-grandmother.

The Morris Canal was built in 1829 to barge Pennsylvania coal to east coast cities. My father learned to swim there in the early 1900s. The Canal ran along the base of Garret Mountain. Its path now serves as the roadbed for Interstate Route 80. He lived on Mary Street below the Canal. The site is now an empty lot. Although I remember visiting it as a child and staring up with awe at the second floor window from which my great-grandmother Eliza Ann (Bertram) Farquhar fell to her death in 1902. A Paterson public school now stands on the site of Sandy Hill Cemetery, where the people of Paterson were interred from 1814. With few extant records of the burials, it is a black hole for genealogists.

All has not been lost, however, and a visit to Paterson today can still be an engrossing experience. The ruins of the old Colt Gun Mill, where James Mayers and John Ryle started silk manufacturing, can still be seen. Raceways, designed by Pierre Enfant, to supply waterpower to the mills, are remarkably preserved. The massive and formidable Doherty Silk Mill stands, in all its faded glory, adjacent to the Garden State Parkway, a stark reminder of the day John Mayers went on strike. The Question Mark Bar, headquarters of the Wobblies, in 1913, has been renamed but was active until recent years. A visit to the graves of Sarah Allison, her husband James Mayers and many of their descendents, at Cedar Lawn Cemetery on the outskirts of the city is an easy side trip.

While gathering data for this history there were many other especially memorable times. In the 1970s I listened to Dorcas Allison in Haverstraw, New York. She was in her 90s and related to me the oral history passed on by her ancestors. Her grandmother lived on a farm in lower Manhattan and as a child walked to the pastures north of Canal Street!

Standing with Dan DeNoyelles on the land occupied by the Allison farms since 1729, he described where Major John Andre, a British spy, had passed over this land in 1780. He was on his way to meet Benedict Arnold on the next farm. It was here that the traitor, Arnold, turned over the plans that could have led to the capture of West Point, the major east coast stronghold of the Continental Army.

The striking scenery in the Hudson River highlands and the rugged hilly landscape of Rockland and Orange Counties in New York State looks much as they did 300 years ago when our Allisons first arrived there. Many descendants of the early families still live in the area. These are places where people take genealogy very seriously.

Adventures and travels to these places of our heritage will continue. I am following the movements of the New York Regiments and walking over the battlefields in the footsteps of John Allison during the Revolutionary War. A trip was made in June, 2004 to visit and research in the Roman and Medieval towns of Yorkshire. This was where the Puritan Lawrence Ellison and generations of his ancestors could be traced back to the 1400s.

In England, church records were often the sole source available before the 18th century. In this country, every possible source of genealogical information was searched to link the generations of these families. Census records starting in 1790 were invaluable in tracing moves and the composition of the families. Land records revealed facts that linked families and generations. Church records, while often missing or incomplete at times provided the only source of baptisms, marriages, deaths and membership rolls.

State archives provided mostly death and land tax information. Cemetery records notably in Paterson and Haverstraw, while not set up for genealogical research, provided evidence of links between people and families. At times, tombstone records also proved to be helpful.

The National Archives are the only source for Revolutionary War military service records. The pension records of John Allison, when he resided in Orange County, New York in 1818, provided the vital clue that he had enlisted in the Continental Army in Rockland County. This was the first proof that the Allisons had come from Haverstraw. NARA also provided the Ship's Passenger List of 1838, showing complete details of James Mayers' voyage to America, on the ship, *Marion*. For later arrivals starting in 1892, Ellis Island records provided an easily accessed, enormous and comprehensive database.

The Internet and email capability have advanced and facilitated genealogical research more than any other factor in history. Traditional research which only a decade ago required expensive travel to historic sites of interest and data sources now can be done quite easily, worldwide, on a personal computer. The ability to view original documents, such as the entire U.S. Federal Census from 1790 to 1930, was especially valuable and provided vital peripheral information on neighboring and related families. Old books and even medieval English parish registers can be read in their original form.

Ancestry.com, Rootsweb.com, FamilySearch.org, Footnote.com and many other online services, each unique in approach, were frequently consulted. These amazing compilations of online research data provided access to hard- to-find materials as well as instructional information on research techniques.

WebPages for towns and historic sites, where this history happened, were surprisingly comprehensive repositories of local history and culture. Many contained beautiful graphics, in full color. The small, medieval villages in Yorkshire, where the earliest Allison ancestry was found, are especially aesthetic and informative.

Message boards on the computer provided me with immediate access to others with similar interests in a common surname or a local geographic area anywhere in the world. I frequently communicated with others on the Mayers, Allison and Ellison surname boards as well as Rockland and Orange Counties in New York and Passaic County in New Jersey for the Paterson research. Difficult 15th and 16th century searching of the Allison line were also found online, on the message boards.

Most genealogical records are still not available on the Internet. The world's largest and most comprehensive collection is the Family History Library, sponsored by the Church of the Latter Day Saints in Salt Like City, Utah. All its sources can be accessed through thousands of branches in local Mormon Church facilities. I was a frequent visitor to Morristown, the branch nearest my home where a vast collection of information can be easily procured on microfilm. What is really astonishing is that it is possible to locate and contact anyone who has had interest in your ancestor, anytime in the past and anywhere in the world. Rare and obscure information not available anywhere else in its original form is found here. The records of St. Michaels Church in Macclesfield, dating back to the 1500s, Paterson marriage records from 1838 and the notes of an itinerate, circuit- riding Methodist minister in 1820s Orange County were among the treasures I found in this astounding collection.

Two studies of the Allison family deserve special mention. Jonathan Barlow in 1890 and Leonard Allison Morrison, in 1893, published extensive genealogical histories of the family. Morrison's ambitious work attempted to cover most large branches of the Allisons in America, tracing each to its roots in Great Britain, Scotland and Ireland. This work devotes an entire chapter to our Allisons of Rockland County New York starting with a brief coverage of Lawrence the Puritan. The book is generally acknowledged as the primary reference on the family.

While providing extensive family tree data, the enormous span of coverage allows only for very limited personal history of the hundreds of people included. With the exception of omitting a Long Island generation, this work is very accurate. Most vital statistics were derived from George S. Allison of Haverstraw, 1792-1884. He gave the data to David Cole for his *History of Rockland County* published in 1884. George Allison's data was essential since most original records have vanished over the preceding hundred years. Allison descendents are fortunate to have this encyclopedic source of family history.

From 1719 to1800, the original Haverstraw family of John Allison expanded to over thirty descendent families. With the pattern of large families and geographic dispersion in that era, the history became impossible for anyone to track. The quality of information in Morrison's work diminishes with the early 18th century and most lines, including the Rockland and Orange branches, simply disappear at that time. Unfortunately, this was the critical period where I encountered the most difficulty in connecting generations.

The Genealogy of the Barlow Family written three years before, contains more detail on several of the more prominent family members and a few interesting pictures of the 18th century Allison home in the Haverstraw area. Morrison used it as a source. An original copy at Chicago's Newberry Library has copious hand written additions and corrections in the margins, entered by some unknown researcher in the past. No similar genealogy studies exist for the Mayers Family.

Another source of early information is from family members who are proving they are descendents by a worldwide DNA analysis project. The Allison/Ellison DNA project under the direction of Mary Allison Yonan, was begun in 2001 and officially organized as a surname DNA project with the Family Tree DNA Website, (FTDNA). The Y-Chromosome is passed from father to son, therefore only men who have surnames with the variant spellings of Allison/Ellison can participate. The Allison/Mayers ancestry can be linked to Lawrence Ellison, the Puritan, through his descendants of Haverstraw line.

The greatest challenge encountered was with the early 19th century, a brief and relatively recent period when viewed in the entire context of this study. This was due mostly to the geographic moves of our direct ancestors during that time.

I think you will be proud of what our ancestors have accomplished, but you will detect that many mysteries still remain here. Is this the end of this family saga? I hope it's only the beginning. As new research sources and techniques emerge in the future, I'm sure fresh information will be uncovered. Those brick walls can come tumbling down when you least expect it.

MASTER TREE:
ALLISON FAMILY FROM 1400, MAYERS FAMILY FROM 1670

MASTER TREE:
ANCESTRY OF ALLISON, MAYERS AND RELATED FAMILIES

ALLISON

GENERATION:

1. Robert Ellisse, born about 1400 AD.

2. Edward Ellisse, born 1440.

3. Anthony Ellisse, born 1470.

4. John Ellisse, born 1500.

5. Thomas Ellisse; married Jenett _____ 23 October 1550.

6. Edmond Lawrencius Ellison; married Jane Clynton 24 August 1590.

7. Lawrence Ellison; married Mary Riston 8 June 1617.

8. Thomas Ellison, born 1622; married Martha Champion.

9. John Ellison, born 1652; died about 1720; m. _____.

10. John Allison, born about 1670; died 1754; m. _____.

11. Joseph Allison; married Elizabeth Benson 10 March 1743.

12. John Allison; married Sarah DeNoyelles about 1778.

13. William Allison, born about 1791; married _____.

14. Sarah Ann Allison, born 1823; died 1869; married about 1841.　　James Mayers, born 1820; died 1887.

Descendants continue on Mayers Tree

MAYERS

GENERATION

1.   Hugonus Meare, born about 1670; married Mary _____.

2.   William Mears; married Margaret Shelmerdine 8 June 1714.

3.   William Meare; married Mary Littlewood 23 September 1751.

4.   Thomas Mayers; married Elizabeth Hough 19 June 1778 _____.

5.   Thomas Mayers; married Betty Brown 6 September 1807.

6.   James Mayers, born 1820; died 1887; married Sarah Ann Allison, born 1823; died 1869.

7.   John Mayers; married Margaret Bertram 1881. Nine children listed below.

GENERATIONS 8. And 9.

1.   James Bertram; married Lillian Tylee. No children.

2.   John Allison; married Susan Van Orden 1905. Children: Anna Margaret, born 1906, died 1918; Elizabeth Jane, born 1919 (Tree 1).

3.   David; married Elizabeth Kupferer 1912. Children: David Jr., born 1913, died 2004; Jane, born 1916; Mary Louise, born 1924 (Tree 2).

4.   Grace Winifred; married Fredrick Andrew Wood 1919. No children.

5.   May; married Joseph Thompson 1918. Children: Alice Eileen, born 1921, died 2001; Howard, born 1923, died 1925; Warren, born 1925, died 1925 (Tree 3).

6.   Margaret; married Arthur Benson Wickham 1924. Children: Alan Arthur, born 1935 (Tree 4).

7.   Perry Bascom; married Nora Kelly 1921. Children: Margaret Ann, born 1922; Eileen Elizabeth, born 1924; Dorothy Bertram, born 1926; Mildred Grace, born 1934; Perry Bascom Jr., born 1936, died 2008; George, died 1899, age two years (Tree5).

9.   Robert Edmund; married Minnie Kievit 1927. Children: Robert Adrian, born 1930; Peter Allison, born 1939 – 1942; Joyce Ann, born 1945 (Tree 6).

Section I: Ellisse – Ellison - Allison

Ellisse / Ellison / Allison Family History - Beginning About 1400 AD

The early ancestry of our Allison forebears leads back through the centuries to the East Riding of Yorkshire, England. Our earliest ancestors are found in Howden, Saltmarshe and Hukersal, the mysterious place whose name has disappeared from history. These are along the banks of the Ouse River, which flows north twenty miles to the ancient City of York. These rich lowlands nurtured early man. The river, with access to the North Sea, served as a corridor for invaders through the ages. Our American blood is enriched by Celts of the Bronze Age, Romans, Vikings, Anglo-Saxons and Normans. This heritage can be proudly passed on to those who follow us in the future.

This area of Yorkshire is unusually rich in history. By 71AD, the Roman 9th Legion had conquered the local Celtic tribes and had set up their capital in York. It became one of the leading cities in the Roman Empire. The Romans mixed with the local population over the next 250 years until 400AD when they were hastily recalled to Rome to join the struggle against invaders from the north.

In the 5th century, Germanic tribes of Anglo-Saxons invaded the region and established the country of Northumbria. They were conquered by Viking plunderers who sailed up the Ouse in their long ships to raid villages and eventually settle in places along the river.

The Norsemen made York their capital in 866, ruled the area and were absorbed into the population over the next two hundred years. Christianity was introduced here in the 7th century. They were finally subdued by the Saxon King Harold II at Stamford Bridge, only twenty miles north of Howden, in 1066. But this victory was short-lived as Harold was defeated only three weeks later at the Battle of Hastings by the French Normans under William the Conqueror. Yorkshire was occupied by the Normans in 1069.

In 1085, William the Conqueror commissioned the Domesday Book which lists all English settlements south of the Scottish border. Howden is shown in as a town with a church. In the 1400s we first begin to identify the names of our direct linear Ellisse ancestors. They are the progeny of these diverse and turbulent cultures.

In 1538, the English church established a system of registration of baptisms, marriages and burials. These are the only vital records we have there for the next 300 years. The parish registers are the only evidence that exists of the birth of an ancestor except those of nobility or gentry. Transient families in England can be traced in wills. Few early property deeds exist in England since the nobility and landed gentry owned most of the land for centuries.

What is amazing is that many of our forbears were truly exceptional people who were driven to go beyond the norms of their time in history. Strong economic, religious and patriotic motivation caused them to venture into the unknown, travel to new lands and start new lives. They personally participated in some of the most significant events in American history.

In 1841, in Paterson New Jersey, Sarah Ann Allison the Granddaughter of John Allison our Revolutionary War hero married James Mayers, an emigrant silk dyer, from Macclesfield, England. This union merged the Mayers and Allison Families. They are the progenitors of the family in America.

The First Three Generations:
Robert, Edward & Anthony Ellisse - Ca. 1400-1500 AD

References to this family's direct ancestors in the 1400s in a place called Hukersal, Yorkshire, England, appear in many Allison/Ellison family histories. Latin parchment scrolls are the source of this information from that early period. These documents are stored at the archives at the town of Beverly in the East Riding of Yorkshire, England.

The original ancient vellum records that have survived from that period show legal and land transactions. These are the primary sources of the family's early history. It is unlikely that anything else was passed down through records or oral tradition over the next 600 years. Parish Registers, providing vital statistics by name, did not begin until about 1550. Research to find the specific references to the Ellisse family in the scrolls was done at some time in the past but has been lost. Further effort is needed to verify this provenance.

Hukersal was likely situated near Howden and its nearby manor, Saltmarshe, on the banks of the Ouse River, about 20 miles below the city of York. Original Anglo-Saxon settlers chose these sites because the land was fertile and slightly raised above the surrounding marshes. The raised terrain was above the flood plain, making it easier to defend from the frequent marauders who sailed up the river. A manor and church were on this site as early as 705 AD, and there is documentary evidence of a settlement at Howden in 959 AD.

A visit to this area of Yorkshire in 2004, and a search of the records there for place name sources in England, did not disclose any town called Hukersal. The English Place Name Society at the University of Nottingham researched this information. They concluded that it could be old English for a rounded hill, possibly combined with a personal name like Hook or it might be a derivation of "halh" meaning a minor or secluded patch of land. Therefore, it could be a description of the land rather than a place name. After examining an early map of the area, Christopher W. Schieffer, an 18th generation descendant of the family, suggested that the name Hukersal could be derived from the towns of Hook or Hook Hall. These towns are directly across the river from Howden and Saltmarshe and were connected by a ferry in early times.

The lives of the first three generations of our known ancestors, Robert, Edward and Anthony Ellisse, span the 1400s. Their lives must have been touched by major historical events of that century. England invaded France and defeated the French forces at the Battle of Agincourt in 1420. Over half of France was occupied by England during the early part of the 15th century. If our Ellisse ancestors were at Agincourt, they may have fought side by side with the famed long bowmen of Cheshire, who could have included our Mayers forebears.

The War of the Roses, a civil war in England, swept over the Yorkshire during this time. The bloodiest and final decisive battle was fought there at Towton, in 1461, only 25 miles from Howden Parish. The Yorkshire area sided with the defeated House of Lancaster and was punished by Edward IV. During this dark period epidemics struck the population and the wool trade was decimated. In the later years of the century, there was peace under Henry VII who extended English justice, based on the common law, throughout the country. Restored wool production in Yorkshire brought prosperity to Howden Parish during Henry's reign.

ROBERT ELLISSE 1. (EARLIEST ANCESTOR IDENTIFIED), BORN ABOUT 1400

Robert Ellisse 1. (Earliest ancestor identified), born about 1400, Hukersal, Yorkshire; died unknown; married unknown. One child: Edward Ellisse.

EDWARD ELLISSE 2. I., BORN ABOUT 1440

Edward Ellisse 2. i, born about 1440, Hukersal, Yorkshire, England; died unknown; married unknown. One child: Anthony Ellisse.

ANTHONY ELLISSE 3. I, BORN ABOUT 1470

Anthony Ellisse 3. i, born about 1470, Hukersal, Yorkshire, England; died unknown; married unknown. One child: John Ellisse.

JOHN ELLISSE 4. i, BORN ABOUT 1500

John Ellisse 4. i, born about 1500, Howden, Yorkshire; died unknown; married Margaret _____. One child: Thomas.

John is the first ancestor identified by the Allison Genealogies as living in Howden. His son Thomas is shown in the Parish Registers in Saltmarshe, Howden. Saltmarshe Manor is described as "the seat of the Saltmarshe family who date back to Norman times." It is likely that the family was engaged in farming and sheep raising on this feudal manor. All references to the Ellisse family are found in The Registers of the Parish of Howden (1543-1702). The index to these records shows the name also as Elice and Elysse.

This area was known as Howdenshire or Howden Parish and encompassed about 20 smaller towns and manors. It was dominated by the Town of Howden itself with the central marketplace and fairground. Howden Minster, a large magnificent cathedral dating back to the 8th century served the surrounding countryside. Its tower can be seen from many miles away. It was used as a sanctuary during floods and to watch for invaders.

The life of the family would have been directly affected by historical events in England at that time. King Henry VIII became King in 1509; and after subduing the Scots at the Battle of Flodden in 1513, he ruled for the next 38 years. His reign was marked with a renaissance and a revival of learning which some say was brought about by the suppression of the Catholic Church. The cathedral, Howden Minster, fell into disrepair during the Reformation when all revenues went directly to the crown and became a ruin over the next 100 years.

During John's lifetime the practice of "enclosure" caused great unrest. In the farmlands of Yorkshire, open land, used by small farmers was confiscated by landlords to create more profitable grassland for sheep raising. The resulting increase in wool production and flourishing cloth export market created prosperity and the birth of industry in England.

The lives of John and Margaret Ellisse also spanned the years when The Protestant Queen Elizabeth I ascended to the throne in 1558.

Howden area, East Riding, Yorkshire, England

THOMAS ELLISSE 5. I, BORN 1525/29

Thomas Ellisse 5. i, born 1525/29, Saltmarshe, Howden, Yorkshire; died November 1603/04 Gargrave, Yorkshire; married (1) Jenett _____ 23 October 1550 Howden, born 1529 Howden; died 1566 Howden; wife (2) unknown. Nine children, all born Saltmarshe, Howden, East Riding, Yorkshire (Howden Register):

	i	Janeta, baptized 4 January 1553.
	ii	Elizabetha, born 1555; baptized 21 August 1555; died 30 March 1604.
	iii	Thomas, born 1 March or May 1561; married Allison _____ May 1589.
	iv	Isabella, born 4 January 1567; baptized 4 January 1567/8.
6.	v	Lawrence (Edmond Lawrencius), born 28 October 1570; married Jane Clynt(on).
	vi	Hugo, born December 1572.
	vii	Agnes, born January 1573; baptized 1573.
	viii	Christoferrus (Xpofferus), born 1576; baptized 10 November 1576.
	ix	Johannes, born 1578; baptized January or "Jun" 1578; died 7 February 1578.

After the death of his first wife, Jenett, Thomas migrated 50 miles north from Saltmarshe, Howden Parish, to Gargrave, North Yorkshire. This picturesque medieval farm village sits astride the river Aire along the Pennine Way. Since his youngest son, Hugo, was born in Howden, Thomas's move occurred after 1572. It is likely that his son Edmond Lawrencius was the son of a second wife, since Jenett died in 1566. The family name evolves to Ellison after this generation.

At that time, the move from Howden to Gargrave could have been caused by "enclosure." Enclosure is the process by which common land, to which many farmers had traditional rights for farming, cutting hay or grazing livestock, was restricted to the use of one owner. The practice was often accompanied by resistance by force and bloodshed. It was one of the most controversial issues of architectural and economic history in England. It caused many small farmers to move north where more open land was available, or to become landless laborers. These displaced laborers created a working class that provided the workforce for new industries that were developing in the north of England.

Moves to other towns also occurred when a younger member of the family learned a trade from his father and not enough of that kind of work existed to support both within the same village. Entire estates were often inherited by the eldest son. This also forced younger males in the family to move.

Thomas lived during the reign of Queen Elizabeth I, a prosperous golden age for England. Her strong rule, which lasted for 44 years, provided stability for England and a sense of national identity. She established the English Protestant Church. During her reign, military campaigns were conducted in the Netherlands, France and Ireland. The Spanish Armada was defeated in 1588. This was the age of Shakespeare and the seafaring adventurers Francis Drake and John Hawkins.

A high level of prosperity prevailed throughout the country and industry and commerce grew from wool exports. Yeoman farmers, commoners who owned and cultivated their own land, could acquire more parcels of land and live in villages in small houses. The rise of Puritanism, which aimed at breaking from the ritual practices of the Anglican Church, began in the 1580s and had a profound influence on the generations of the family that followed.

EDMOND LAWRENCIUS ELLISON 6. v AND JANE CLYNTON

Edmond Lawrencius Ellison 6. v, born 28 October 1570, Saltmarshe, Howden, Yorkshire; died unknown; married Jane Clynt (Clynton) 24 August 1590 Gargrave, Yorkshire; born 24 August 1569 Gargrave; died unknown. One child:

> 7. i, Lawrence "Goodman," born about 1599.

After their marriage in 1590, Edmond Lawrencius and Jane moved from Gargrave, Yorkshire to Colne, a cloth producing town about 10 miles south. Their son Lawrence was born here about 1599. The family next appears in Blackburn, Lancashire, 30 miles to the Southwest. This town's history dates back to the time of the Romans. It was located on an ancient military highway that lead from Manchester to Ribchester, the site of a first century Roman fort. The church of St. Mary the Virgin was erected there in the 14th century on the site of an earlier church built in 596 AD. It was rebuilt in the prosperous 16th century and demolished in 1820.

A review of Blackburn Parish Registers shows several other Ellison families living in Blackburn between 1600 and 1630. Based on the pattern of given names and ages they could have been sons or brothers. Many references to Edmond, Thomas, John, Ralphe and Henry Ellison and their families are found in these records. From this we can assume that Edmond and Jane had more than one son when they migrated to Blackburn, or they had joined other family members.

The likely reason that the young couple left the rural life of Gargrave at this time was to better their lives by finding work in the cloth weaving industry. Cloth production started in Blackburn in the early 1300s. The industry was brought from Holland by Flemish weavers. Starting as a textile center based on wool and cotton, it became the predominant industry by the middle if the 1600s. Cloth weaving and the wool trade gave rise to great prosperity and a surge in commerce. Edmond may have become skilled in weaving or acquired property as a merchant.

During the lives of Edmond and Jane, Latin was still the language of the literate. This was the age of William Shakespeare, Bacon, Marlowe and Spencer. The gun had still not replaced the longbow as the most widely used small arm. The Ellison family lived in a half-timber framed house with a thatched roof.

News about the defeat of the Spanish Armada in 1588 must have been celebrated in Blackburn. Reports of exploration in the new world, the exploits of Francis Drake, John Hawkins and Walter Raleigh, and the colonization in America must have thrilled the young Edmond. The nationalist spirit that arose during the Protestant Reformation under Queen Elizabeth gained momentum during his life. Lancashire leaned toward the fast growing spirit of Puritanism, which the Ellisons seem to have enthusiastically embraced.

Blackburn Parish Church, Lancashire, England

NOTES & SOURCES

Sources for first three generations: Allison Genealogies: www.familysearch.org, www.gencircles.com, members.lycos.co.uk/house of burgess-Howden, An East Riding Market Town; Butler and Powls, 1994.

(FOR JOHN Ellisse) Allison Genealogies, A Guide Book to Howden Minster Rev. Barry Keeton, 2000, Great Britain to 1688, Maurice Ashley, 1961, Imperial Gazeteer of England and Wales, 1872, A Roots Search Trip to England, Robert A. Mayers, 2004.

(FOR THOMAS Ellisse) Parish Records, Howden, Parish Records, Gargrave, 1558-1812.

(FOR EDMOND LAWRENCIUS Ellison) Parish Registers; Howden 1543-1659, Gargarve 1558-1812, Blackburn 1600-1660.

St. Mary the Virgin parish registers start in 1568 for baptisms and marriages. Burials start in 1600. The Lancashire Parish Register Society has published two volumes: Vol. 41 1660-1660, which also includes baptisms from 1568, and Vol. 93 1653-1680.

A ROOTS SEARCH TRIP TO YORKSHIRE, 2004

In early June 2004, I traveled to England with my grandson, Christopher Schieffer, a history major at American University. Our mission was to research our Allison line of direct ancestors, which have been identified back as far as about 1400, in Yorkshire, England. Over the past six hundred years, the family name has evolved from Ellisse to Ellison and finally to Allison by 1720. Our plan was to meet a cousin, Alan Wickham, of Las Vegas, in the city of York. Alan, an accomplished genealogist, shares this ancestry through his mother Margaret Mayers Wickham.

After taking a few delightful, sunny days to visit most of London's main attractions and an especially interesting side trip to Windsor Castle, Stonehenge and Bath, we left for the City of York to begin our work. Historically, England's second city, York lies about two hundred miles north of London. It was a pleasant two-hour train ride through Midlands pastures lush with a thick carpet of spring grass.

Evidence of our Yorkshire roots has been traced back to our earliest known ancestor, Robert Ellisse. According to family history he was born about 1400 in a place called Hukersal. After three generations, or about one hundred years, Robert's Great-grandson, John Ellisse is found in Saltmarshe, in the Parish of Howden the year 1500. These towns are located on the Ouse River, which flows north twenty miles to York. Saltmarshe is mentioned in the Domesday Book, England's earliest census Taken in1086. This part of Yorkshire is known as the East Riding and we surmised that Hukersal might be in this general area.

By about 1590, the family had migrated to Gargrave, another Yorkshire town, 50 miles north of Saltmarshe, where the name had evolved into Ellison. Only 10 years later, they are found in Blackburn, Lancashire which lies about thirty miles southwest of Gargrave. It was from there that the Puritan, Lawrence Ellison, and his family migrated to America with the John Winthrop Fleet, in1632.

We had specific objectives for this journey into our past. We wanted to try to verify the sources of the recorded genealogy of the family in England, compiled in past years by Allison family members. These records provide names, locations and some birth, death and marriage information on the seven generations of our Ellisse/Ellison ancestors from 1400 to 1632. Most of this widely accepted information is undocumented and without reference to primary sources. Genealogy, without documentation, is just a myth. We believed that local archive collections could reveal these sources.

Actually, visiting sites identified in the family history could provide us with an insight into the culture, history and geography of this part of Yorkshire. Placing our early ancestors in the context of this history, in places where they had lived for over two hundred years, would go beyond records and would help us understand their world and much about their lives. The quality of our family history will be enhanced by creating people from simply names and dates.

We also needed to find the location of Hukersal, identified in the family histories as the home of the first three generations of our earliest direct ancestors. Before the trip we made extensive searches of the English town records for the place. Even an ambitious Internet effort failed to find the location in Yorkshire, or anywhere in England.

The City of York was an exciting setting to begin our research. This fascinating, medieval, walled city was founded by the Roman Ninth Legion who set up camp on the bank of the River Ouse there, in 71AD, after conquering the local Celtic tribes. It served both as fortress and city for successive waves of invaders through the ages. The Britons, Romans, Vikings and the Normans all ruled the region from here.

York Minster, the largest gothic church in northern Europe, dominates the city. First built in 627, it stands on the site of the crowning for Emperor Constantine, the world's first Christian ruler of Rome. He happened to be in York when his father died. We explored the vault and crypt beneath it and saw artifacts" in situ" from levels of excavation down to the Bronze Age. Digs, to uncover more evidence of the rich past buried beneath the city, were actually taking place as we walked through the streets.

Our research began at York's Main Library. Evidence of our family's ancestral records was immediately discovered in the parish registers of Howden. These church archives were begun in 1543, and list births, deaths, baptisms and marriages. This village is the site of the Howden Minster Cathedral which served about 20 surrounding towns and manors, including Saltmarshe, a few miles away.

The next day we took a train ride from York to this ancient East Riding market town in the Yorkshire lowlands. Howden traces its origin to a manor established on the site in 959 AD. The Anglo-Saxons, Romans, Vikings and Normans had all lived here over the centuries.

We got off at a small, deserted, Victorian train station, but there was no town there! Spying a steeple in the distance, we surmised that this was the village. On a long trudge, along an empty highway, the steeple finally grew larger. We learned later that the railroad, built in 1840, had bypassed Howden by several miles. While having a severe effect on the economic growth of the town over the next century, this fortuitously preserved the medieval appearance of the town. Many of its ancient buildings still stand. A pattern of narrow winding streets lead from a town square rimmed by Tudor, timber-framed buildings

Howden, and the surrounding low-lying country, is dominated for miles around by the magnificent church of St. Peter and Paul, Howden Minster. Dating back to the eighth century, generations of our direct ancestors worshipped here. A tour of the Cathedral, noted for the ruins of its lofty chancel, was conducted by an enthusiastic and knowledgeable parishioner. He was even willing to abandon his active table at the annual cake sale when we explained that we were a family returning home after four hundred years.

Our next stop was the town library, a modern facility, where we learned that all old records for the area were kept at the Records Center at Beverly, another East Riding town, about twenty miles east of Howden. We were told that there was little of interest to see at Saltmarshe. It was now a park with a few buildings from a time long after our people had left the area. They had never heard of Hukersal. Disappointed and without transportation we decided in favor of a pint and a hearty pub lunch on the town square We had seen all of Howden and it was only lunch time.

There were few trains scheduled to return to York, and we had more than a little concern when we found no public transportation to take us back to the station. In desperation, we entered the Post Office where the staff of two, neglecting a long line of patrons, made frantic calls, unsuccessfully attempting to arrange some type of ride for us. Had nobody left the town since1840?

Finally, a compassionate lady, with a Margaret Thatcher accent, overhearing our plight, offered to drive us. Fortunately she was an avid local historian. We reviewed our Yorkshire roots in Howden Parish as we waited for the train and she recounted the rich history of the successive waves of invaders who had swept through the area. She emphasized the strong Viking influence here. Plunderers, who sailed up the Ouse River in their long ships to raid the villages, had settled in places along the river on the way to Jorvik, or York, which became their capital in 866. She observed that our genealogy must be accurate since my grandson, tall and sandy haired, appeared to be the perfect personification of a Scandinavian warrior. She was very familiar with the geography here but had never heard of a place called Hukersal.

Our next side trip from York was to the Archives and Records Center at Beverly. Most early records for the East Riding are there. This would be the best place to verify information from the 1400s to 1543, before parish registers were begun. The archives for Howden Parish consisted of about 50 original parchment scrolls, most relating to legal proceedings. These included Saltmarshe and twenty other surrounding towns. The scrolls, of course, were in Latin and many were in an archaic variation of Latin script.

While it was interesting to examine a few of these ancient documents, it was immediately apparent that it would be impossible to discover evidence of any name or place that would provide a link to our Ellisse ancestors. This would require an enormous amount of effort by a linguist skilled in translating the classical Latin of this period.

Researchers of the Allison/Ellison family history have done this in the past. These scrolls are the source of the existence of the earliest generations of our family tree. These early names appear repeatedly in many genealogies of the family and even provide approximate birth dates and references to the mysterious Hukersal. The search for specific references in the scrolls should be continued by researchers of the family. Since much of the data comes from the extensive LDS (Mormon Church) collection, the answers may also be found there.

The visit to Beverley also gave us an opportunity to confer with Yorkshire archivists about the location of Hukersal. The patient staff reviewed all of their indices of historic place names, but could find no evidence of it.

While examining an old map of the area, Christopher noted that towns of Hook and Hook Hall are directly across the river from Howden and Saltmarshe. Records show there was a ferry at that site in the 1400s. Hook Hall, a baronial manor, dates from 1743, a much later period. Could Hukersal be a variation of these names garbled by Yorkshire dialect? While possible, it seems unlikely that the name could have been passed down in any form, through 600 years of oral tradition in the family. Historical Societies at Hook and Goole, the nearest large city, could not identify or link this place name to the area.

Another interesting theory was provided by Dr. Paul Cavill, Research Fellow, English Place Name Society, School of English, University of Nottingham, who was intrigued by my inquiry. He states that Hukersal may not be a town at all, but a description of a plot of land.

> "I've looked long and hard for Hukersal, but can find nothing convincing. The probability is that the last bit is an Old English word, halk, a corner of land and the first a personal name like Hook, or an element like hocer, a rounded hill meaning maybe Hoc's nook or corner of land by the rounded hill. None of these elements has a remarkable distribution that might help to localise the name. The second element is, as I suggest, halh, that tells us that the name was given to a minor or secluded patch of land, and that, in turn, might explain why the place-name itself has not survived."

We learned a great deal from this visit to Yorkshire. Discoveries in Parish Registers of Howden, Gargrave and Blackburn served to verify our data from the mid 1500s until Lawrence Ellison, our Puritan progenitor, came to America in 1632. Many new names of long forgotten people in our ancestry were found and will be added to the repository of knowledge of the Ellisse/Ellison/Allison Family.

Family history cannot be isolated from historical events. A closer study of Yorkshire history will create people from these names and dates by revealing many details of their lives, and why they moved to Gargrave, Blackburn and finally to America. Exploring the lowlands of the East Riding of Yorkshire has given us an insight into the history and culture of an area during the time of our earliest known ancestors.

LAWRENCE ELLISON "GOODMAN" 7. I AND MARY RISTON
PURITANS TO AMERICA, 1630

Lawrence Ellison 7. I, born 22 January 1600, Colne, Lancashire; died 2 January 1664 Hempstead, Long Island, New York; married Mary Riston 8 June 1617, St. Mary's Parish Blackburn, born 1596/00, Blackburn; daughter of Gefferye (Galfride) Riston and Maria Pemerton; died 2 January 1665/6 Hempstead, NY. Eight children, all born Blackburn, Lancashire, England:

	i	Richard, baptized before 30 March 1618; died 1683 Hempstead L.I.; married Thomasina _____; died after 1714. Eight children, seven eldest born in Braintree, MA.
	ii	Katheryne, baptized 19 December 1623; married Henry Linington 1656.
	iii	Samuel, born about 1624.
	iv	John, born 1614; baptized 16 March 1625; will 8 November 1684, proven 1688 estate to brother Thomas. No known children.
	v	A child of Lawrence was buried 10 October 1628.
	vi, vii	Twin daughters, baptized 29 November 1629.
8.	viii	Thomas, born about 1631; died 1697; married Martha Champion. Six children.

Lawrence and Mary are the Puritan progenitors of this family in America. "Goodman" was a name taken on by skilled artisans and freeholders, which Lawrence could have assumed as a cloth weaver or a merchant. According to family histories and genealogies, they migrated to America with the Winthrop/Saltonstall fleet of Puritans in 1630. Both were about age 30 in that year. Their children, all under the age of12, came with them on the voyage.

What caused this courageous young family to leave their home and many relatives in Blackburn, Lancashire to embark on a perilous voyage to an unknown land? They may have immigrated for reasons of religious faith or just a better life in the new world. To travel with the Puritan fleet, religion must have been an important issue.

After the English Reformation, the Church of England differed little from the Catholic Church except for the issue of allegiance to the Pope. This similarity was a matter of deep concern for the Puritans who felt that the Reformation had not gone far enough and wanted to eliminate all semblances of the Roman Catholic Church. Their beliefs along with the persecution they suffered from King Charles I (who wanted to keep more traditional church ritual) caused many Puritans to leave England. The ones that remained overthrew the crown in 1649. Idealistically, they envisioned establishing "a city upon a hill" as an example of how godly people should live. They believed that they could make this dream come true in the new world.

Most Puritan immigrants were from the middle classes and were craftsmen, not farmers. They were weavers, tailors, coopers, brewers, shopkeepers and shoemakers who became farmers in the new world. Most were middle-aged and married, and had a few young children. They were the pioneers who were robust and courageous enough to conquer an unknown wilderness.

Many families were related, and were either from the same town or church congregation. While worshiping as they pleased was a primary motivation, economic conditions were also a driving force for many. Severe winters, commercial depressions and bad harvests had left many in poverty in these years. For these reasons, and with so many young children to feed, the Ellisons probably believed that it was time to leave their homeland.

The Winthrop Fleet left Yarmouth, Norfolk, in the spring of 1630 with 11ships and 300 families. With 700 passengers, this was the largest Puritan fleet to leave England. No original complete lists survive that name the passengers of the ships in the fleet. While the ship the Ellisons sailed has not been identified, other people who were in their congregation and were with them on their travels from place to place in the Massachusetts Bay Colony were passengers on the ships, Plough, James, Frances and Elizabeth.

The average family of eight persons paid about 30 pounds for the trip. This is the equivalent of $5,600 today. Shipping household goods was expensive. The cost of shipping a horse or cow was ten pounds. Navigation was done with a cross staff; the sextant would not be used until the latter half of the next century.

Soon after leaving port they spotted six sails astern and believed they were enemy ships. Women and children were sent below and armament was run out to prepare for battle, but the ships proved to be friendly. About half way across they spotted a spouting whale a few yards from the ships. Closer to land, they stopped to fish for cod. Many large fish were easily caught and provided the first fresh food of the voyage. Religious services were held each day.

Replica of Arabella, flagship of the Winthrop Fleet of 1630.

The ships reached Salem, Massachusetts, on June 13, and briefly stopped there to pick strawberries. A curious Indian was allowed to board the Arabella, perhaps to allow the apprehensive passengers assess the affability of the Native Americans they would soon meet.

Seeking a better site, the ships continued on about six miles to the Charles River, to what is now Charlestown. Boston was not inhabited at that time. The new arrivals fanned out to set up towns in the greater Boston area. Only about half survived in the new world to raise families. Those who did often saw most of their children die in infancy. Of the 700 colonists in the fleet, 200 perished and another 100 returned to England within six months of their arrival.

Most of the Puritans had left in groups, often with their minister and other members of the congregation. The Ellison family followed Reverend Richard Denton, a small one-eyed man from Yorkshire. He had graduated from Cambridge, a hotbed of Puritanism. Denton also came to the colonies with the Winthrop Fleet in 1630 on the ship James. For the next 14 years, Denton led the Ellisons and others in his small flock in seeking a permanent place to settle. Records show Lawrence Ellison and his family did first settle in Braintree, on the outskirts of Boston. It is likely that this was their first home in the new land. Richard, the oldest son, remained there until 1663.

From Braintree, the Ellisons moved to Watertown, another suburb of Boston, in 1633. A 1644 record shows that the lands of Lawrence Ellison in Windsor, Connecticut were forfeited because by not occupying the land he did not fulfill residence requirements. Windsor was the first settlement in the state. This indicates that they may have lived there for a brief period before moving 10 miles south to Weathersfield, Connecticut. They reached Weathersfield in 1635. It was a new plantation in the fertile valley of the Connecticut River. Lawrence Ellison is shown there as being a member of the Connecticut Colony, which was under the leadership of Reverend Richard Denton.

Dissention among the Puritan congregations due to leadership, land distribution and religious issues soon set in. Rivalry with a congregation from New Haven caused problems for Denton's congregation. They favored a church modeled on the Presbyterian form and not the Church of England. The issue caused Denton, Ellison and 33 families to move to Stamford, Connecticut, in 1643. The New Haven opposition wasted no time in confiscating the land of those who had left.

The land for the Stamford settlement was bought in 1641 or 1642 from the Indians for a few coats, hoes, hatchets, knives, kettles and some white wampum. The Ellisons were living in Stamford by 1643. That year, Lawrence obtained a verdict of damages, cause unknown, from Thomas Marshfield in a Connecticut court there.

In 1643, anticipating problems in Stamford, Denton's people sent two emissaries, Robert Fordham and John Carman, across Long Island Sound. Their mission was to acquire land rights from the Dutch and purchase title from the Indians in west Long Island. In December, they met with representatives of the local tribes and were able to negotiate a deed with them. These Indians had slaughtered the few scattered Dutch settlers who were in that area only a year before.

A dispute over the land franchises granted by the rival New Haven Colony soon caused Denton's flock to break away and leave English land. The group of 30 settlers and their families sailed from Stamford over to Long Island in early 1644 and established the

Puritans arrival in the New World

Town of Hempstead. This land, acquired by Fordham and Carman, was called Mantinecock. It was surrounded by in Indian country and still under control of the Dutch.

The Ellisons and others in Denton's group had to pledge allegiance to the Dutch Government so they would not be driven out. They were forced to pay a tax of one-tenth of the value of their harvest. Some of the settlers accompanying Denton were from the town of Hemel Hempstead, about twenty miles from London, and named the town after it. Hempstead was Long Island's first settlement. When they arrived in 1644, they founded a church. It is the oldest continuing Presbyterian Church in the United States.

Lawrence and Mary remained in Hempstead for the rest of his lives, with their children, John, Thomas and Katheryne. Their son Richard, who had stayed behind in Braintree, joined the family in Hempstead in 1663.

Hempstead records show evidence of his activities of Lawrence:

- In 1647, he is listed as one of 66 proprietors of the town. This shows that many others followed the original settlers of 1644.

- In 1657, he was taxed in Hempstead for 29 acres and 10-200 acres.

- In 1658, the town records show that Lawrence and John Ellison became sureties for the good behavior of Lawrence's son-in-law and John's brother-in law, John Ellington.

- On November 29, 1658, Lawrence had 10 acres of land allotted to him in Hempstead.

- In 1659 he was chosen a "townsman" (councilman).

Reverend Richard Denton fell out of favor with his parishioners. After not having been paid for a number of years, he returned to England in 1659 leaving four sons and their families.

Lawrence Ellison died in Hempstead in 1664, the same year that the Dutch gave up New York to the English. At the Court of Sessions, held in Hempstead on January 2, 1665, letters of administration were granted on his estate to his three sons, Richard, Thomas and John Ellison, at which time his land was divided among them. This is the second oldest document recorded in the Surrogates Office of the City of New York. Early church records for Long Island have not survived and no mention of Mary Riston has been found.

Lawrence and Mary Ellison were truly incredible people who with strong faith and unusual courage risked many dangers to travel to a new land and start new lives. Early settlers such as these built our nation. No one should ever forget their strength and principles.

NOTES & SOURCES

Anderson Robert Charles, *The Great Migration Begins, Emigrants to New England, 1620-1633*, New England Historical Genealogical Society, Great migration study project, (three Volumes), 1988.

Anderson, Virginia DeJohn. New England's Generation: The Great Migration and the formation of Society and Culture in the Seventeenth Century, Cambridge, England: Cambridge University Press, 1991.

Letter of Administration for Lawrence Ellison, January 2, 1665, Liber 1, 9. Abstract of Wills NYHS.

Blackburn Parish Reg. 1600-1660, 1547-1812 on LDS film 0599249, Dates for Lawrence Ellison and Mary Riston.

Banks, Col. Charles Edward, *The Winthrop Fleet of 1630*, Genealogical Publishing C. 1930, reprinted 2003. This is a list of the 700 passengers who are believed to have come to New England with John Winthrop in 1630. Based on research in England and America, it provides as much information as can be verified on each passenger name, place of departure and residence, occupation, dates of birth, marriage and death and relationship to other passengers. It also lists passengers for the Mary, John and Lyon, ships that sailed with the fleet. Banks made many unwarranted assumption and this study should not be considered completely reliable.

Note: The Lawrence Ellison family does not appear on any extant passenger lists of the fleet that I have found. Banks and other compilers point out that these are incomplete and family historians should not be discouraged since and most are reconstructions from other sources.

The Topographical Dictionary of 2885 English Emigrants to New England, 1620-1650, Banks lists the English homes, names of ships and where they settled in New England and identifies the manuscript sources of the information.

Barlow, Jonathan Genealogy of the Weed and Allied Families, C. A. Weed 1971.

Betlock, Lynn, *New England's Great Migration*, new England Historic Genealogical Society, 2001-2008.

Denton, Daniel, *A Brief description of New York: formerly called New Netherlands*, John Hancock and William Bradley, London, 1670: reprinted, Gowans, New York, 1845.

Daniel Denton was the son of Rev. Richard Denton. He wrote this promotional brochure to encourage English settlers to come to the territory taken from the Dutch a few years before. This account describes geographic features and the economy of the country surrounding New York, City. It also relates the customs of the Indians and offers advice and incentives to new settlers.

Hawke, David Freeman, *Everyday Life in Early America*, Harper and Rowe, NY, 1988.

Hinman, R.R., Catalogue of the Names of the First Puritan Settlers of the Colony of Connecticut, Hartford, 1846, reprinted, Genealogical publishing Co., 1968.

Hotten, John C. John C. Original Lists of Persons of Quality who went from Great Britain to American Plantations, London 1874, New York 1880; rpt. Baltimore 1962, 1968.

This comprehensive list of migrants to America was compiled from customhouse, seaport records and the archives at the Tower of London. It focuses on the years after 1634and does not contain Winthrop fleet passengers. Lawrence Ellison, Richard Denton or any of their group are not found here, which lends credence that they arrived earlier with Winthrop.

Mather, Frederick G., *Refugees from Long Island To Connecticut*, J. B. Lyon Co. NY, 1913.

Moore, Charles B., *The Early History of Hempstead Long Island,* The New York Genealogical and Biographical Record, New York, January, 1879, 10.

While omitting Lawrence Ellison, this source lists his son John Ellison as one of the original proprietors of Hempstead in 1647.

Morrison L.A., History of the Alison or Allison Family in Europe and America AD 1135 to 1893. (Boston: Daniel A. Upham, 1893.)

Onderdonk, H.O., Annals of Hempstead, Lott Van de Water, Hempstead, NY, 1878.

Queens County Land Records, Deeds, Isaac Smith deposition, August 10, 1747 declaring that he knew Lawrence Ellison and his sons.

Silversmith, Herbert F., *Colonial Families of Long Island and Connecticut*, Vol. II, privately published 1939-58.

Stocks, M.A., Tait, James, *Dunkenbalgh Deeds c. 1200-1600,* Cheltham Society, Manchester, England, 1921. Describes early history of the Riston family in the Parish of Blackburn.

Thompson, Benjamin F., *History of Long Island*, Vol. II, E. French, Nassau St., New York, 1839.

Weed and Allied Families, C A Weed, 1971.

Winthrop Journal and Papers, Winthrop Society, Boston, 1922-1925, www.winthropsociety.org.

The Lawrence Ellison family does not appear on any extant passenger lists of the fleet that I have found. Banks and other compilers point out that these are incomplete and family historians should not be discouraged since and most are reconstructions from other sources.

Wood, Charles B., *The Early History of Hempstead, Long Island*, The New York Genealogical and Biographical Record, New York, January, 1879.

THOMAS ELLISON 8. VIII AND MARTHA HONOR CHAMPION

Thomas Ellison 8. viii, born 1622 St. Mary's Parish, Blackburn, Lancashire; baptized 27 February 1630/31; died 11 October 1697 Hempstead, New York; will dated 7 April 1697, proved at Jamaica, L.I. 11 December 1697; married Martha Honor Champion 1659, born 1642, Stamford, CT; died about 1698 Hempstead, New York; daughter of Thomas Champion, born 1615 and Frances Jacocks, born 1617, both of Ashford, Kent, England. Nine children, all born Hempstead, Queens, Long Island, New York:

9.	i	JOHN, born about 1652.
	ii	Mary, born about 1660; died 25 February 1731; married George Baldwin/Benham.
	iii	Elizabeth, born 1668/78; m. _____ Finch.
	iv	Eleanor/Ellinor, born about 1674/80; married John Hicks.
	v	Martha, born 1676; unmarried; "incompetent".
	vi	Thomas, born 1670; died 1739 of Shrewsbury, NJ; married Cornelia Johnson 7 July 1698.
	vii	Lawrence, born 1672; died after 1678.
	viii	Grace, born 1664; married John Rogers.
	xi	Hannah, born 1674; died after 1698.

Thomas was eight years old when he migrated with his parents, Lawrence Ellison and Mary Riston, from Blackburn, Lancashire, England to America, with the John Winthrop Puritan Fleet in 1630. His youth was spent traveling south from Massachusetts with his family as they sought a place where they could settle, live in peace, and worship as they pleased. They moved from place to place, for over fourteen years, with a group under the leadership of Reverend Richard Denton until they reached Hempstead, Long Island In 1644.

After landing at what today is Boston, the Ellison family moved to their first home, a few miles away in Braintree. Disputes with other church groups caused them to move several times. These problems seemed to be about land rights rather than liturgical matters. They moved to Watertown, Massachusetts in1633 and then to Weathersfield, Connecticut, in 1635, but left there because of a "lack of democracy in politics and religion." They arrived in Stamford in 1639. Martha Champion's family appears to follow the same route with Rev. Denton. She was born in Stamford, in 1642, and later moved to Hempstead, Long Island, as did the Ellisons.

When Thomas was 22 years of age, Denton's congregation finally settled down in Hempstead. This was an area of rich grassland, more suitable for raising livestock than farming. The town had the appearance of an English community and the first permanent homes were the saltbox type. There were less than a dozen Dutch families in this part of New Amsterdam. English customs and traditions prevailed.

Thomas Ellison lived his entire life in Hempstead. He and Martha were a very enterprising family and actively acquired land and other assets. He is listed with his father, Lawrence, and brothers, John and Richard, on records and legal documents in the town, beginning in 1654.

1656: Thomas signed his mark to a land document. His signature appears on later documents, which indicates he later learned how to write.

1658: He had ten acres of land, in Hempstead, allotted to him on November 27, from the town fathers, probably because he married that year and become the head of a family.

1659: Thomas married Martha Champion. Her parents had also come from England and had migrated south through Stamford, Connecticut, during the same period as the Ellisons. It is likely that the families were acquainted.

1661: Thomas bought land from George Mills.

1662: He was chosen a "townsman" (councilman) for Hempstead succeeding his aging father, Lawrence who three years before had held this office. Town meetings were the life of the community. Neither the Dutch nor the English government interfered with these local councils to any great extent. They had the power to settle disputes, grant and lease land, grant mill rights, provide for the poor and make changes in the common land usage. Serious crimes were uncommon during this time and most problems were over land rights.

1663: Along with his brother John and Thomas Hicks he was granted the entire tract of land known as Mad Nan's Neck which later became Great Neck. It is believed that that the peninsula was named after Nan Heatherton, a feisty leader of early English squatters who in 1640 repulsed both the Dutch and Indians from the land. Others believe that the name is derived from the Indian name mad-nan-nock, which means hilly land.

1665: On January 18, Thomas and his brother, John, of "Hempstead, Long Island, in the North Riding of New Yorkshire" sold Little Neck, in Hempstead to Thomas Hicks and Samuel Denton, witnessed by Richard Gildersleeve and Thomas Jones.

1667: Land in Hempstead was allotted to him at a public meeting. In the same year, land was given to him on Hempstead Plains.

1673: Thomas signed an oath of allegiance to England when New York passed from Dutch to English control.

1675: Matthew Bedle claimed that Thomas owned him pay "for two days work during harvest."

1676: Thomas owned land in Cow Neck, Hempstead.

1689: In May, Thomas and his wife Martha, made a "reversion" (the return of an interest paid mortgage) to Samuel Denton Jr. the son of Reverend Richard Denton.

1683: Thomas sold a meadow on "Cose Neck" to John Treadwell. Cows Neck was the name of the peninsula on which the Town of Port Washington is now located.

1685, Thomas and his son John are listed as freeholders. In that same year he was taxed on 60 acres and another 270 acres.

1688: On January10, Thomas inherited the entire estate of his brother John.

1696: In December, he conveyed lands in Hempstead to his brother Richard.

All of this activity occurred in turbulent times. Hempstead was constantly threatened by the Indians who demanded additional payments for land for which they had previously been paid. In 1656, Governor Peter Stuyvesant negotiated a peace treaty with Taackapousha, the chief sachem (chieftain), to put the town under Dutch protection and to build a trading post. Harassment by the Indians still continued after this. The unfriendly Dutch continuously pressured their English subjects for excessive taxes.

Hempstead was in disputed territory during the struggle between the Dutch and English over control of New Netherlands. The Dutch surrendered the territory on September 8, 1664. Conditions did not improve for the Puritans at Hempstead under the flag of their own country. The first English governor, Richard Nicolls, attempted to extract even heavier taxes from the town.

Despite this adversity, Hempstead was a pleasant and bountiful place. In 1670, Daniel Denton, son of the minister, wrote a lyrical description of the area:

"The island is most of it a very good soyle, and very natural for all sorts of English grain, which they sow and have very good increase of, besides all other fruits and herbs common in England, as also tobacco, hemp, flax, pumpkins, melons etc. Yea in May you shall see woods and fields so curiously bedecked with roses and an innumerable multitude of delightful flowers, not only pleasing to the eye, but smell, that you may behold nature contending with art and striving to equal if not excel many gardens in England."

Thomas died on December 11, 1697, and Martha died one year later. Their burial site is unknown. The will of Thomas Ellison Sr. of Hempstead is dated April 7, 1697, (Liber, A, 120) and proved at Jamaica, Long Island. This detailed document covers extensive acreage, houses, livestock and grazing rights. It mentions his wife, Martha, his sons, Thomas and John, and his daughters, Grace Rogers, Mary Baldwin and Elizabeth. Unfortunate daughter Martha, disabled in some way, is provided with "sufficient maintenance of diet and apparel and all other necessities fit for one in her condition, not long capable of maintaining herself out of ye estate." His wife Martha, and son, Thomas are executors. Captain John Jackson and Nathaniel Pearsall, of Hempstead, were appointed as overseers.

Thomas Ellison and his wife had very successful lives. Confronted by many obstacles, they were brave, vigorous and very entrepreneurial and politically astute. They were and able to acquire large tracts of land and many other assets to provide a substantial legacy for their family. This was accomplished despite frequent threats from hostile Indian tribes, antagonistic Dutch rule and an oppressive English government.

*Entred for Mr Thomas Hicks of Hemp-
stead, this following Deed ye 20th of Febry 1666.*

Bee it knowne to all men, whom these puts
may concerne, That wee John Ellison,
and Thomas Ellison, of Hempstead on Long
Island, in the North Riding of New York
=shire, have Alienated and Sold, all that
our Right Title and Interest, of ye Little
Neck which was given to us, by the Towne
of Hempstead, wee say wee have Sold the
fore mentioned pmisses, from us, our heires.
and Successors for ever, to Thomas Hicks, ―
and Samuell Denton, of the same place,
to them, their heires and Successo. for ever,
as wittness Our hands and Seales, this
18th of January Anno 1665. And in the
sth yeare of his Ma:ties Raigne, Charles the
Second, by the Grace of God, of Great Brit=
=taine, ffrance and Ireland King, Defen.
of the faith &c   Thomas Ellison (Seal)

                                   John Ellisons] Marke

Sealed & delived in the   (Seal)
psets of us
Rich Gildersleve.
Thomas Jones, ⊙ his Marke.

On January 18, 1665, Thomas Ellison and his brother John sold "Little Neck"
in Hempstead, Long Island to Thomas Hicks and Samuel Denton.

JOHN ELLISON 9. i

John Ellison 9. i, born 1652 Hempstead, Long Island, New York; died about 1720; married unknown. One child:

> 10. i, JOHN Allison, born about 1697 Hempstead, Long Island; died 6 June 1754; married unknown, wife died before 1754; migrated to Orange now Rockland County, New York in 1719. The name changes to Allison after this generation.

This generation was completely omitted from the Morrison and Barlow family histories, the monuments at Mount Repose Cemetery in Haverstraw and all other sources that recount Allison/Ellison genealogy. For two centuries, a gap in dates between Thomas the son of Lawrence, the Puritan, and John, who migrated from Hempstead to Haverstraw in 1719, has caused difficulty in tracking the continuity of generations.

In recent years Allison family researchers believed they solved the mystery of this missing Long Island generation with an abstract of the will for John Ellison of New York, dated 1721.[1] After examining the full text of the original will, I conclude that this was not the will of John Ellison, our Hempstead farmer. While the birth and death dates of this person match the missing years, the document does not mention land holdings or any given names of the Hempstead family. Heirs include the nationally famous printer William Bradford Sr. who receives 100 pounds. With generous sums also provided to family members, the will seems to be that of an affluent city dweller. This John, and his wife Eleanor, is found with a group of Ellisons who appear to be related, in the Dock and South Wards of New York City according to the census records of 1673 and 1703. These people are found in the same wards on the New York City tax lists of 1695 to 1699.[2]

The difficulty and confusion in tracing the missing generation in the past has been caused by existence of three men from Hempstead, all named John Ellison, whose lives overlapped in the last half of the 17th century. To identify which of the three was the family's direct ancestor it was necessary to search all existing Hempstead municipal, land and court records for this period for references to John Ellison. The references were then linked to each of the three men by comparing relationships with other family members, land locations and other factors. It was then possible to differentiate between them and to identify the ancestor, the son of Thomas and Martha Champion and the father of John Allison, the progenitor of the Haverstraw Allisons.

Most documents during the period refer to this man as John Ellison Jr. to distinguish him from his older uncle, John and not because he is the son of a John, This was a common practice at the time. To eliminate confusion for future genealogists the three men are designated here as John Jr., John Sr. and John son of Richard.

- John Jr., refers to the missing generation ancestor, the son of Thomas Ellison and Martha Champion and the grandson of Lawrence, the Puritan.

- John Sr., born in England about 1624, was the son of Lawrence, the Puritan, who arrived in Hempstead Long Island in 1643. This John was a prominent landowner and office holder in the town. According to a book published in 1893 by Morrison, he did not have a will. Morrison shows him with two sons but this is an error. After he was chosen constable in 1678 no further references to him are found in any records. Both John Sr. and John Jr. often appear on the same record.[3]

- John, born August 26, 1780, was the son of Richard and grandson of Lawrence, arrived with his father in Hempstead from Braintree, Massachusetts, in 1662. Morrison show that he never married. His will dated November 8, 1684, was proven in 1688.[4]

When John Jr. was twelve years old, the Dutch under Peter Stuyvesant surrendered New York to the English. The years that followed were peaceful in Hempstead and demands from the Mantinecock Indian chiefs for more payments for the land they had sold to the Dutch in 1653 diminished. This tranquility was disturbed only by aggressive tax collection and growing animosity toward the Presbyterian descendants of the Puritans by the new Anglican English government.

Threats from the Indians completely disappeared by 1670. In that year, Daniel Denton, son of the Hempstead minister, wrote this poignant justification for the demise of the Native Americans.[5]

> *"There is now but few Indians and those few in no means hurtful, but rather serviceable to the English; and it is to be admired how strangely they have decreased, by the hand of God since the English first settling in their parts. Their six towns are now reduced to two villages. Where the English come to settle, a divine hand makes way for them by removing or killing off the Indians, either by wars with one another or by some raging mortal disease."*

Daniel Denton's account in 1670 was written to encourage settlers from England to come to the territory recently taken for the Dutch. He extols the opportunities of colonial life in Hempstead, in what may be America's first promotional real estate brochure.

> *He appealed to "those which fortune hath frowned upon in England.... Who may procure here inheritances of land and possessions, stock themselves with all sort of cattle, enjoy the benefit of them whilst they live, and leave them to the benefit of their children when they die." How many poor people in the world would think themselves happy if had they an acre or two of land, whilst here is hundred, nay thousands of acres, that would invite inhabitants. .... Here one may furnish himself with land, and live rent free, yea, with such a quantity of land, that he may weary himself with walking over his fields of corn and all sorts of grain."*

A list of the Inhabitants of the Town of Hempstead in 1673 shows both John Jr. and his uncle, John Ellison Sr., on a list of those citizens of Hempstead who signed an oath of allegiance after New York passed from Dutch to English control.[6] Hempstead enjoyed continued peace and prosperity after this time and for nearly a century in an idyllic setting. These references of John Ellison Jr. were found in the records of that time:

1679: In a land grant to patentees, the town of Hempstead granted 22 acres to John Jr. and 42 acres to John Sr.[7]

1683: John Ellisson Jr., Hempstead, estate valuation, 81 pounds, 10 shillings.[8]

1685: John Ellison is taxed for 125 acres and his uncle, John Sr., for 60.[9]

c.1688: John and John Ellison Sr. receive land that is distributed to the patentees of Hempstead. The same year John Jr is shown owning land that bounds on the east side of land sold to Thomas Ellison Sr. by Thomas Martin.[10]

1692: John Allison is one of 16 men provided by Queens County to Captain Peter Schuyler's company.[11]

1697: John Jr. was generously provided for in the will of his father, Thomas, in 1697. He inherited carts, plows, tools, horses and oxen and land. The property included a twenty acre lot of meadow on great neck, an upland lot of fifty or sixty acres near Mantinecock Hollow and another 50 acres, "that I had right to take up on the commons."[12]

1698: Census of Hempstead, taken a year after his father, Thomas, died, shows John living with his mother, Martha; brother, Thomas and sisters Grace, Martha and Hannah and an unknown person whose given name does not appear. This may have been his wife.

What was daily life like in Hempstead for the John Ellison family in the last half of the 17th century? The farming and pastoral community was governed by the Town Meeting. Social life centered on the church and taverns. Church attendance was compulsory and failure to attend was punished by fine or banishment for repeated offenders.

Clothing was coarse fabric made from yarn, made on a spinning wheel. Food was grown in a garden lot near each house. Bays reaching miles inland from Long Island Sound provided fish, clams and oysters. Nearby marshes and forests teemed with game that supplemented the meat from domestic animals.

All farmers raised cattle that were herded together in the town's common pasture. The livestock was watched over by a "keeper" who was appointed each year at the town meeting. Ordinances were constantly being enacted for the care of the cattle, fence construction, earmarks and penalties for straying. A "hay warden" kept cattle from straying into cultivated fields.

During the next generation, the sons of John Jr. and the great-grandchildren of Lawrence, the Puritan, would leave Hempstead for new frontiers after 75 years and three generations. They would depart for the same reasons that Lawrence had left England in 1630- the opportunity to improve their quality of life and freedom to worship as they choose.

NOTES & SOURCES

Seversmith, Herbert F., *Colonial Families of Long Island and Connecticut*, Vol. II, privately published 1939-58; *Early History of Hempstead, Long Island*, Vol. II, 1948.

Blackburn Parish Registry, 1600-1660; LDS film 0599249Abstract of Wills NYHS.

Hempstead L.I. Deeds.

Colonial Families of L.I. NY and CT.

O'Callaghan, Edmund Bailey. *List of Inhabitants of Colonial New York, Excerpted from the Documentary History of the State of New York* Genealogical Publishing Co. Inc, 1979, 26.

Combes, D. A. *Genealogy of the descendant of Reverend Richard Denton*, Ann Arbor: University microfilms, 1980.

Kerr, Frank Melville, *The Reverend Richard Denton and the Coming of the Presbyterians*, New York History, April, 1940.

Thompson, Benjamin F., *History of Long Island*, Gould Banks, New York, 1843.

Hicks, Benjamin D., *Record, of the Towns of North and South Hempstead*, Long Island.

Onderdonk, Henry, *Annals of Hempstead*, Jamaica Long Island June, 188(?).

Hempstead Census of 1698, State Library, Albany, NY.

---

[1] Old Liber, NYC Surrogates Court, 330. Abstract, 330, Old Liber, NYC Surrogates Court.

In the name of God Amen, the twelfth day of October 1718, I John Ellison being sick in body but of good and perfect memory, ... [Traditional religious introductory wording] I make my loving wife Eleanor and John Ellison Junior my son my whole and sole executors. I bequeath unto my loving sister Elizabeth Finch, if alive at my demise 100 pounds and her two daughters if alive each 50 pounds. To William Bradford senior, printer, 100 pounds (not 10 as in abstract). To my loving brother William Ellison in England, 50 pounds. All the remainder of my estate real and personal as goods, chattels, houses and debt monies I leave[1] to the disposal of my loving wife Eleanor Ellison with the advice of John Ellison my son and my other executor, to be divided at my decease amongst my four sons or as many of them as shall be alive. Namely, John Ellison Junior, William Ellison, Thomas Ellison and Joseph Ellison. John Ellison (LS).

Witnesses: Abraham Messier, Peter Messier, Peter Ferrand (Ferrand added). Proved December 13, 1721, approved, January 8, 1722/23 by William Burnet, Esq., Captain General and Governor in Chief of the provinces of New York, New Jersey and territories thereon in America and Vice Admiral of the same. Signed I. Bobin, Deputy General.

[2] Tax lists New York City,1695-1699, New York Historical Society, 1910.

[3] Morrison, Leonard Allison, *The History of the Allison Family in Europe and America*, Daniel A. Upham, Boston, 1893, 1645, 249.

[4] Morrison, 1632, 249.

[5] Denton, Daniel, *A brief description of New York: Formerly Called New Netherlands*, London: printed for John Handcock and William Bradley, 1670, New York Gowans, 1845, 2.

[6] Translation of Vanderekemps Dutch Record XXII.

[7] *Records of North and South Hempstead, Long Island*,Vol. VIII edited by Benjamin O Hicks, Long Island Farmer Print, 1900.

[8] O'Callaghan, Edmund, Bailey. *Lists of Inhabitants of Colonial New York*, Genealogical Publishing Co. 1979.

[9] Thompson, Benjamin F., *History of Long Island*, E. French, 1839, 350.

[10] Hicks, Vol. VIII, 241.

[11] Onderdonk, Henry Jr. Queens County in Olden Times, Charles Willing, 1865.

[12] Liber A, page 16 April 7, 1697. Abstract, NY Genealogical and Biographical Soc. Vol Vl. 65, 246.

JOHN ALLISON 10. i: PROGENITOR OF THE HAVERSTRAW, NEW YORK, ALLISONS

John Allison 10. i, born about 1697, Hempstead, Long Island, NY; died 6 June 1754 Haverstraw, New York, will dated 6 June 1751, proven 21 October 1754; married unknown, wife died before 1754. Ten children, all born in Haverstraw except Benjamin:

i	Benjamin, born about 1717 Hempstead NY; married (2) Leah Ackerman in 1769; will 1796.
ii	John, born about 1719; died 1782; married Amy _____. Ten children, some loyalists to Canada after the war.
11.iii	JOSEPH, born 3 August 1721; married (1)Elizabeth Benson (2) Elsie Parcells; died January 1796.
iv	William, born about 1723; died 1758. One child, Edward.
v	Elizabeth, born about 1725; married _____ Cuyper/Cooper.
vi	Deborah, born about 1727; married John Johnson.
vii	Mary, born about 1729; married _____ De Grough.
viii	Hannah, born about 1731; married John Taylor.
ix	Richard, born about 1733; physician, died 1749; unmarried.

John was probably the most enterprising and audacious of this family's direct ancestors. With this generation, the family name changed to Ellison from Allison. He was born and raised in Hempstead, Long Island, a town founded by his grandfather, Lawrence Ellison, and other Puritan settlers in 1643. He inherited a substantial amount of land from his father, John Ellison. It had been passed down in the family for the past three generations.

John did not remain in Hempstead. In 1719, he migrated northwest with his family and a company of others from his town. They moved to what today is Rockland County, New York.

They were motivated to leave for both economic and religious reasons. The frontier was west of the Hudson River, only 40 miles from Hempstead. Boundless tracts of fertile land, uninhabited except for a few Dutch settlers, could be easily and inexpensively acquired there.

At this time, the English government was determined to crush Presbyterianism in New York and to make the Church of England dominant. In 1704, Lord Cornbury, Governor of New York, put into effect a law that unified church government under the Church of England (Episcopal) in all territory owned by the Duke of York. The Episcopal Reverend John Thomas was appointed minister for Hempstead Parish. The enraged townsmen had no voice in his selection. They started meeting in private homes and negotiations to find a new place to live began in 1711. For the same reason that their Puritan forefathers had left England, 90 years before, the more radical citizens, a group of 35 families, began leaving the town before 1720.

Most of the migrants had the surnames of the original Puritans settlers of Hempstead, Long Island. Denton, Halstead, Woods, Coe, Cuyper, Hutchins, Seaman, and Conklin were names that would become common in Rockland County as their descendants multiplied over the next two centuries. The fugitives from Long Island bought a huge tract of land known as the north part of the Kakiat Patent. It covered what today is the northern half of Rockland County, New York.

This group founded a village and named it New Hempstead after their Long Island home. This is the present town of Ramapo. The Indian name for the area was Hackyackawek, corrupted by the settlers to Kakiat. A homestead of 400 acres adjoining the town was given to each family. Soon after their arrival they built a Presbyterian Church, which became known as the English Church. This name was chosen because sermons were preached in English and not in Dutch. It was to remain the only English speaking church in Rockland County until 1781. For the next three generations, Allisons worshiped, married, and were baptized there, but few records have survived from this time.

John Allison arrived at New Hempstead in 1719 with his wife, who has never been identified, and first born son, two-year- old Benjamin. John Allison began to acquire more acreage soon after settling his allotted homestead. He probably financed acquisitions with funds realized from land sales on Long Island. In April 10, 1722, he bought land from Jonah Halstead for 100 pounds. Halstead was one of the original settlers from Long Island.

In 1729, he began to acquire large contiguous tracts of land along the banks of the Hudson River at Grassy Point, Haverstraw. This land, in the wilderness, was about five miles north of New Hempstead in the De Harte Patent. Balthazar De Harte, a Dutch settler, originally purchased the tract from the Indians before 1666.

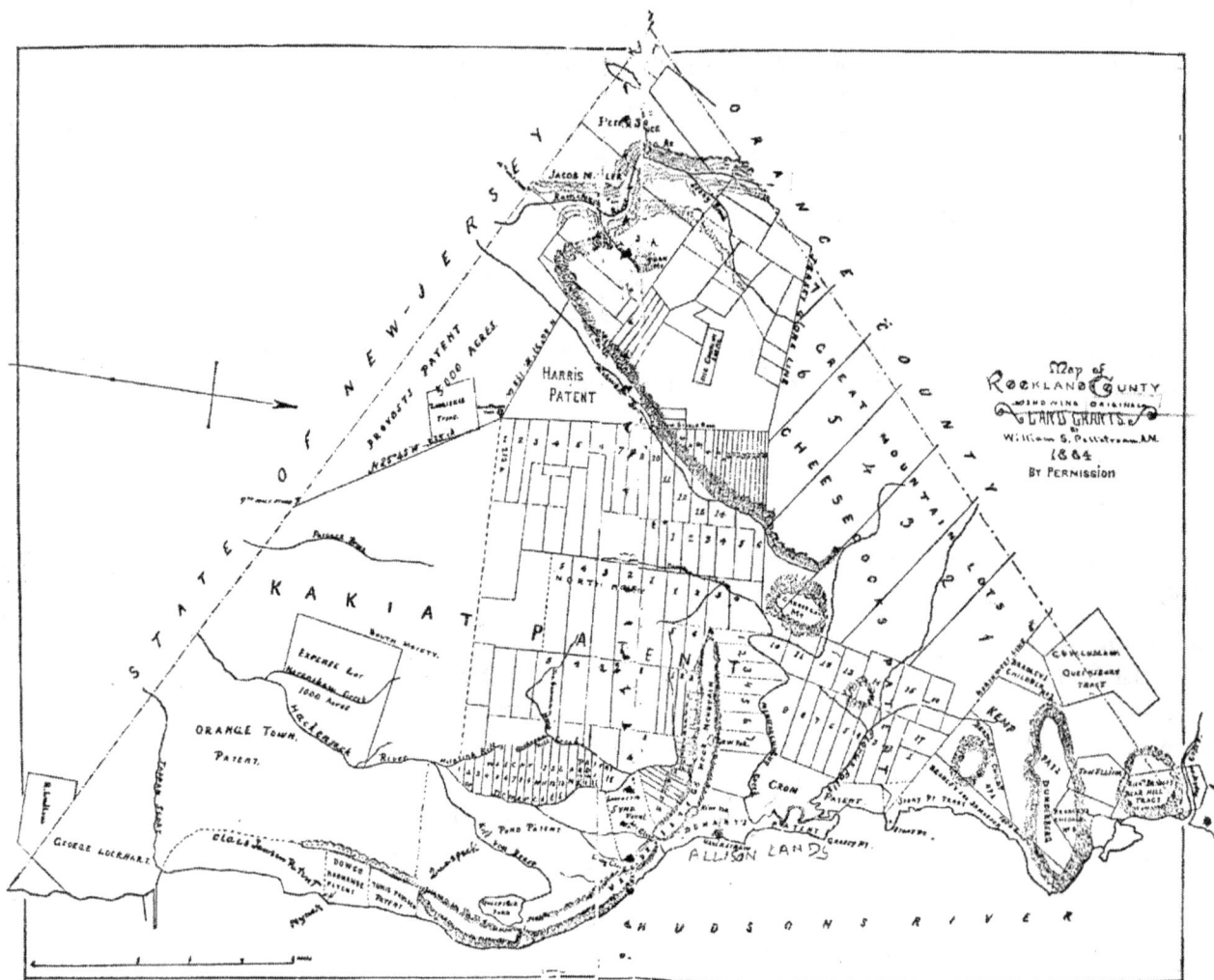

On May 14, 1729, John Allison bought another 150 acres from James Osborn for 400 pounds and in the same year added another 100 acres from Albert Minnie for 270 pounds. He added to these lands on June 16, 1741, with a purchase from Nicholas Kupyer and a final acquisition from Matthew Benson in 1742. The entire tract extended about three miles along the bank of the Hudson River and encompassed all the land now covered by the Town of Haverstraw. It was described as "bounded north and east by the Hudson River, south by the mountains and running westerly by Minisceongo Creek and the mountains." The land extended south along the river and included a neck of land called Grassy Point. The Point was green and fertile in appearance, with level fields and groves of great trees. It was described in the early 19th century as a pleasure to gaze upon.

John Allison built his house on a bluff overlooking Grassy Point and the river. It was a small two story building with a large kitchen attached. The house must have been small for his large household, that included slaves. It was located in Haverstraw on the west side of what today is still called Allison Street. It was about eight rods (forty yards) north of present day Main Street. The gate to the farm was at the corner of Broad Street and Broadway. It led straight up a lane to a large orchard and a grove of oak and chestnut trees that surrounded the house.

John Allison's land covered a long a stretch of riverbank and was frequently crossed by travelers and haulers of produce from the west who had to gain access to the river. In later years, Haverstraw would become an important Hudson River port. This traffic prompted John to open a public house and general store at Grassy Point.

Numerous accounts of his brash and politically incorrect activities in the Orange Court of Appeals and in the New York Supreme Court are found during this time.

In 1729 he was indicted by a grand jury for using false weights and measures. The charge read:

"That he the said Allison died on January 6, 1729, and other days, sell to Joseph Wood, then of Haverstraw, Blacksmith, several parcells of iron for greater weight than the same did in fact contain, and that he did also sell to Joseph Wood a parcel of Duffells for nine yards whereas in truth the parcel was but eight yards and a quarter and half a quarter of a yard.

That John Allison had and kept one false measure called a yard which was very much burnt at both ends and had been broken near the middle and was pieced by being laid over and tied near the middle with a string.

Further that he the said John Allison on June 7, 1731, at Haverstraw kept a public house and sold sider, punch, rum and other liquors and that (several names), his majesty's subjects were in said public house and then there called for, had and drank, sider, rum, punch and other liquors for which he the said John Allison fraudulently demanded, exacted, had and received of and from said subjects much more money than the liquors were worth or ever usually sold for."

The same year, Thomas Pullen, a neighbor, complained that John Allison and Thomas Hughes said, "The Pope of Rome was a good Christian." One can imagine this incident occurring during a spirited discussion at the Allison pub.

In 1736, after John Allison lost a lawsuit against Jonathan Seaman, "he called the jury abusive names and declared that there was not above two or three honest men in the county." For this, he was charged by the New York Supreme Court "with being a daily stirrer up of strife and discord among his neighbors."

During the same period he was charged with obstructing a road near his land with "force and arms" to prevent travelers from crossing to the river.

When John was assigned as administrator for his son, Richard's, will in 1750, the creditors objected and "prayed that administration be granted to his son John Allison Jr."

John Allison died in 1754 leaving most of his land to his sons, Benjamin and Joseph. Joseph inherited his home site and 200 acres along the river. Land that John continued to own in Hempstead, Long Island, was left to his son William. He left his daughters, Elizabeth, Mary and Hannah monetary settlements. Phebe Hubbs was directed to "stay with my slaves and family in my house and receive [most] of the produce of the farm for the support of the family." She may have been a surrogate mother to his children after his wife's death. She was also mentioned in the will of his son, Richard. The Hubbs family was a large family in Hempstead, Long Island, but her relationship is unknown.

John's grave on Minisceongo Creek, near the river, has disappeared. In 1890, Barlow reported, "his remains were either buried in the old burying ground on the neck or near the Minisceongo Creek, now all dug up for brick clay, or in the old Allison burying ground located about 1000 feet east of the old Benjamin Allison house, now being undermined for the blue clay beneath it, the headstones have all disappeared." A side of a monument in the Allison plot at Mount Repose Cemetery lists his birth in Hempstead, Long Island, and his move to Haverstraw in 1719. The stone shows his children and their spouses, but does not mention his wife.

While impetuous, aggressive, and outspoken, John Allison was a bold and enterprising pioneer who chose to trek with his family to the wilderness of the frontier for greater opportunity and the freedom to worship as he chose. His courage and that of the others of the brave band of settlers from Long Island led to the opening up of Rockland County, New York, for the thousands that followed over the next two centuries.

CAPTAIN JOSEPH ALLISON 11. III AND ELIZABETH BENSON

Captain Joseph Allison 11. iii, born 3 August 1721 New Hempstead, NY; son of John Allison, mother unknown; died 2 January 1796, will 12 September 1792, probate 4 April 1796, codicil 19 December 1795; married (1) Elizabeth Benson 10 March 1743; born about 1722 New Hempstead NY; died 12 December 1767; daughter of Matthew Benson and Elizabeth Bussing; (2) Elsie Parcells 4 May 1769; born about 1748, Haverstraw; died 16 April 1815. Seventeen children, ten by first wife, eight by second.

Children: Mother, Elizabeth Benson, all born in Haverstraw.

i	Mathew, born 13 July 1743; Revolutionary War veteran; died 12 September 1792.
ii	Elizabeth, born 2 October 1745; married David Ten Eyke, Ferry master, Kings Ferry.
iii	Mary, born 17 October 1747; married Amos Hutchings 14 November 1764; Revolutionary War veteran.
iv	Hannah, born 14 February 1750; married Adrian Waldron; Revolutionary War veteran.
v	Joseph, born 29 May 1752; Revolutionary War veteran.
12. vi	JOHN, born 12 May 1754; Revolutionary War veteran; married SARAH DENOYELLES 1778; died 22 January 1828.
vii	William, born 11 March 1756; Revolutionary War veteran; married Rachel _____.
viii	Thomas, born 11 February 1760; married Abigail Goldthwaite 30 October 1779.
ix	Deborah, born 29 June 1762; married William Willis; Revolutionary War veteran.
x	Benjamin, born 3 July 1764.

Children: Mother, Elsie Parcells, all born in Haverstraw.

xi	Peter, born 19 November 1769; married Margaret Suffern; died 21 February 1836.
xii	Amos, born 29 May 1771; blacksmith/hotel owner Haverstraw; married (2) wife widow Clark.
xiii	Michael, born 3 June 1773; unmarried; lived NYC.
xiv	Parcells, born 25 April 1777; married widowed sister-in-law Nellie Parcells.
xv	Richard, born 23 October 1780; died 26 November 1825; cabinet maker on Vesey St, NYC; married Eliza Ruckel.
xvi	Elsie, born 9 November 1783; married Jacob Archer in 1801.
xvii	Abraham, born 9 November 1783; twin; died in infancy.

Joseph's father, John Allison, one of Rockland County's first English settlers, came to the area in 1719 from Hempstead, Long Island. Joseph grew up on his father's estate, which stretched about two miles along the bank of the Hudson, at Haverstraw. The Allison farm covered the larger part of the De Harte Patent, which included all land now occupied by the town and extended south from the extremity of Grassy Point. Joseph was a Captain in the Orange County Militia and had seventeen children with two wives.

Joseph first married Elizabeth Benson, the mother of his son John Allison, the direct ancestor whose life is recounted in the next chapter. Elizabeth was the daughter of Matthew Benson and Elizabeth Bussing. They owned the large farm adjacent to the Allison lands on the north side. The Bensons were one of the early Dutch families in the area. Elizabeth's brother, Mathew, was in the Orange County Militia during the Revolutionary War.

In 1754, Joseph inherited the home site of his father, John, and the larger part of the Allison estate. In the will, this tract is described as bounded north and east by the Hudson River, south by the mountains, running west along Minisceongo Creek so far as to reach a tier of hundred acre lots, a little to the east of Muddy Brook.

As an affluent landowner, Captain Allison and is shown on a list of officers dated October 27, 1763. This was during the French and Indian War period. The list, from the Budke Collection, was on a piece of parchment that was used as a cover for binding a school copybook belonging to Mary Haring. A note on the fragment reads: "In trimming the sheepskin to suit her purpose, she very nearly destroyed the record."

He seems to have valued his rank as captain and used the title for the rest of his life. There was no military action in Rockland County during this period. During the Revolutionary War, Joseph Allison, in his 50s, served along with his sons and most other male citizens, as a private, in the 2nd Co. Orange County Militia.

In 1760, John DeNoyelles, a young, French military officer who had been in the service of Great Britain, opened a store at a landing along the river and purchased the remainder of the De Harte Patent, south of the Allison farm. Both families were patriots during the War and remained good neighbors for the rest of the century. Joseph's son, John, married Sarah DeNoyelles, but her relationship to the family is unknown. The border between the two estates was never defined until it was amicably settled by the families in 1792.

Joseph's wife, Elizabeth Benson, died in 1767 at about age 45. She was the mother of Joseph's first ten children. Six of them were under age fifteen at the time of their mother's death. Joseph must have had several difficult years managing his large estate and extended family of laborers and slaves. The three eldest daughters may have helped raise the younger children. Two years later, at age 48, he remarried the 21-year-old Elsie Parcells. They had another seven children. Four of these children were conceived during the Revolutionary War and the last was born when Joseph was age 62. Joseph took an active role in the community. In 1770 he was chosen at a town meeting to be a Fire Master and "Highway Master, from the river to the head of the mountain.

The War for Independence was personally, and economically, devastating for the patriotic Allison Family. In April of 1775, Joseph Allison and nine other Haverstraw Allisons signed an "Association," pledging to support the Continental Congress and the cause of liberty. Joseph's son, John, age 21, immediately enlisted in the Continental Army in early 1775 and marched off on the ill-fated invasion of Canada. His sons, Mathew, William, and Joseph, joined the Orange County Militia to defend the banks of the river from an impending invasion by the main British Army from New York City. His son-in-law, Amos Hutchings, became a Captain and William Willis became a private in the New York Continental Line. Over a dozen Haverstraw Allisons served in the regular army or as minutemen during the war.

As with many families at the time, the Haverstraw Allisons were bitterly divided by the war. Joseph's nephews, sons of his brother, John, were loyalists and joined Tory Regiments. Edward became a Captain in DeLancey's 3rd battalion. John was killed in combat opposing the American forces at the battle of Quebec in 1775. Joseph, another of John's sons, fought the American forces at the Battle of White Plains in 1776. Two other sons of the family, Jeremiah and Benjamin, were exiled to Canada when the war ended. For many years, this part of the family was a mystery since they disappear from all records after the war. Most had fled north to Canada rather than join the Patriot cause or suffer

---

110.

LIST OF MILITIA OFFICERS
IN ORANGE COUNTY -- 1763.

A piece of parchment containing the following list of militia officers of 1763 was converted into covers for binding a school copy book belonging to Mary Haring who wrote her own name upon it. In trimming the sheepskin to suit her purpose, she very nearly destroyed the record. I have copied as many of the names as I can decipher.   G.H.B.

Jacob blauvelt   Ditto

Derick vanderbelt Jr, Ditto

Joseph Allison   Captain

Nicholas Conklin   1 Lieut
         his
John D (Johnson ?)   2 Ditto
     mark
          his   EYKE
Hendrick ⊥ Ten ---- k Ensign
         mark
Derick Vanderbilt   Captain

June yo First Day 1763
       gerret eckerson }
                        } Capt
       gerret demarest }
       Abraham A. Haring Jun }
              his   } first lieut
       Peter + -------y   }
             mark   }
              his   }
       Daniel D V --------   }
              mark   } good lieut
              his   }
       Aurie X Blauvelt   }
             mark   }
       Jan J Haring   }
                             } Ensigns
       Thunis Kuyper   }

Oot ye 27 th 1763

32

the harsh treatment that loyalists received after the war, as recounted through oral family tradition that had been passed down over 200 years.

The patriotic fervor that had swept through Orange County and the rest of the colonies in early 1775 soon gave way to apprehension and fear in Haverstraw. In 1776, the war was going badly for the American side everywhere, and the Hudson highlands river corridor was in a vital position. If the British Army, occupying Manhattan, could link up with their troops coming down from Canada, they could split New England from the rest of the colonies and win the war.

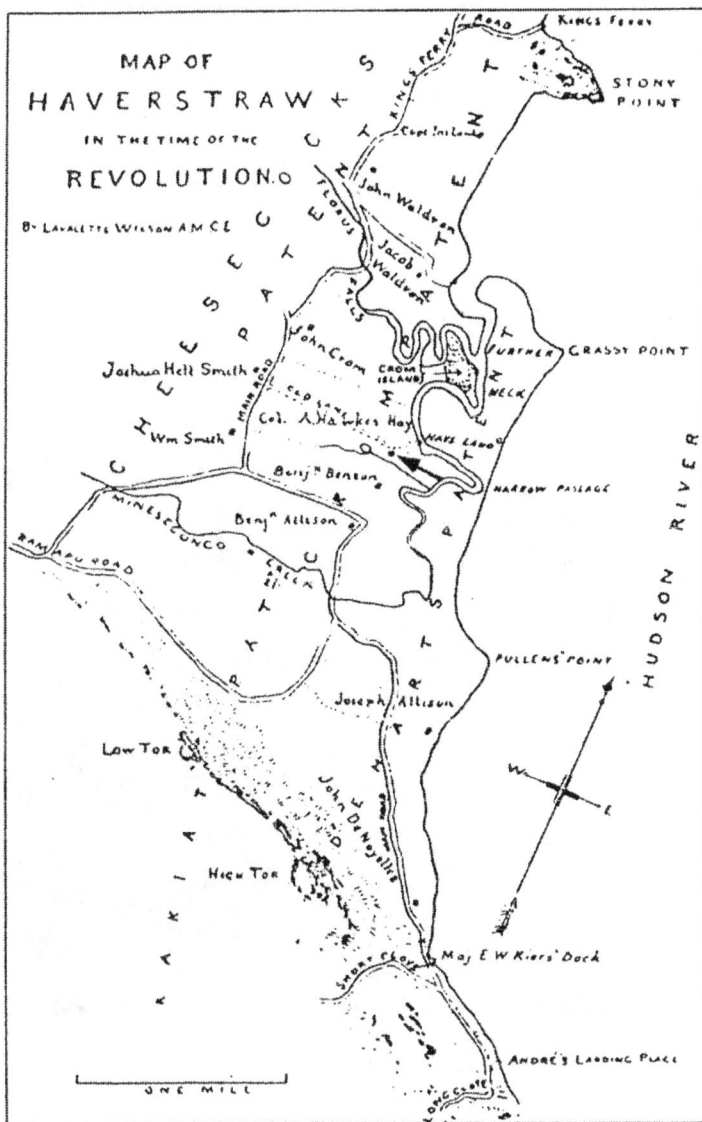

MAP OF HAVERSTRAW
IN THE TIME OF THE REVOLUTION

Joseph Allison and his sons, while attempting to work their farm and feed their families, were constantly pressed into duty to patrol the banks of the Hudson. They served as minutemen in the Orange County Militia, a small force that came from all parts of Rockland County. Colonel A. Hawks Hay, a neighbor, whose land was separated from Joseph Allison by only one other farm, led them. This small group of about 300 men was stretched in a thin line, attempting to guard the many miles extending north and south of the Allison farm.

While rekindling the spirit of the American cause at that difficult time, the Declaration of Independence signed in the summer of 1776 created havoc in Haverstraw. It completely segregated those loyal to the mother county from the patriots. For the Allisons, it brought the war as close as the next farm. With events tilting victory to the English side, loyalists were becoming more aggressive and actually pillaging the farms of their neighbors. The Tory estates of the Lambs, the Smiths, and even Joseph's nephews, who were now enemies, adjoined the Joseph Allison farm.

Joshua Hett Smith, a spy for the British Army, lived on the main road about one farm away from Joseph Allison. The treason of Benedict Arnold took place at his house. Smith brought Major John Andre ashore from the British sloop Vulture, which was moored out on the Hudson, to a landing place about two miles south of the Allison farm. During the night, they traveled past the Allisons to meet Arnold and plot for the surrender of West Point.

Joseph Allison's land along the river remained at the crossroads of much conflict for most of the war. In the summer of 1776, a British fleet sailed 40 miles up the Hudson to anchor in Haverstraw Bay. Shore parties began pillaging crops, burning homes and stealing cattle. Homes on both sides of Joseph were razed by the marauders. The DeNoyelles house on the south and the home of Colonel Hay, Commander of the Militia, were both burned to the ground. Most Rockland Co. men between ages of 16 and 60 were in the militia and continuously dashed from their homes to drive off the invaders. Constantly on duty and expecting an invasion by the main Redcoat Army moving north, they were unable to harvest the grain when it ripened. At the end of the year, it was feared that many of the minutemen would desert to return to their farms. Many had left their families without shoes for the winter and wood and fodder for their cattle.

British raids on Haverstraw intensified in 1777. The precarious position of the Hudson Highlands required stronger defensive action. Regular troops began to arrive to back up the beleaguered citizen soldiers. The Continental Army began building a fortification on the river 12 miles north of Haverstraw' It was called Fort Montgomery, after General Richard Montgomery who fell at the Battle of Quebec.

Grassy Point, Haverstraw, New York at time of the Revolution

Later that year, a British force of two thousand landed at Kings Ferry, only three miles north of the Allison farm, to attack the fort. The American defenders were vastly outnumbered at the incomplete fortifications and expected the attack to come from the river and not from the rear, over land. Joseph's son, John, a corporal in the 5th New York Regiment, was with a company of thirty men who were the first to engage the British force. Before day's end, corporal John and son-in-law Amos Hutchings both narrowly escaped being killed. William Willis, another son-in-law, was listed as missing.

For the next five years, the war seesawed across the Haverstraw area. At times, Rockland was virtually occupied by the British. Joseph's niece, Mary Storms Allison was interrupted at a quilting bee by a British foraging party. She leveled her gun on the lower half of her kitchen door and emptied the barrels of a musket into them. In 1778, American forces under General Anthony Wayne, commanding a Pennsylvania Regiment defeated the British forces in a surprise attack at Stony Point, a fort three miles north of the Allison home. While local patriots served as scouts, no Orange County troops were reported to have taken part in this rare, early, American victory.

American forces often passed along the main road, which ran along the side of Joseph's farm. It was the main highway north to Kings Ferry. Washington's Army camped in Haverstraw Precinct and in Smith's Clove, a mountain pass to the west. In the later years of the war, action shifted from the Hudson Highlands to other parts of the colonies. In 1781, Joseph and his family witnessed the New York troops pass their farm on the way to the final victory at Yorktown. His son John was among them.

In 1781, Joseph and his neighbors founded Haverstraw's first church, the First Presbyterian, and erected a meetinghouse in 1789. For the previous 60 years, residents had the option of going to the Old English Church in New Hempstead, four miles away, or the Dutch Church in Tappan. Joseph Allison, Matthew Benson, Amos Hutchings, and five other Allisons are listed among the founders.

Joseph died in 1796, and his lengthy will provided for everyone in his large family. The surviving sons of his marriage to Elizabeth Benson, John, William and Joseph, were previously given a large portion of his land in 1793, with the proviso that they sell it for 600 pounds. The will also provided for his second wife, Elsie Parcells, and the remaining 12 children and six grandchildren. Elsie and John D. Coe were executors. Joseph was first buried in the old Allison burial grounds on Grassy Point near the river. Remains were later removed to Mount Repose Cemetery. His monument stands high on the hill overlooking Haverstraw and the former Allison estates. The names of all of his children are on the stone.

Joseph Allison's life spanned two wars. He began his military career by serving England but became a staunch patriot for the cause of liberty. The Revolutionary War profoundly impacted his life and that of his sons. They had to defend their homes from the British invaders and served in the Continental Line and as minutemen. During these turbulent times he provided for a large family and served his community and church.

The homes of Joseph B. Allison and Benjamin Allison date from the mid-18th century. These sketches, made in the mid-19th century, include additions to the original houses. From Cole, *History of Rockland County, New York:*

HOMESTEAD OF JOSEPH B. ALLISON.
BUILT 1760.

BENJAMIN ALLISON. HOUSE.
Built 1754.

Treason House. Home of Loyalist Joshua Hett Smith, Route 9W Haverstraw, New York.
Meeting place of British spy Major John Andre and Benedict Arnold in 1780. Razed 1920.

NOTES & SOURCES

Morrison, Barlow Genealogies, Cole, Green Histories of Rockland County.

Historical Record of Rockland A.S. Thompkins 1902, Now and Then and Long Ago" Cornelia Bedell, 1941, Tombstone Mt Repose Cemetery, Haverstraw, New York.

Court of Appeals Records, Orange County. Supreme Court, Surrogates Court, NYC, Haverstraw Indian Deeds - Budke Collection-BC88.

Note: Most of birth death and marriage for the Haverstraw Allisons were provided to Rev. David Cole for his "History of Rockland County" 1884, by George S Allison of Haverstraw, 1792-1884 and William O Allison born 1849 of Englewood, New Jersey.

Cole, Budke-list of militia officers, 1763, Will Abstracts Orange/Rockland 1785-1815: Mt Repose Cemetary, Haverstraw; List of Orange County Soldiers, Loescher; Morrison.

Gleanings From Rockland County History, 1780-1980, The Historical Society of Rockland.

County, 20 Zukor Road, New City NY, 1980.

Talman,Wilfred Blanch. How Things Began in Rockland County and Places Nearby, Historical Society of Rockland County, 1977.

JOHN ALLISON 12. vi (CORPORAL, CONTINENTAL ARMY 1775-1783) AND SARAH DeNOYELLES

John Allison 12. vi, born 12 May 1754 Haverstraw, NY; son of Captain Joseph Allison and Elizabeth Benson; died 22 January 1828 Monroe, NY; married Sarah DeNoyelles/DeNoailles/Noyell/Noll about 1776-1778; born 1751, parentage unknown; died 1821-1828. Six children, born in Haverstraw, all except Elizabeth, moved to Monroe N.Y with parents 1801:

i   Elizabeth, born about 1777; married Peter Hoffman. Heir of John Allison on an 1838 land bounty record with other siblings. Appears to have married before 1800 and did not migrate with family to Monroe. The 1810 Census of Haverstraw shows the Peter Hoffmann family with five children under 10 years of age. Children unknown.

ii   Anthony, born 1780; died after 1850; married Mary _____ born 1791; died 1865 Orange Co. NY; migrated to Paterson, NJ 1820-1825, blacksmith. Four children: Catherine, born 1814, died 1856, married Ephriam Ward; Mary, born 1814, died 1887, married Stephen Cooper; John, born 1811 or 1816, died after 1860, married (1) Eliza Blakely (2) Mahala _____; Isaac, born 1821, died after 1860, married Mary Jane Clark.

iii   John Jr., born about 1782; died after 1840, Monroe NY; married Deborah _____. Private Orange County Militia, War of 1812. Four sons and one daughter, born before 1820 names unknown.

iv   Sarah, born about 1782; died 4 August 1863; married Matthias Brooks born 14 March 1780; died 16 May 1842, Orange Co Militia, War of 1812. Both buried at Cemetery of the Highlands, Rt. 32, Woodbury/Monroe NY Tombstones still there. Matthias was son of John Brooks and Martha Burndage. He owned Lot 19, previously owned by his father-in-law John Allison. Eight Children: Andrew, born 1808, married Mary Thorne; John, born 1809/10, married Emmeline Thorne; Peter, born 1813; Hannah, born 1815, married Nathan Pembleton; William, born 1817, married Phebe Jane Rumsey; Elizabeth Ann, born 1820, married Jesse Ryder; Charles, born 1824, married Sarah Case; Catherine, born 1826, married William Case.

13. v   WILLIAM (direct ancestor), born 1791; died after1840; married _____, born about 1800 Orange Co. Migrated from Monroe, NY to Paterson, NJ in 1827. Six children.

vi   Alexander, born 1792; died July 1867 Monroe, married Catherine E. _____, born 1807, NY, living in Colchester, Delaware Co. NY in 1810. Orange Co. Militia, War of 1812 (1814) Belnaps Regiment. 1850 Census of Monroe shows six children: John J., Catherine, William, Charles E., Sarah J., George O.

John Allison was a patriot who joined the Continental Army in 1775, a year before the Declaration of Independence was signed. He served for the entire eight years of the war. In 1801, he moved with his family from Haverstraw, Rockland County to Monroe in Orange County. He also served in the Orange County Militia in the War of 1812. Before 1798, Rockland was part of Orange and all records refer to the area as Orange.

ANCESTRY AND EARLY LIFE

John grew up on the large farm of his father, Captain Joseph Allison. The land was on the banks of the Hudson at Haverstraw, about 30 miles north of New York City. Joseph was a Captain in the Orange County militia during the French and Indian War in the late 1760s. He inherited the extensive tract from his father, John Allison (Sr.), one of the original English settlers who came over from Hempstead, Long Island, in 1719. This land, known as Grassy Point, extended about two miles along the riverbank and covered all the area now occupied by the town of Haverstraw.

John Allison had nine brothers and sisters and seven half-brothers and sisters. He was probably baptized at the "Old English Church" in Hempstead, about two miles away. It was the only English-speaking church in the area at that time. Few records for this church have survived. His birth date has been passed down from nineteenth century family records. His mother Elizabeth died in 1767 when he was age 13.

On July 17, 1775 John, together with his father, Captain Joseph Allison, and several other Allison family members, signed an "Association" pledging support for independence. At this early stage in the war, with the American victories at Lexington, Concord and Ticonderoga, a patriotic fervor was sweeping through the colonies. The news quickly reached Haverstraw that the American Army was advancing north, unopposed, up the Hudson Valley to invade Canada. It was the first offensive campaign for the new nation. The colonies were winning the war and had proven that untrained farmers could stand their ground against the seasoned professional soldier of the British Army, considered to be the best in the world at that time. Unfortunately, these events, which portended an early end to the war, were short-lived.

A CALL TO ARMS, 1775

On July 20, only three days after signing the "Association," John Allison joined the 10th Company of the 3rd Regiment of Foot, New York Continental Line, at Clarkstown, about five miles from his home in Haverstraw. The company of seventy-two soldiers was led by Captain Robert Johnson. Colonel James Clinton commanded all four New York Regiments. Enlistments at the time extended only to the end of the year, so new recruits only committed to a little over six months of service. This short enlistment time would devastate the new army at the end of the year when, at a critical time, large numbers of the volunteers simply walked home.

John, the son of a local militia captain, was the perfect recruit. He was young, single and physically fit from a strenuous life of farming without the labor saving implements of later years. A muster roll, from August 4, 1775, describes him as a laborer. At five-foot-ten inches, he was one of the tallest men in the company. He had brown hair and eyes and a complexion deeply tanned from toiling in the fields since early spring.

The 10th Company appears to be a hastily cobbled together group with some out of town men and late arrivals. This may explain its lack of cohesion in the months that followed. It consisted of mainly laborers and farmers, but about one third had trades or skills. All but a few were between ages 18 and 25. Three of John Allison's cousins, another John, age 35, and Thomas, age 28 and Richard appear on the 10th Company muster rolls.

John Allison does not fit the profile of the typical enlisted soldier of the time. His signature on military and land records during his lifetime is evidence that he was literate and he was in position to inherit substantial property from his father, Joseph. Although having the accepted credentials, he chose not to become an officer. Perhaps this was because of the five-year commitment that was required.

CONTINENTALS — 1775.

A Muster Roll of the men Raised and Pass'd Muster in the County of *Orange* for Capt. *Johnston's* Company 4th August 1775

Robert Johnston Captain   [Misc. papers, 34–137.]   *Jnᵒ. Mavritius Goetschius* } Lieutenants
                                                  Philip Dubois Bevier

MENS NAMES.	Day of enlistment.	Age.	Where born.	Trade.	Officers who enlisted.	Feet	Inches	Complexion.	Eyes.	Hair.
W'm Martin	July 17	20	Jersey	Carpenter	Capt. Johnston	5	10	Sandy	Blue	Sandy
John Ackerson	do 16	24	Orange Co.	Farmer	do	6	....	Fresh.	do	Fair, marded with the Small Pox
Zephaniah Miller	do 24	26	do	Blacksmith	do	5	10	Brown	do	Black, a few Small Pox
Philip McQueen	do 20	24	do	Labourer	do	5	7	Fair	do	Brown, Smooth fas't
John Lesler	do 24	24	Pennsilvania	Shoemaker	do	6	...	do	do	Fair, Smooth fas't, a scar on right cheek
David Babcock	do 13	22	Orange Co.	Farmer	do	5	9	Fresh.	do	Brown, Smooth fas'd
Peter Carmichel	do 25	21	Pensilvania	Cooper	do	5	7	Fair.	Brown	do, a scarr on his right face & neck
John Ozburn	do 19	18	Orange Co.	Farmer	do	5	8	do	do	Brown Freckled
Corn's Bradley	do 12	23	N. Britain	do	do	5	5	Brown	do	Black
John Clark	do 11	18	Orange Co.	Fuller	do	5	8	do	do	do
Isaac Monnel	do 22	22	Orange	Farmer	do	5	9	do	Blue	Brown, A Scar above ye Right Eye
Tho's Fergyson	do 16	26	Westchester	do	do	5	11	do	do	Black, A Scar on Left upper Lip
Ruttes Stephens	do 22	31	Orange	do	do	6	11	Fair	do	Black, Smooth Fas't
Andw Cable	Aug. —	27	Germany	Cooper	do	6	1	do	Brown	Brown
Edle Ackerman	July 22	27	N York	Weaver	do	5	6	do	do	Fair, Pock marked
And'w Houser	do 27	21	Orange Co.	Blacksmith	do	5	8	do	Blue	Black
Abr'n Blauvelt	do 15	22	do	Weaver	do	5	8	do	Gray	Brown
Dao'l Ward	do 16	22	East Jersey	Cordwainer	do	5	7	Sandy	Blue	do
Tho's Jackas	do 11	39	England	Taylor	do	5	10	Fair	Gray	do
W'm Yeomans	do 17	28	Orange	Farmer	do	5	8	Sandy	do	Sandy
Benj'n Ackerson	po 25	23	do	do	do	5	11	Fair	do	Brown
Stephen Bloks	do 20	21	W. Chester	Blacksmith	do	5	11	do	Blue	Sandy
Tho's Ackerson	do 27	23	Orange	Farmer	do	5	7	Brown	Brown	Black, A mole on left side of chin
Tho's Kelley	do 27	26	do	do	do	5	5	do	Blue	Brown, Scar above left eye brow
Abr'n Van Kempen	do 31	23	Pensylvania	B Smith	do	5	10	Fair	do	Fair
John Bogard	do 27	22	Orange	Farmer	do	5	11	do	do	do
James Secaur (?)	do 14	23	do	Cordwainer	do	6	0	do	do	Brown
John Cooper	do 16	32	do	Farmer	do	6	1	do	do	do
Sam'l Conklin	do 29	28	do	do	do	5	9	do	do	do
John Ellison	do 20	35	do	do	do	5	11?	Brown	do	do
Sam'l Garitson	do 29	24	do	do	do	6	...	do	do	Black, Pock mark'd
Dan'l Parker	do 17	20	W. Chester	do	do	5	7	Fair	do	Brown
Stephen Conklin	do 20	21	Orange	do	do	5	8	do	do	do
John D. Coe Sr	do 17	21	do	do	do	5	9	do	do	do
Garit Cole	do 29	20	W. Chester	do	do	5	6	do	do	Light brown
Peter Retan	do 20	22	M. County, Jersey	Mason	do	5	8	do Red	do	Brown curled, Pock Pitted
John C. Cooper	do 20	32	Orange	Cordwainer	do	5	6	do	do	Fair
Tompkins Odle	do 19	26	W. Chester	Laborer	do	6	4	do	do	Black, Scar in Forehead
David Morgan	do 21	20	Connecticut	do	do	5	10	do	Blue	Fair
Abram Cooper	do 20	27	Orange	Cordwainer	do	6	..	Brown.	do	Black
Jacob Mott	do 26	23	do	Farmer	do	6	4	Fair.	do	Fair
Peter Ellison	do 25	23	do	do	do	5	10	do	do	Black, A Scarr on ye Right Cheek
Mordica Mott	do 25	30	do	Blacksmith	do	5	9	do	do	Fair
John McVey	do 31	26	Ireland	Laborer	do	5	3	do	do	Brown
David Huffman	do 31	24	Orange	do	do	5	5	Brown	Black	Black, Scar in ye forehead
Edward Cone	do 16	25	Ireland	do	do	5	9	Sandy	Blue	Brown
James Burges	do 20	24	Orange	Weaver	do	5	7	Fair	Darkish	Black
Edward Warren	do 22	21	East Jersey	Mason	do	5	4	do	Blue	Fair
Jabez Fowler	do 22	21	do	Blacksmith	do	5	4	do	do	do A Scarr near ye Left Eye
Egbert D. Van Zall	do 24	45	do	Cordwainer	do	5	7	do	do	Fair & Pock Pitted
Cornelius Smith Jr	do 16	26	Orange	Carpenter	do	5	7	do	do	Fair
Rob't Frayer	do 29	30	England	Schoolmaster	do	5	6	Black	Black	Black, One Scarr on ye Left Cheek
Joseph Wood	do 19	20	East Jersey	Laborer	do	5	9	Fair	Blue	Fair
John Ellison	do 20	21	Orange	do	do	5	10	Brown	do	Sandy
John Conelio	Aug. 4	10	East Jersey	do	do	5	..	do	do	Black
Isaac Secaur	July 22	19	Orange	do	do	5	8	Brown	Black	Black, a Scarr in ye forehead
Simon Trump	do 16	48	Germany	Carpenter	do	5	6	do	Blue	Black
James Tenuer	do 25	19	W. Chester	Weaver	do	5	8	Sandy	do	Red
John Haycock	do 20	46	N. York	Laborer	do	5	8	Fair	do	Fair
Corn's Nicks	Aug. 1	20	East Jersey	do	do	5	9	do	do	Black
Jacob Hallstead	July 19	21	Orange	do	do	5	5	Brown	do	do Pock Pited
Pawles Milcbier	Aug. 4	33	Germany	do	do	5	8	do	Black	do
John Springsteel	July 26	33	Orange	do	do	5	7	do	Blue	do
Timothy Town	do 26	18	do	do	do	5	5	do	Black	do
David Condum	Aug. 3	50	Ireland	do	do	5	7	do	do	do
Rich'd Dawson	July 4	26	England	do	do	5	4	do	Brown	do Hair Lipp
Pater Burges	do 18	22	Orange	do	do	5	8	Fair	do	do
Harmanus Kisler	do 28	18	do	do	do	5	9	do	Blue	Brown
Tho's Ellison	do 20	28	do	do	do	5	8	do	Black	Black
John Stuert	Aug. 5	34	Ireland	do	do	5	8	Brown	Black	Black
John Jiffler	July 17	23	Jersey	Carpenter	do	5	6	Fair	Blue	Brown
Tho's Alver	Aug. 1	28	Ireland	Laborer	do	5	7	Brown	Black	Black

(handwritten note beside John Ellison row: "COUSIN OF JOHN")

CANADA MUST BE OURS, 1775

There was an urgent need for fresh troops to move up the Hudson Valley to the front. The invasion of Canada, led by Generals Richard Montgomery and Philip Schuyler, had already begun. After only two weeks of training, and lacking weapons, uniforms and equipment, John's company trudged north on a two -week, 200-mile forced march. The new soldiers passed through Albany and headed for the staging area at Fort Ticonderoga. Food was already in short supply and the more aggressive of John's hungry comrades were raiding farms along the way to supplement their meager rations.

Desertions began as the troops moved further north. Many of the new soldiers, although still far from the enemy and without firing a shot, became disenchanted with the discipline of military life and started to go home. By the time the 10th company reached Ticonderoga on September 21st, it had already lost 23 men, almost one-third of its total. Among those who went missing were John's cousins, Thomas and Richard Allison. Richard, a corporal, had two brothers who were loyalists fighting with the British Army in Canada. Did he dread facing them in battle?

During the first week in October, John's untested unit moved into combat. Clinton's regiments traveled 80 miles north of Ticonderoga by bateaux, 30 -foot boats, rowed by eight men. They attacked the well-fortified Fort St. Johns, at the northern end of Lake Champlain. Here they joined 1,300 other American troops. The 200 "Yorkers" were immediately sent to build a new battery that was under constant heavy cannon bombardment. Led personally by James Clinton, they were able to erect a new emplacement in spite of taking heavy casualties, but. Cannons were immediately mounted into position to break the stalemate and turn the tide of the battle. This valiant action by the New York Brigade led directly to the unconditional surrender of the fort by British forces two weeks later.

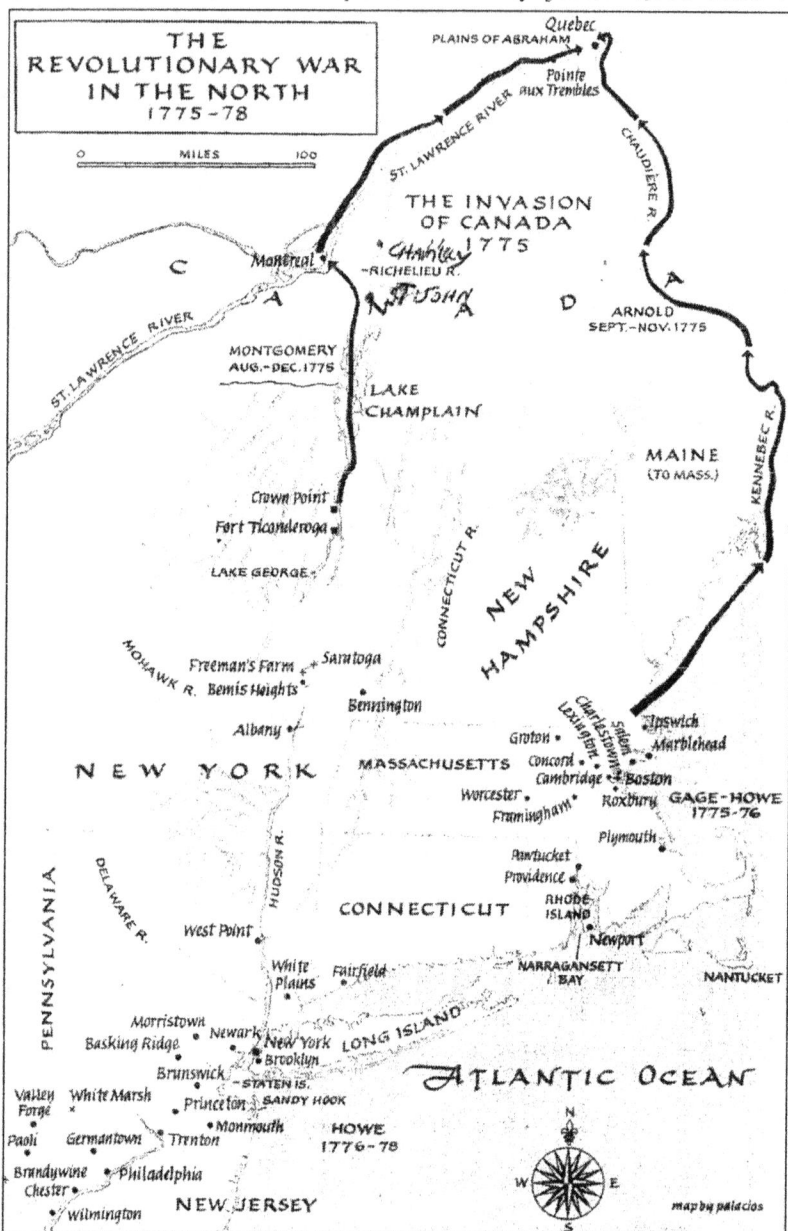

After the fall of St. John, Private John Allison's 10th company, led by Captain Robert Johnson, was probably merged with other undermanned units. It disappears from the military records of the Canadian Campaign at that time. Tracking units and individual soldiers is difficult during this early and turbulent period in the war. Colonial troops were constantly on the move and companies and regiments were often reorganized as troop strength diminished. It is likely that John Allison, with other survivors of the 10th, continued to march north from St. John through ice, snow, and mud, to occupy the City of Montreal, in November of 1775.

John's pension application, written in 1818, shows that he fought at Fort St. Johns but does not mention Montreal or the major battle of Quebec that followed. This indicates that he may have remained in Montreal as part of the Garrison left to defend the City, while other troops continued up the river to attempt to capture the City of Quebec. Some evidence indicates that he did reach Quebec. The name of company commander, Captain Robert Johnston appears on a list of New York officers in Canada on February 28, 1776. Another document shows that Robert Johnston was appointed Captain of the 4th Company, Colonel Nicholson's Regiment, on April, 15 1776 at "Headquarters before Quebec." The men of the 10th company may have remained with their leader.

42

The attack on Quebec was a tragic American defeat. The popular General Montgomery was killed attempting to storm the walls of the city during a raging snowstorm. This setback stopped the American advance and ended Patriot hopes of annexing Canada. British forces received reinforcements from England and over the next year could move back south, down the lakes and the Hudson Valley, to divide the colonies and put an end to the American rebellion.

The patriotic euphoria that had swept the colonies, when John had enlisted, less than a year before, soon turned to gloom and helplessness. About a third of the 3rd Regiment soldiers did not reenlist at the end of the year. At that time, John Allison and his comrades, considering their enlistment obligation over, left Montreal for the long trek south to their homes in Orange County. During the spring of 1776, entire companies, from the New York Regiments, with enlistments expiring, were released from service.

MINUTEMEN AT WAR, 1776

Back home around the fireside in the early months of 1776, he must have recounted his adventures on the ill-fated invasion of Canada to eager family listeners. He probably described the long sail up the lakes, his days on the east battery at the 50 day siege of Fort St. Johns and the triumphant march into Montreal. His enthralled audience probably included Sarah DeNoyelles. She was from the large Patriot family that owned the southern half of Grassy Point.

He married Sarah in 1776. This time estimate is based on the birth of their first child, Elizabeth, in 1777. John DeNoyelles or DeNoailles was an officer in the British Army who served in New York in 1754. In 1760, after he left the army he purchased the land on Grassy Point and shared the three-mile stretch on the Hudson with the Allison farm.

Sarah was too old to have been his daughter and was likely his niece. John's brothers Pierre and Edward also migrated to America and she was probably the daughter of one of them. She was born in either France or New York City in 1751. Her age is based on John Allison's pension application in 1821. It states that, "he had a wife about seventy." The exact details of her birth remain a mystery.

John DeNoyelles died in 1775 at age 41. He left his widow, Rachel Shatford, with five children, which included three sons less than 10 years of age. Rachel must have warmly welcomed her 23-year-old niece, Sarah, into the household to help with the family. During this time Sarah met the young soldier John Allison.

John may have remained in the regular army during the spring of 1776. Captain Robert Johnson was stationed at nearby Clarkstown. This indicates that John's company may have stayed together after returning from Canada. At some point during 1776, John left the Continental Army and joined the Orange County Militia.

His service as a minuteman allowed little time to spend with his family or help with the spring planting or fall harvest. The frequent absence of his father, Joseph, and his eldest brother, Joseph, who were also minutemen, left the family short-handed. Most able-bodied were drafted into the militia to patrol the banks of the Hudson. John Allison was in the 2nd Company, Orange County Militia. Colonel A. Hawks Hay, a close Allison neighbor, commanded this small force of 300 men. These civilian soldiers were charged with defending the 24 miles of riverbank, from Stony Point, New York, to Fort Lee, New Jersey. Half of them were without weapons. Those that were armed were probably veterans of the Continental Army who had left with their weapons, a problem that frustrated Washington.

The Orange County Militia was constantly engaged against the British forces that were headquartered in New York City. They British threatened occupation and sent raiding parties to steal cattle and pillage and burn homes in Haverstraw Precinct. In 1777 they invaded the Hudson Valley. Loyalists from the area joined the British and served as scouts for the enemy. While the Allison home was spared, but homes on both sides of their farm were burnt to the ground. John's uncle, Benjamin Benson, was killed by marauders while repairing his roof on the adjoining farm. With no respite to tend their farms, the families of the minutemen had little food or winter clothing.

Because of the pivotal position of New York and the Hudson Highlands, George Washington decided to build forts to defend the river above Haverstraw. He also added a new fifth regiment to the existing four from the state. Colonel Lewis Dubois was appointed to command the New York 5th Regiment, Continental Line. Dubois chose Amos Hutchings, the leader of the Haverstraw Militia, as captain with a warrant to raise a company of 90 men. Amos was the husband of John Allison's older sister, Mary. As a local hero, he must have been a mentor for John, his 22-year-old brother-in-law. John's father, Joseph, also a former militia captain, was also a role model.

Recruiting lagged painfully for Hutchings. After two months he had only enlisted 46 men. The hardships, cold and hunger of the Canadian Campaign were still fresh in the minds of the veterans who may have discouraged new recruits. John Allison was a seasoned combat veteran and a prime prospect for Amos. He must have used strong persuasion on his younger relative to convince him to reenlist. Another brother-in law, William Willis, and his cousin, the other John Allison, also joined Amos Hutching's company as privates.

John was probably motivated to reenlist in the Continental Army again because of the deteriorating situation, which endangered his family and home. The Tory enemy was as far as the next farm and the entire British Army was poised to invade the Hudson River valley from the north and the south. The main American Army under Washington was losing battle after battle in 1776 as it was driven from Brooklyn to Harlem to White Plains and across New Jersey.

REDCOATS CLOSE THE TRAP, 1776-1777

On February 12, 1777, John Allison again went to Clarkstown and reenlisted for "three years or the duration of the war." Soldiers signing up during these early years of the war interpreted these vague terms as whichever event occurred first. With his combat experience and literacy, he was appointed corporal in Hutchings 2nd Company and ordered to report to the new twin forts of Montgomery and Clinton, six miles north of Haverstraw.

These forts, undermanned and still under construction, were at a narrow point where the Hudson River was only a few hundred yards wide. This was a very strategic site for the defense of the new nation. The Hudson and the lakes north of it formed a water highway that stretched all the way to Canada. If the British could occupy this corridor, New England would be split from the other colonies and the patriots could be easily beaten. Colonel Dubois, with 600 men of the 5th New York and nearby militia troops, was all that stood between Manhattan and the St. Lawrence River.

When he reported at Fort Montgomery, John was greeted by Amos and old comrades, neighbors and relatives. Many of them had been with him in the Canadian Campaign. Many in the company bore the names of early settlers of Rockland County. Despite their precarious position, the troops at the twin forts enjoyed a good quality of life during the spring and summer of 1777. John could visit home, less than a day's wagon ride away. Archeology at Fort Montgomery has uncovered the remains of two story barracks, complete with fireplaces and glass windows.

During this time, the men of the 5th Regiment were kept busy patrolling the riverbank and constructing the outer defenses and apprehending Tories. Militia, from the nearby countryside, also stationed at the forts and often went home to take care of their crops and families. Some were considered deserters but most returned and were accepted back without question or with token punishment.

THE SKIRMISH AT DOODLETOWN, OCTOBER 6, 1777

At this critical time in the nation's history, Corporal John Allison and his fellow patriots of the 2nd company played a key role in the ensuing Battle of Fort Montgomery. On the morning of October 6, 1777, 2,100 British assault troops, shrouded by dense fog, landed at Stony Pont, six miles south of the forts. This was a surprise attack by land to strike at the rear of the forts and not from the river, as the defenders had expected.

At 10:00 AM, John Allison's company of about 30 men was sent on a reconnaissance patrol to find out the location and size of the British forces. 34-year-old Lieutenant Patton Jackson led the unit. They moved south along Old Haverstraw Road to try to learn the enemy movements and strength. The 2nd Company had been selected for this perilous mission because of its high number of seasoned combat veterans such as John Allison. Most of the men lived in this part of Orange County and knew the terrain and mountain passes through the rugged wilderness. John had often passed through here on previous patrols and on visits home.

The small detachment moved cautiously, about two miles down the road, where they reached a stream at the crossroads hamlet of Doodletown. Here, they came upon advanced elements of the British army, hidden in the heavy foliage. Facing overwhelming numbers, in an amazing display of courage the brave little band stood fast and from only 25 yards away attacked with a withering barrage of musket fire. When the enemy saw that there were so few men, they returned the gunfire from their concealed positions. Three of John Allison's comrades fell in the sharp exchange of musket fire. At that moment, the surviving 27 Patriots learned that they were facing the large Redcoat Army.

These were the first shots fired in the Battle of Fort Montgomery. When the sounds of this gunfire were heard back at the forts, it immediately alerted the defenders that the assault had begun. Drums were ordered to beat to arms and defensive measures were taken to shift men and artillery to the unfinished rear of the forts. Patton Jackson and his men also observed that the British were following the advice of local Tories by dividing their force at Doodletown to strike the forts on two fronts. This critical intelligence was quickly relayed back to the defenders. The enemy had lost the advantage of surprise.

As the 2nd Company fell back, they made another stand from behind a stone fence, less than a mile from the rear of the forts. For a brief time they stood alone, holding off the 1,200 Redcoats who had split off at Doodletown to attack Fort Clinton.

AT THE TWIN FORTS, OCTOBER 6, 1777

Back at the forts, John Allison and other survivors of the 2nd company joined other defenders stretched out in a thin line and clustered in redoubts. The battle raged throughout the day. The 5th Regiment and supporting militia troops drove back massed bayonet charges by disciplined British regulars, Hessian, and Loyalist units, by spraying them with grapeshot from their cannons. Unable to dislodge the outnumbered patriots, British commanders offered the beleaguered defenders a chance to surrender at 5:00 PM. The terms were "surrender or die by the bayonet." American General George Clinton, not to be intimidated, made the enemy a similar counter offer. By early evening, the defenders had taken heavy losses and were finally overwhelmed by a massive bayonet charge.

FORT MONTGOMERY
LAST STAND OF AMERICAN MILITIA, IN THE DEFENSE OF FORTS CLINTON & MONTGOMERY AGAINST THE BRITISH, OCTOBER 6, 1777

By nightfall, the British had killed or captured about half of the 5th Regiment and militia troops. The intrepid 2nd Company was decimated. Eighteen of the thirty men were listed as missing. Patton Jackson was taken prisoner, as was the only other Lieutenant, John Furman. Of its eight sergeants and corporals, four were lost. General James Clinton and Colonel Dubois were wounded while escaping. John Allison luckily escaped by falling back into the surrounding woods in the darkness or sliding down the steep cliff to the river.

While the capture and destruction of the Twin Forts was viewed at the time as a devastating defeat, actually it was a strategic success. History credits the event as having a significant effect on the outcome of the entire Revolutionary War. If the British forces had not been delayed at the Twin Forts, Sir Henry Clinton coming north from New York City could have swept up the Hudson Valley to join Burgoyne at Saratoga. These reinforcements could have tipped the scale and cost the Americans the great victory at the Battle of Saratoga. Many historians regard this triumph as the turning point of the American Revolution and the reason for the political decision in France to enter the war. Could the skirmish at Doodletown have changed history?

For over a century and a half, the site of the Twin Forts, which now is along Route 9W, at the approach to the Bear Mountain Bridge, became buried in underbrush and completely disappeared. Substantial archeology, begun in the 1930s, revealed surprisingly intact remains of the fortifications. A reenactment of the battle, attended by hundreds of people, is held in October of each year. In 2004, on the 227th anniversary of the battle, I received much unsolicited attention as the only person present descended from a veteran of the battle.

FORT MONTGOMERY BY WILLIAM WADE

From Stony Point to Fort Montgomery was only a short distance; but the route which Clinton determined to pursue, in the hope of taking the Americans by surprise, was one of the roughest and most laborious that can be conceived: it was impassable to artillery, and therefore no guns were brought; though they were marching against fortified places. It was a path across the Dunderberg, steep, winding, and so narrow that in many places not more than three men could march abreast. Two hundred resolute Yankees, posted across the path, and on the hills and rocks above it, might have checked and even destroyed the two thousand British; but the daring Putnam was away on the other side of the Hudson, and the garrisons of Forts Montgomery and Clinton never conceived it possible that regular army would take so dangerous a road. The British thus got to the crest of the mountain, and began to descend it on the other side before they were discovered, though they were many hours in performing that toilsome march. At the foot of the mountain the advanced guard stumbled upon an American detachment, which was advancing much too late for the defence of the pass. This detachment quickly retreated to the forts, and destroyed Clinton's hope of capturing them by surprise, at the approach of night; he resolved, however, to go on and trust to his muskets and bayonets. He divided his forces into two columns, one of which he sent under Colonel Campbell against Fort Montgomery, while he advanced in person to storm Fort Clinton. The attacks were made upon the two forts about sunset, at the same time, and precisely as agreed upon. The garrison of Fort Montgomery made a short resistance, in which Colonel Campbell was killed, and then abandoned their works...

The enemy had advanced to the charge in the dusk of the evening, and before they had completed their conquest it was night. But the darkness was soon partially dispersed by a most brilliant illumination, which proceeded from two frigates, two galleys, and a sloop, which the Americans had drawn up in a little inlet under the guns of the fort, and to which the crews now set fire, to prevent them from falling into the hands of the conquerors. It was a part of Clinton's plan, that Hotham should have secured this flotilla while he was engaged in storming the forts; but his scheme was baffled by another exercise of the ingenuity and great industry of the Americans, from which he suffered so much during the war.

THE HARSH YEAR, 1778

After the tragic defeat at the forts, the remnants of the 5th regiment attempted to regroup at New Windsor a few miles north and remained in the Hudson Highlands through the early months of 1778. In April, John was within a mile of his home at Kings Ferry on his way to join the main army in White Plains. Amos Hutchings probably never recovered from the slaughter at Fort Montgomery. With only 22 men left in his 2nd Company, he resigned from the army in May. The company would not have any officers for the next two years.

John Allison was reduced in rank from corporal to private on June 22, but was reinstated in August. This punishment appears to be for some minor infraction such as missing roll call or returning late from a visit home. John Wilson the only remaining corporal in the group was listed as "sick all year" and later deserted. The 5th Regiment returned to West Point in September. By the end of 1778, only 185 enlisted men remained in Colonel Lewis Dubois' Regiment.

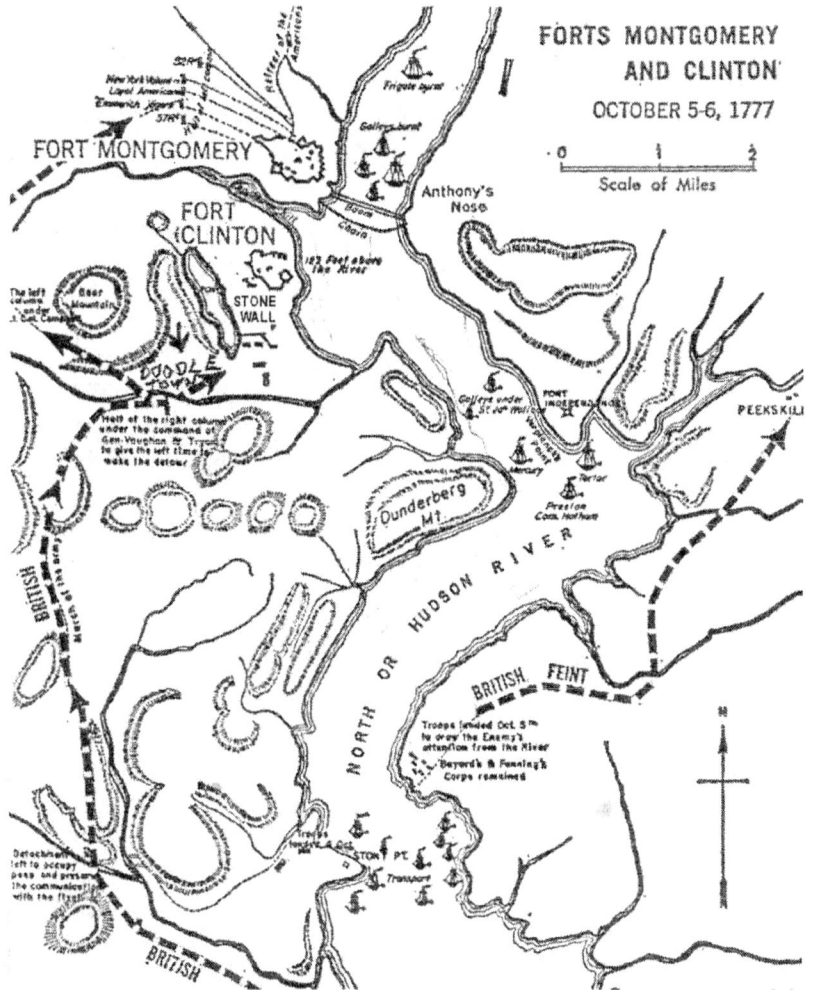

FORTS MONTGOMERY AND CLINTON
OCTOBER 5-6, 1777

THE SULLIVAN-CLINTON CAMPAIGN, 1779-1780

In 1779, brutal attacks and atrocities on settlements along the western frontier of New York by the Indians of the Iroquois Nations were increasing. The Native Americans openly sided with the British. They correctly perceived that they would have a better chance of protecting and keeping their lands under Great Britain. Washington ordered a major offensive to counter this terrorism by destroying the homes, crops, and cattle that the Indians used to sustain these raids.

To accomplish this he gambled a detachment of 5,000 men, about one third of the entire Continental Army. The force consisted of 2,300 troops under Major General John Sullivan with 1,500 men of the New York Brigade under

Brigadier General James Clinton. The two brigades would join up at Tioga, present day Athens, Pennsylvania. The New York Brigade included John Allison's 5th Regiment of 383 men. With no officers, its 2nd Company would be led through the entire campaign by Corporal John Allison and two sergeants.

The New York Brigade boarded bateaux and sailed 140 miles down Lake Oswego and the Susquehanna River to the rendezvous point at Tioga. They destroyed Indian towns along the way. The combined force then marched westward into the heartland of the Indian Nations. At the village of Newtown, six miles from Elmira, New York, the Indian defenders decided to make a stand. Commanded by their most able leaders, a force of 1,200 warriors plus Tory units and some British regulars, set up an ambush.

At the battle of Newtown, the Americans succeeded in surrounding and entrapping the enemy who retreated to the top of a hill where they were in a good position to confront the American advance. John Allison's Regiment struggled up the rear of the hill into a steady barrage of gunfire from screaming and well-armed Indians who fought from tree to tree. Terrified by the onslaught of a bayonet charge, the outnumbered Indians and Tory defenders along the ridge finally broke.

John survived the battle and his unit pressed north. The American forces continued their path of destruction until they reached the northern end of Lake Seneca. Here they turned westward toward their final objective, the capture of the Indian Nations capital at Genesee, New York. After burning 100 houses and destroying crops and fruit trees at Genesee, the victorious Americans marched 130 miles back to Tioga. With their infrastructure and unity shattered, the power of the Indian Nations was permanently destroyed.

The rigors of the Indian campaign took a toll on the men of the 5th Regiment. The Continental forces were constantly devastated by outbreaks of dysentery. By the fall of 1779, many are listed as sick on the muster rolls. John Allison is shown as "sick in the hospital" in October and November. He was probably at the field hospital in Wyoming, (Scranton), Pennsylvania. The weakened soldier then had to trek an arduous 200 miles over the mountains to winter camp, in New Jersey.

WINTER AT JOCKEY HOLLOW, 1779-1780

John Allison spent the winter of 1779-1780 at Jockey Hollow, Morristown, New Jersey. The incredible hunger and suffering that he and his comrades endured during that harsh winter, the most severe in a century, is well recorded. Twenty-eight blizzards blasted through the camp and supply roads were blocked by six-foot snowdrifts. Food supplies dwindled and starvation set in, resulting in many deaths. Desertions were rampant. Men left their posts and attacked officers. Orderly books at Morristown show that during the winter, twenty-one men received floggings of one hundred lashes. Eighteen were sentenced to be hung but most were reprieved. These appalling facts do not appear in history books. The Connecticut 1st Brigade marched out of camp, claiming their enlistments had expired.

Small huts offered little protection from the wind. The sick were covered by only a single blanket after their clothes were given to those fit for duty. Most of the officers of the 5th Regiment are shown as being on leave during the winter. The location of the huts and parade ground of the New York Brigade, where John Allison spent the winter, are clearly marked at the north end of this national park. In December, Colonel Lewis Dubois, Commanding Officer of the 5th New York, who led John Allison and his comrades for the past four years, resigned over a rank dispute.

By the spring of 1780, the American cause was on the verge of collapse. Enlistments were expiring and new men could not be recruited. Washington's entire army at Morristown was reduced to only 4000 men fit for duty. They had not been paid for five months and the paper money they would receive was almost without value. Both soldiers and those at home were completely discouraged and everyone began to doubt the success of the patriot cause.

Enduring the Morristown winter while his wife Sarah was back in Haverstraw most likely expecting their first child, prompted John Allison to send a personal letter to General Washington. He requested a discharge, claiming his enlistment had expired. His enlistment papers, and those of thousands of others, bound him to serve "for three years or until the end of the war." This was widely construed by the recruits as limiting service to whichever event should occur first. But Congress later decided that the terms required service to the end of the war.

The letter was sent on April 16, 1780, from "Camp near Morristown, to his Excellency General Washington Commander in Chief of the United States of North America, The Humble Petition of John Allison Soldier in the fifth New York Regt. In the late Captain Hutchings Company---." The request included affidavits by his former company commander, Amos Hutchings, now a civilian, and John's brother Thomas. Both claimed that his intention was to enlist only for three years. There is no evidence that the letter was ever acknowledged.

From Morristown, the 5th New York marched north through Pompton and Ramapo, and then passed by John's home near the main road through Haverstraw. He hadn't seen Sarah for several months and this may have been the first time he saw his first child, Anthony, who was born that year. The regiment continued up the Hudson River Valley by sloop from Kings Ferry to Albany and then north to the Mohawk Valley frontier.

Camp near Morristown April 16th 1780

To His Excellency Genl Washington Commander in Chief
of all the United States of North America &C. &C. &C.

The Humble Petition of John Allison Soldier in the fifth New
~~York Reg. in the late Captain~~ Hutchins Company

Most Humbly Sheweth

Whereas your Excellancies Petitioner, having only Inlisted
for the Term of three years, and that time being Expired the
first day of January last past, and Whereas I made application
to the Commanding Officer of the Reg. for my Discharge, but
Could not Obtain it, though I produced Evidence Sworn in

Writing that I was only Inlisted for three years and
no longer — which Depositions I Enclose that your Excellency
may see the fairness and Clearness of my Inlistment —
Now Please your Excellancy I implore that you would do me
Justice done in this affair and your Petitioner as in Duty
Bound shall Pray ——

N.B. As the Commanding Officer of the Reg. would give no attention to the
affidavits produced and Sworn, without the Evidences personally —
appeared — I produced them personally and yet would not
Accept of them ——

John Allison's request for discharge. 1780

50

SEASON OF DOUBT, 1779-1780

For the next two years, the war was a stalemate without any major engagements. Neither side had the strength to attack the other. During this time, John's regiment moved back and forth from the Hudson Valley to the Mohawk frontier, depending on where the enemy pressure was greatest. Attacks could come from an invasion from New York City, or from the frontier by the British-Indian alliance.

In June of 1780, the 5th New York was hastily recalled to repair the defenses at West Point, to counter a possible invasion up the Hudson. Lieutenant Colonel Marinus Willet was appointed to replace Dubois. From August through October, they were in Haverstraw and the Bergen County, New Jersey area.

In November, the New York Regiments marched north again to counter constant attacks on the New York frontier by Chief Joseph Brant's warriors, Tories and British Grenadiers. They passed through West Point and Albany to arrive at Fort Schuyler, which is now Rome, New York, in November. This fort was the furthest outpost into hostile territory. At the end of 1780, sickness, early discharge and desertion had depleted the 5th Regiment to only 263 men, with only 127enlisted men available for duty. It would be their last campaign together as a unit.

On January 1, 1781, the 5th New York was merged into the 2nd New York Regiment and ceased to exist. From the valiant stand at Fort Montgomery, the subduing of the British and Iroquois Nations on the Mohawk frontier, the brutal winter at Morristown and the confrontation with the British in New York City, the 5th New York had served honorably for the most critical four-year period of the war. John continued to serve with his new unit, the 2nd New York, commanded by Colonel Phillip Van Cortlandt, until the end of the war.

During the winter, provisions to the beleaguered Fort Schuyler, which was at the end of the supply chain, were often cut off by the enemy. The defenders there lived on half rations. Parties foraging for firewood were captured and scalped. The outpost was finally abandoned. In July of 1781, the 2nd New York marched south to Albany, and through West Point, to join General Washington and a combined American and French force of over 9000 men at Dobbs Ferry, New York.

A LONG MARCH TO YORKTOWN, 1780-1781

In August, the entire army received orders to move out. Both officers and men believed their objective was to attack New York City. After a week of secrecy, to everyone's amazement, their route turned south. When they reached central New Jersey, they learned that their destination was Yorktown, Virginia, 600 miles south. Corporal John Allison was on his way to fight in the most decisive battle in American history. It took seven days for the men, horses, wagons and cannon of the American and French forces to cross the Hudson at Kings Ferry at Haverstraw. John again passed by his home and waved at what could have been a final farewell to Sarah and his family.

The 2nd Regiment, part of General James Clinton's New York Brigade, was assigned to escort heavily loaded wagons, which included thirty flatboats. The boats, part of the feigned attack on New York City, served as an unexpected reward to the regiment. They boarded them at Trenton and sailed down the Delaware River while the rest of the army marched over land. Two weeks later, they arrived at Head of Elk (Elkton, Maryland). From there they sailed to Baltimore and boarded ships to complete the journey 175 miles down the Chesapeake Bay.

By September 24, the entire army was assembled at Williamsburg, Virginia, poised to entrap the main British Army under Lord Cornwallis on the York Peninsula. The combined American and French Armies, now totaling 16,000, encircled heavily fortified Yorktown. A French Fleet blocked any British escape to the sea.

The Battle of Yorktown was a siege with frontal assaults on the redoubts (fortified cannon emplacements). Corporal John Allison and Van Cortlandt's New Yorkers were in the thick of it. They worked day and night digging trenches

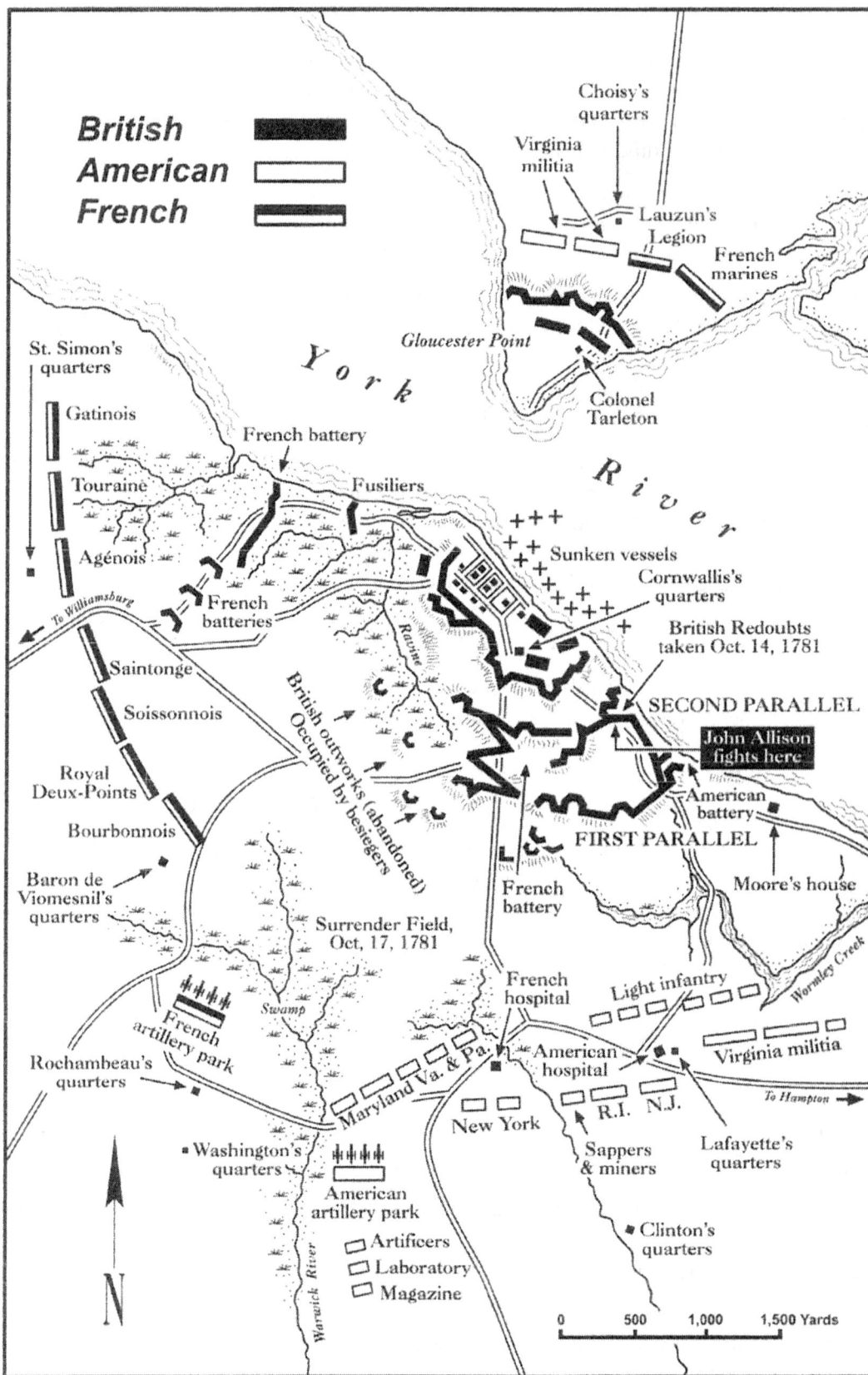

British

American

French

Choisy's
quarters

Virginia
militia

Lauzun's
Legion

French
marines

Gloucester Point

Colonel
Tarleton

Y o r k

St. Simon's
quarters

Gatinois

R i v e r

Touraine

French battery

Fusiliers

To Williamsburg

Agénois

French
batteries

+ + +
+ + +

Sunken vessels

+ + +

Cornwallis's
quarters

+ + +

Saintonge

British Redoubts
taken Oct. 14, 1781

Soissonnois

SECOND PARALLEL

Royal
Deux-Points

John Allison
fights here

Bourbonnois

American
battery

FIRST PARALLEL

Baron de
Viomesnil's
quarters

British outworks (abandoned)
Occupied by besiegers

Moore's house

Surrender Field,
Oct, 17, 1781

French
battery

Swamp

French
hospital

Light infantry

Wormley Creek

French
artillery park

Rochambeau's
quarters

Maryland Va. & Pa.

American
hospital

Virginia militia

To Hampton

New York

R.I. N.J.

Washington's
quarters

Sappers
& miners

Lafayette's
quarters

American
artillery park

Clinton's
quarters

Artificers

Laboratory

Warwick River

Magazine

0   500   1,000   1,500 Yards

N

that moved ever closer to the enemy line. The exhausting work, on the second siege line, was done under threat of sudden death from continuous cannon and small arms fire and in the midst of an outbreak of smallpox.

The battle reached a climax when a detachment of the New York Brigade, led by Colonel Alexander Hamilton, captured redoubt number 10. John was less than 100 yards away from this engagement. His 2nd Regiment waited in reserve in the event Hamilton's attack failed. American artillery then pounded the town into submission. On October 17, 1781, the British surrendered. John stood proudly in the ranks as more than 7,000 Redcoats laid down their arms and became prisoners. The surrender at Yorktown ended the last major battle of the Revolutionary War. Although it destroyed the political will in London, the British side still had two thirds of their army intact. Hostilities continued for another year and a half.

THE ROAD TO PEACE, 1781-1783

The victorious 2nd New York Regiment was assigned to escort 460 British and German prisoners north to Fredricksberg, Virginia. They then retraced their route back to New Jersey and reached winter quarters at Pompton in late December. It was a mild winter encamped on the sunny slope on the banks of the Pompton River. There were warm huts and enough food and clothing. John may have been allowed to take a brief furlough. In March he witnessed a visit to the camp by General and Mrs. Washington. On April 2nd, the New York troops were inspected by Baron Von Steuben and received high praise.

That same month John was "on Command at Smith's Clove." Where he was assigned on a patrol into the 23- mile long valley through the Hudson Highlands. The Clove served as the main line of movement and communication for the Continental Army between New Jersey and West Point. It ran parallel to the Hudson River and was regarded by Washington as equally important as controlling the river. The Clove was destined to play an important part in his future life. He would migrate with his family, over the mountains from Haverstraw, to settle there in later years.

In August 1782, Washington found time to provide recognition to the soldiers who had made such great sacrifices over the last seven years. He awarded chevrons to those who had served with bravery, fidelity and good conduct. One "hash mark" was awarded for each three years of service. John was entitled to two white stripes that denoted six years of meritorious service.

The Regiment then joined the main Continental Army at Verplanck's Point, on the Hudson, near Peekskill, where it massed for a possible attack on New York City, the last major British stronghold. John passed his home in Haverstraw once more on the way to Kings Ferry. This anticipated campaign to recapture New York City never occurred since preliminary peace negotiations had begun.

In October, the 2nd Regiment crossed back over the river again to set up camp for the winter at the New Windsor Cantonment at Newburgh, New York, about 20 miles north of Haverstraw. At New Windsor, 7,000 troops and 500 women and children built log huts and kept ready for a possible spring campaign if peace efforts failed. Grievances over back pay, land bounties and pensions brought the Army close to rebellion during this time.

Washington issued cease -fire orders on April 19, 1783, and brought the eight-year war to an end. John Allison spent seven months at the Cantonment and remained on the muster rolls through April. According to his pension application, he was finally discharged from New Windsor in June, 1783 "by General Washington." He then marched home to Haverstraw with the other proud veterans of the 2nd New York Regiment.

The Cantonment is now a state park. It has a restored headquarters area with a small museum, replica huts and Temple assembly hall. The park is also home to the National Purple Heart Association. With their ragged appearance, the tattered New York 2nd Regiment was not billeted at this center, but in a remote swampy area. Visitors at the time saw only the showpiece New England troops in their crisp new uniforms. The location of the New York huts is out of sight, along the base of I 87 the New York Thruway. I found the site in 2008 after walking several hundred yards through dense woods. Apparently, I was the only person who had been there in several years.

THE SOLDIER RETURNS, 1783-1800

After the war, John Allison age returned to Haverstraw to rejoin his wife Sarah, now with three young children, and resumed working on his father's farm for the next ten years. The life of the Allison family, from that time, is better related chronologically.

1786: On April 16, John Allison, "formerly a corporal in the 2nd Regiment, sold his land bounty rights to Samuel Coe of Haverstraw for eight pounds." Although the acreage is not given, the sale was likely for both congressional and state grants received by John and totaled 600 acres. The document was witnessed by his neighbors, Peter DeNoyelles and John Roberts. Eight pounds is the equivalent of about $16.00 today. On August 12, 1790, a patent was issued, giving Coe the right to settle on the bounty land purchased from John Allison. The land belonged to the Indians and was in Onandaga County, New York.

1790: On July 8, John Allison received a bounty land grant for another 600 acres in Montgomery County in the township of Tully, near Syracuse, designated as Lot 37. The Certificate was signed by Governor George Clinton and approved by the New York Land Office on August 12, 1790. This grant contained a provision that the land had to be settled on within seven years. There is no evidence that John had any intention of moving to this area. It was on the frontier, 140 miles west of Haverstraw and populated by hostile Indian tribes who believed they owned the land.

The year of the first Federal Census was 1790. The John Allison family was living in Haverstraw, close to several other Allisons including his father, Joseph. Other neighbors have familiar names: DeNoyelles, Benson, Hay, Smith and Crom. John Allison was recorded in the documents as the head of family with two males under age sixteen: his sons, Anthony, age ten, and John, Junior, age eight. A female over 16 was John's wife, Sarah DeNoyelles. The two other females were their daughters Elizabeth, about age 13, and Sarah, age three.

1793: John's aging father Captain Joseph Allison, conveyed to his eldest sons, John and his brothers, Joseph and William, a 103-acre parcel of the ancestral Allison farm. This land, the northern end of Grassy Point, had been in the family since 1729. It was purchased by the original Haverstraw settler John Allison Sr. Joseph retained most of his holdings for his second wife, Elsie, and numerous other children and grandchildren from both of his marriages.

The inheritance provided that the brothers sell the land and that any sum received over 600 pounds was to revert to Joseph. On April 9, 1793, the land was sold to Jacob Sabriska for five hundred and ninety pounds, about $1,200 in today's money. Even when divided into three parts, it was enough for each of the brothers to become financially independent.

Only a month after receiving his share, John bought his own 55-acre farm. The land was purchased from Peter DeNoyelles for 132 pounds. John is described in the deed as a yeoman. The document refers to "Sally" (Sarah) as the wife of John Allison. The farm bordered his father's land on the northwest.

1799: A Haverstraw tax roll for this year shows that John Allison owned a house and farm valued at $484 and had personal property of $84. His tax that year was 56 cents or one per cent of his total assets.

1800: The second Federal Census shows John and Sarah living in Haverstraw. John, age 46, appears with his wife and five children. Elizabeth apparently left the household to marry before this year. The family still lived in close proximity to other Allisons and DeNoyelles.

MIGRATION WEST, 1800-1828

1801: The Allison children were coming of age, and the 55-acre farm in Haverstraw could not support the growth of what would soon become multiple households. Over the mountains, in a sparsely settled locale of western Orange County, acreage was available at low prices. The Allisons decided to leave Haverstraw to find enough land to support the anticipated growth of their family. "John Allison, Yeoman," appears on a list of jurors that year. This is the last evidence we have of him in Haverstraw.

The reason for the migration of John and Sarah appears to be economic. It must have seemed right for John Allison to move at that time. He had four sons of working age, and may have had funds from the sale of his land in Haverstraw. No document for this sale has been found. In the early months of 1801, they loaded a wagon with their household possessions, tethered their farm animals and headed west.

They moved 50 miles to what today is Monroe, New York. It was a hard three-day wagon ride from Haverstraw. They traveled south around the mountains to Suffern and then turned north up Smith's Clove. The Clove formed a corridor between the mountains to the west of Haverstraw. The road is now Routes 17 and Interstate 87. John knew the rugged country well from leading patrols through the area when he was in the army.

The Allisons bought a 150-acre tract of land, 12 miles north, up the Clove. The land is designated lot 19 on maps of the period. The site is on the northern end of Monroe, New York, close to where the town now borders Woodbury. Their new tract was large enough to support the anticipated growth of the family.

The lot appears on the first map of the area in 1736. Surveyor, Charles Clinton, drew it. He divided Monroe into 150-acre lots and described and graded the quality of each. In his Marble Book, Clinton describes Lot 19 as being of "middlin" quality because it was stony, had little level ground and lacked a meadow. The lot appears on maps of the area for the next 200 years. It straddles the abandoned Whitman/Hadley Farm Road, a one-lane dirt road, along which the house was located. In 2007, the road became a street in the Woodbury Junction housing development.

The land lies on the side of a slope that descends down to Dunderberg Road at a point where the Central Valley School buildings are located. No document for the purchase has been found, but an 1812 mortgage on the land shows that it was purchased from Hopni Smith.

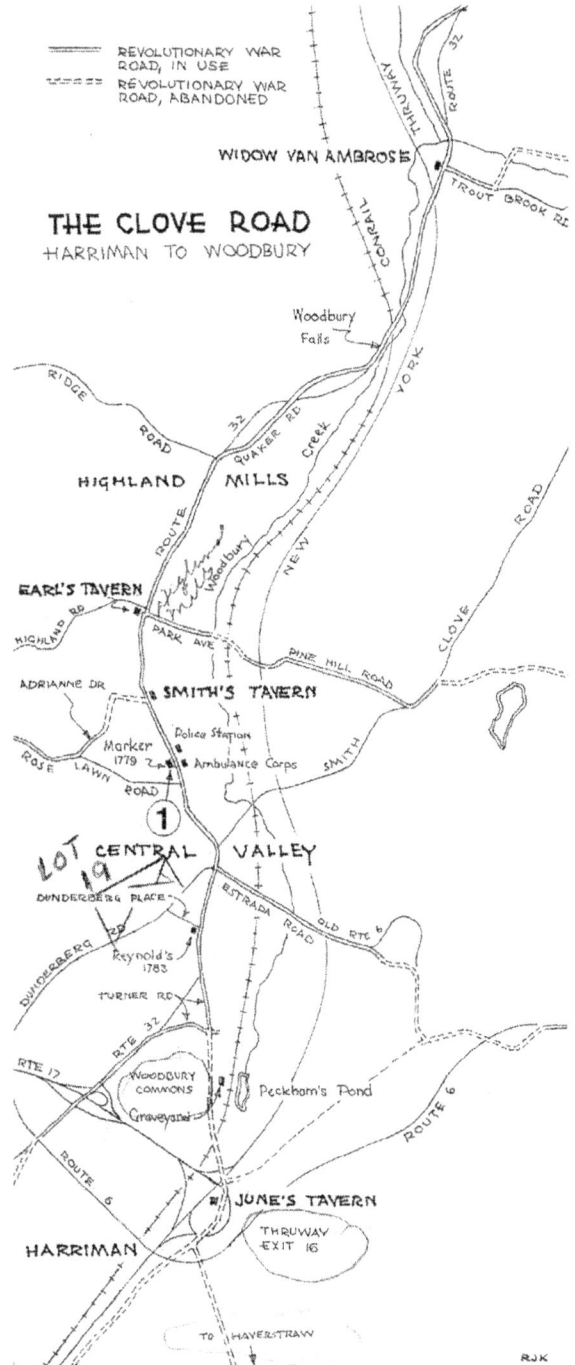

THE CLOVE ROAD
HARRIMAN TO WOODBURY

The first evidence of the family in Monroe was an 1801 Tax Record, which showed that John Ellison was taxed on property valued at $600 and had personal assets of $70. This tax record indicates that the area was sparsely settled.

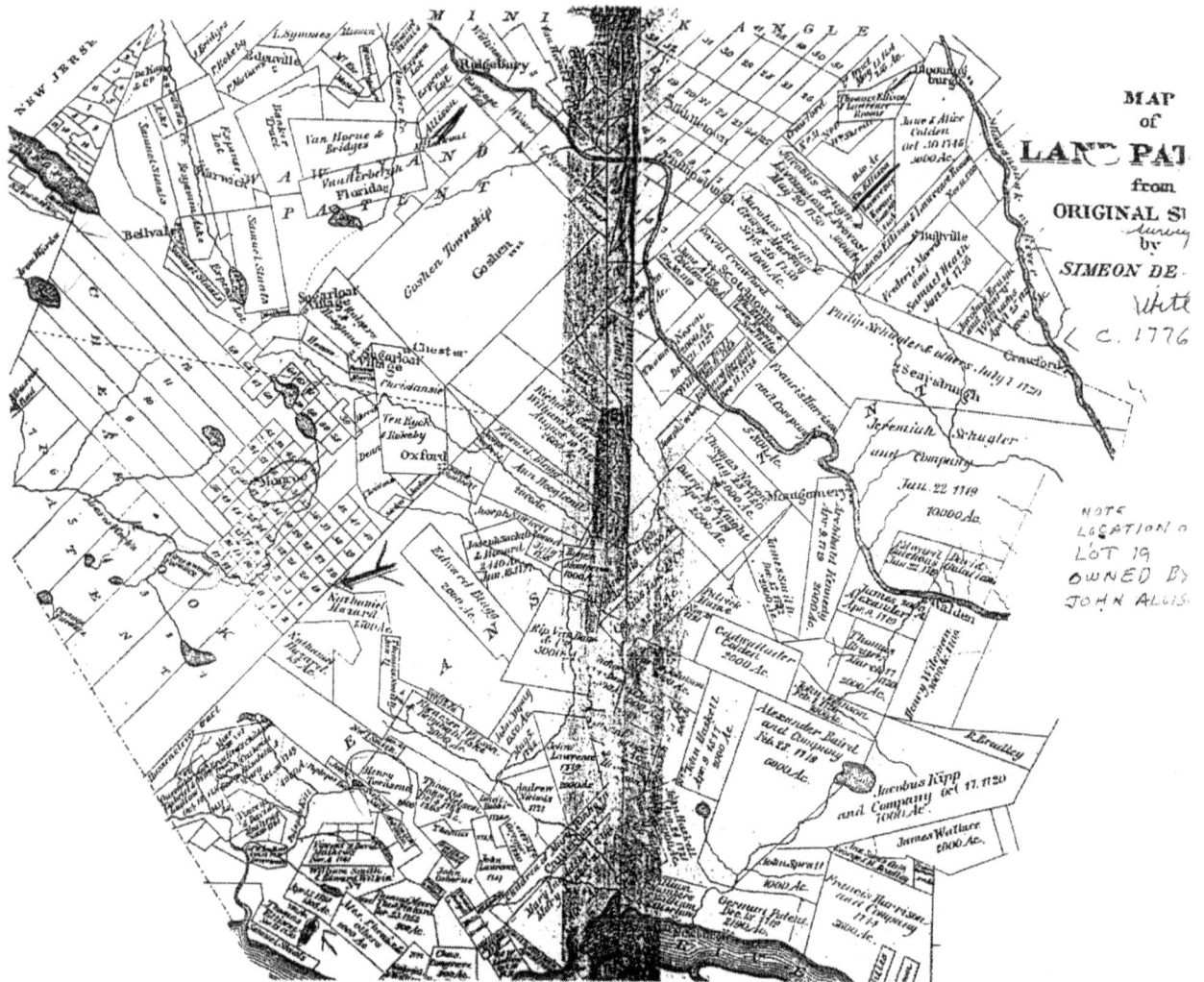

Map of Land Patents from Original Survey by Simeon De Witt, Monroe, Orange County, New York. c. 1776.

A flourishing iron industry existed in the area around Monroe. Dozens of mines were found in the mountains around that part of the Clove. The iron furnaces required huge amounts of charcoal, which was supplied from nearby forests. The land acquired by the Allison family was heavily forested. It is likely that the family produced charcoal to sell to the forges as they cleared timber from the virgin woodland. This opportunity appears to have been the reason for their relocation. John or his older sons may have worked at one of the nearby forges.

1807: Sarah, the 20–year-old daughter of John and Sarah Allison, married Matthias Brooks. The Brooks family owned a farm only a few hundred yards away from the Allison land.

1810: The Allison family does not appear in Orange County in the 1810 Census. After an extensive online search they were found in Colchester, Delaware County, New York. The census page there shows John's sons, William and Alexander, with a male 45 or older and a female 16 to 26. The older male was likely their father, John, age 56. The younger female was William's wife.

Colchester, located 60 miles northwest of Monroe, was a frontier-logging town. Timber was cut here and formed into rafts, which were floated 200 miles down the Delaware River as far as Philadelphia. With the hardwood forest on Lot 19 stripped after nine years, this would have been a natural place for John and his sons to go to find an alternate source of income. This move seems to clearly indicate that during his early years in Monroe, John was a lumberman and charcoal maker, not a farmer. The work in Colchester appears to have been temporary, and the Allisons were back in Monroe two or three years later.

1812: According to oral tradition from the Brooks family, John Allison served in the Orange County Militia during the war of 1812. Muster Rolls at the National Archives name John Allison in Belnaps and Gurnees Regiments in Orange County. His sons, William, Alexander and John, also are listed in military records of the period, as is his son-in-law Matthias Brooks. This second war with England did not touch Orange County, although Alexander was on active duty in Harlem Heights in 1814 at a coastal fortification.

During this year there is the first evidence of the family enduring economic hardship. On December 12, 1812, John Allison defaulted on his mortgage on lot 19 and Hopni Smith, also the constable and tax collector for Monroe, foreclosed on the property for $100. John was able to keep the property at that time, but other claims on the land followed. John, then age 58, and by experience a soldier and lumberman, must have struggled desperately to scratch out a living by farming on the stony mountainside.

1818: Congress passed a law providing pensions for Revolutionary War veterans who were in need of financial assistance. John Allison applied for a pension for his service. The handwritten application states, in his own words, that he was 64 years old and a resident of Monroe and "that he is in reduced circumstances and needs a pension from his country for support." It shows that he enlisted in 1777 at Clarkstown, in the company commanded by Captain Amos Hutchings, in Colonel Dubois Regiment of the New York Line. It tells that he was at St. John in the Canadian campaign and fought at the battles of Fort Montgomery and Yorktown. It further states that he served to the end of the war and was discharged at New Windsor, Orange County, "by the commanding officer whose name I now forget" (Van Courtlandt) and General Washington. John signed his name on the document. He was declared eligible to draw a pension of eight dollars a month commencing on April 15, 1818.

Because many applicants were feigning poverty, all pensioners were required to reapply in 1821 and list their property and income. His second application, dated May 29, 1821, adds more details on his personal life and military service. It shows that he enlisted at Clarkstown, in 1775, and that he went to Canada under Captain Johnson and Colonel James Clinton. He certified that he did not dispose of any property to make himself eligible and that he had no income other than the bare subsistence he earned as a farmer. As was the common practice, veterans tried to prove they were in a state of abject poverty in order to qualify. John lists his only possessions as "one cow, one bed, three knives and forks, four old chairs, which he bottomed with bark and one corn hoe. The revised application adds that he had a wife (unnamed) "about age seventy."

John Allison's application for military service pension, 1818

1820: The Federal Census of Monroe for this year shows John and Sarah with a male age 26 to 45. This was probably their youngest son, Alexander, age 28, who was still at home. Their adjoining neighbors, Brooks, Taylor and Bloom, allow the exact positioning of the Allison land on lot 19. Their sons, Anthony and William, are in another part of town on small farms. They later migrated to Paterson, New Jersey, by 1827.

From 1820 to 1825 John and Sarah Allison began having financial difficulty, which eventually led to their losing their land. Court records show five minor lawsuits, averaging about $100 each, brought against John Allison and his sons, Anthony and John, by their in –laws, John and Matthias Brooks, and a Samuel Webb.

On September 2, 1820, in a sheriff's sale, a small lot of about 18 acres, on or adjacent to lot 19 and owned by John and Anthony Allison was foreclosed to satisfy the judgment for Samuel Webb. Webb was a large landholder and sawmill owner in Monroe. An option to buy John Allison's land was granted to Matthias Brooks, his son-in-law, for $257. Matthias would gain possession in 1822 if the debt were not paid. It was a common practice for relatives to assume debt in this manner to save property from foreclosure.

(The sheriff's sale document provided the most important evidence in the many years spent researching this family history. It was the missing link that connected Anthony Allison of Paterson New Jersey, with his father, John Allison of Monroe, and provided the tie that joined the Allison and Mayer's family history. The Allison financial problems seem to have continued.)

The same week, September 7, 1820, a mortgage for $1,300 was granted by William and his wife, Keziah and Joseph and Alexander Allison, to John Allison. This appears to be an effort by family members to save John's farm. It involved 90 acres. An adjacent neighbor, James Wygant, acquired the remaining 60 acres. The mortgagors, Alexander and William, are two of John's sons. Joseph may have been his brother, still living in Haverstraw. It is also likely that his son, Anthony, moved to Paterson, New Jersey, in 1820 to escape the debts and find employment in that flourishing manufacturing center.

1821: On March 7, John Allisons', lot 19 was auctioned off to satisfy the $100 mortgage held by Hopni Smith. The highest bidder was Matthias Brooks, who bought rights to the lot for $199. On June 22, 1822, Matthias Brooks and his wife, Sarah, John's son-in law and daughter, acquired the land. This transaction was handled by Beverly Robinson, a lawyer and mortgage broker from New York City.

1825: The New York State Census of that year shows John, then age 71, and his wife, Sarah, now without their farm, living alone near their son, John Jr., in Monroe. Judging by the names of their neighbors, the location is near lot 19. Matthias and his wife Sarah continued to live on the Allison land for many years. They developed a prosperous farm and raised a large family.

1828: John Allison died at age 74 on January 22, 1828. He did not leave a will, but a letter of administration names "a friend," Charles Townsend as administrator. His son Alexander rescinded this duty. His assets totaled less than $40.00. Of this amount, $36.00 was pension arrears due him from the "New York Pension Office." The letter states that the deceased left no widow. (This proves that Sarah died between the 1825 census and John's death in 1828.)

The burial places of John and Sarah are unknown, but it is likely they rest in one of the many small private cemeteries in the area of lot 19. Most of these have disappeared over time as fields turned into woods. Another possibility is the Methodist Cemetery of the Highlands in Highland Mills about two miles from their farm on lot 19. The church was erected there in 1829, a year after John Allison died, but the burial ground may have started earlier. A Daughters of the American Revolution publication states that Corporal John Allison is buried in the Allison plot at Mount Repose Cemetery in Haverstraw. This is unlikely: that study contains many errors.

1830: Sarah Brooks, John's daughter, applied for a 100-acre bounty land grant provided to her father for his military service during the Revolution. In 1833, script was issued to heirs for unsatisfied land warrants. Her request was approved, but not enough land had been purchased for the purpose, which caused a delay. Finally, in 1838, 20 years after his death, John Allison's heirs received script entitling them to 100 acres. No evidence has been found that the land was ever claimed. "Sarah Brooks, John, Alexander, William Allison and Elizabeth Hoffman" are listed as heirs.

FINDING LOT 19, MONROE, NEW YORK

2005: The location of lot 19 was found on Hadley Farms Road in Monroe. There are several buildings on both sides of the abandoned road that appear to be of 20th century construction. The land slopes down from Bloom Hill and has a large level field that may have been cultivated. Stone outbuildings built into the hillside appear to be early structures. There is a stone- lined well on the corner of a larger abandoned house. Lot 19 overlooks Smith's Clove and has a beautiful, panoramic view of the valley. (This site was discovered and visited by Harriet Mills Chesi, Alan Wickham, Ted Jones and Bob Mayers, all direct descendants of John Allison.)

This land, and thousands of acres in the adjacent area, was purchased in 2004, by William Brodsky, a developer. He employed archeologist George Price to identify any sites of historical interest on the tract. Lot 19 and its buildings were designated as site #6. Digs here, which included a midden next to the larger house, the probable site of the earlier Allison/Brooks dwelling, failed to turn up any 18th century artifacts. In 2007, the tract, named Woodbury Junction, was subdivided into 450 single-family home sites, and construction started.

John Allison began fighting for the cause of liberty a year before the signing of the Declaration of Independence. He personally participated in some of the most pivotal events of the Revolutionary War in the presence of many of its top leaders. John and Sarah Allison were exceptional people. Their sacrifices during the most critical years of American history, typify the people who gave birth to our great nation.

NOTES & SOURCES

Mayers, Robert A., *The War Man*, Westholme Publishing, Yardley, Pa., 2009. The entire life of Corporal John Allison is reviewed in detail in this full biography.

Cole, David, *History of Rockland County, NY*, L.B. Beers, 1884, Reprinted by the Historical Soc. of Rockland Co. 1986, 1992.

Ruttenber, E. M. and Clark L. H., *History of Orange County NY*, Everts and Peck, Philadelphia 1881.

National Archives. Source for pension, pay, bounty and other service records of John Allison. Muster rolls and pay records for 1775-1783 and War of 1812 bearing his name, rank and status of and the military units he served in during the Revolutionary War.

Roberts, James A., *New York in the Revolution as a Colony and State*. Lists names of all soldiers and officers by unit, serving in the Continental Army, militia and levies in the State of New York.

Historians of recreated regimental units- Stephen Gilbert 3rd NY, Richard McGuinness, 5th NY Analysis of their regiment's history through muster rolls, orderly books and other primary sources.

Aimone, Alan C., Senior Librarian, West Point Military Academy. This Author, Historian and one of the nation's leading scholars on the Revolutionary War reviewed all of the author's biographical material on John Allison to ensure accuracy of military details.

Fitzpatrick, John C., Writings of George Washington from Original Manuscript Sources. 1741-1799.

Talmadge, Samuel, *Orderly Books of the 4th New York Regiment, 1778-1780*. University of the State of New York, 1932. Records include the 2nd New York Regiment from 1780 to 1783. Orders apply to all NY regiments brigaded together during these periods. A treasure trove of information on troop movements, locations, punishments and many other details of military life.

Van Cortlandt, Philip, The Revolutionary War Memoir and Selected Correspondence of Philip Van Courtlandt, Sleepy Hollow Restorations, Tarrytown, NY, 1976.

Budke Collection, George H. Budke (1868-1948) spent most of his life researching and collecting document s relating to the history Rockland County and the genealogy of its families. New York Public Library.

Brooks Family History, Harriet Mills Chesi Collection, Kerrville, TX.

Many of the personal history dates for the Allison family of Haverstraw, including births and deaths were provided by George S. Allison (1792-1884). His data was used by Morrison, Barlow and Cole for their accounts on the family.

Cole, "Association" signed by citizens of Orange County, July 17, 1775. 28, 29.

DeNoyelles, Daniel, Birth of an American Family, Charles E. Decker, Publisher, Newburgh, NY, 1971.

Koke, Richard J., Carr, William H. *The Twin Forts of the Popolopen, Forts Clinton and Montgomery, New York, 1775-1777.* Bear Mountain Trailside Museums, Historic Bulletin No. 1, July 1937, 26.

Fisher, Charles I., Ed. *The Most Advantageous Situation in the Highlands-An Archeological Study of Fort Montgomery State Historic Site,* New York State Museum, Cultural Resources.

Survey, Project No 2. Albany 2004.

Report into the Loss of Forts Clinton and Montgomery, Court of Inquiry April 5, 1778.

Extracts-General Alexander McDougall Papers, Vol. III, New York Historic Society.

Talmadge, Samuel, Orderly Books. Detailed accounts are often kept from day to day for the entire period of the Sullivan-Clinton Campaign.

Budke Collection, New York Public Library.

BC 81 - January 17, 1780 - Affidavit of Thomas Allison concerning the enlistment of John Allison son of Joseph Allison.

BC 81 - January 19 ,1780 - Affidavit of Amos Hutchings concerning the enlistment of John Allison son of Joseph Allison.

BC 81- April 16, 1780 - Petition of John Allison concerning his enlistment.

BLWT No. 7109-100-12, 1790, Issued to John Ellison, Pvt., New York Line, assigned to Samuel Coe. National Archives.

Bounty Land Grants-State of New York, No. 32, July 8, 1790, signed by Governor George Clinton.

Will of Joseph Allison, September 12, 1792, probated April 4 1796, Orange Co. Probate records, Liber A. Orange Co. Mortgage Books, Liber C, 83.

Taxable Property, Town of Haverstraw, September 20, 1799, State of New York, Archives, Albany. Page six of nine.

Clinton, Col Charles, *Marble Survey book of Cheesecocks*, 1736. Orange Co. Courthouse.

Proceedings of the County Board of Supervisors and Tax Records-tax assessment rolls 1799-1993, microfilm Ara 4482, NY State Archives, Albany.

Ruttenber and Clark provide a comprehensive description of events and people in Orange County during the War of 1812, 73-78.

Lot No. 19 from Hopni Smith to John T. Allison, December 21, 1812, Orange County Mortgage Book, Liber P, 368.

Allison, John, Pension Application, District of New York, Certificate No. 1652, May 29, 1821. Certified by D. M. Westcott, Clerk. National Archives.

Court of Common Pleas of Orange County, September 1820.

Sheriff's sale-Land Book 1, Orange Co., 1820.

Mortgage- Land Book Q, Orange Co. September 1, 1820, 26.

Auction- Land Book P, Orange Co. March 7, 1821, 168.

Chesi, Harriet Mills, *Allison/ Brooks Farm History*, Unpublished Manuscript, 2005.

Traces the ownership of Lot 19 from 1800 to 1947 from original documents. Eight pages.

Letter of Administration for John Allison. Liber F-43, Charles Townsend, Administrator.

Application for Land Bounty Grant No. 1657, of John Allison under Act of Congress, September 16, 1776, by his daughter, Sarah Brooks.

Dumont, William H. *Some Revolutionary Soldiers and the Heirs*, Washington, D.C., New England Historical and Genealogical Register, 1960 Vol. CXIV, 177-179, 184.

Pierce's Register of Certificates issued to Officers and Soldiers of the Continental Army under Act of July 4, 1783, 17th Report of the National Office of the DAR, Genealogical Publishing Co., Baltimore, 1987.

WILLIAM ALLISON 13. v (First Direct Ancestor In New Jersey)

William Allison 13. v, born about 1791 Haverstraw, Rockland County, New York; died between 1832 and 1840; married (1) Unknown, born about 1791; (2) Possibly Keziah or Jane, born about 1802, Monroe, NY. Six children, all born Monroe, Orange County, New York, migrated with parents to Paterson, NJ in 1826. All resided in Paterson:

   i   William, born 1811; married Mary _____, son William, molder, born 1835; married Emma Hocket 31 December 1856, born 1835 England. Three children.

   ii   John, born about 1811; died unknown; married Effie _____, born about 1814 New York. One child: Jane, born 1834; married Robert Houston 4 March 1855.

   iii   Eliza, born 1814; died 7 November 1873; married Alexander Anderson 31 March 1831, born 1811 Scotland; died 1863. One child, Charles; baptized 1856 Prospect St. M.E. Church, age 2 yrs 6 mos.

   iv   George, born 1819; died between 1841 and 1850; married Phoebe Ann Lane 4 March 1840, born 1820 Pennsylvania. One child: Sarah, born 1841.

   v   Isaac, born 1821; died after 1860; moulder; married Mary Jane Clark 17 September 1844, born 1825 NY; died 21 March 1856. Four children: Harriet, born 1844; Sarah, E, born 1845; married Andrew Clark; Amelia, born 1849; will 1864; Issac Jr., born 1854; died 1856.

14. vi   SARAH ANN, born 1823 NY; died 3 August 1869; married JAMES MAYERS about 1841; silk dyer; born March 1820 Macclesfield, Cheshire, England; died 1 May 1887.

William and his wife are a generation of the family that is difficult to trace. No documents have been found that record dates for their birth, marriage or death. William was born in Haverstraw about 1791. This estimate is based on his being age twenty when his first child, William, was born. He was the son of Revolutionary War veteran Corporal John Allison and Sarah DeNoyelles. As a child in 1801, he moved with his parents from Haverstraw to Monroe, Orange County, New York. He grew up on his father's land on Lot #19 in Smith's Clove, in Monroe.

It appears that he married twice but no marriage records have been found for either of the marriages. In rural Orange County, at that time, most weddings took place at home and clergy who traveled from town to town kept few records. The old Methodist Church, in nearby Highland Mills, where the family attended in later years, was not built until much later, in 1829.

His sister, Sarah Allison, married Matthias Brooks in 1807. This is the only evidence we have of the family in Monroe between 1801 and 1810. We assume that during these years William assisted his father and brother in cutting timber on Lot #19 to produce charcoal for the iron forges at Sterling and Woodbury. The only Allison of the family in the 1810 Monroe census is John Allison Jr., his brother, age 28, with a wife and two children.

After an extensive on line search the missing family members were found in Colchester, Delaware County, New York in 1810. This census shows John's sons William and Alexander together with a male age 45 or older and a female 16 to 26. The older male was likely father John the Revolutionary war veteran, age 56. The younger female was William's wife. William was about age 20 at the time and Alexander about 19.

The frontier town of Colchester was a center for the logging industry on the east branch of the Delaware River. It was located 60 miles northwest of Monroe, near present day Downsville, It could be reached by traveling directly up a wagon trail, which today is New York Route. 17. The area was a heavily forested, mountainous upland, broken by narrow stream valleys. Hills rose hundreds of feet on each side of the creeks. Timber was cut and formed into rafts that were floated 200 miles down the river as far as Philadelphia.

With the hardwood forest on Lot 19 stripped after nine years of harvesting this would have been a natural place for John and his two sons to go to find an alternate source of income. This move is further proof that the Allisons, during those years, were lumbermen and charcoal makers, not farmers. The stay on the frontier was temporary and the Allisons were back in Monroe on Lot 19 by 1812. William's first wife who accompanied him to Colchester died before 1820. In that year his family appeared in the census and showing a female age 16 to 18. She is apparently his younger second wife and the mother of his three youngest children.

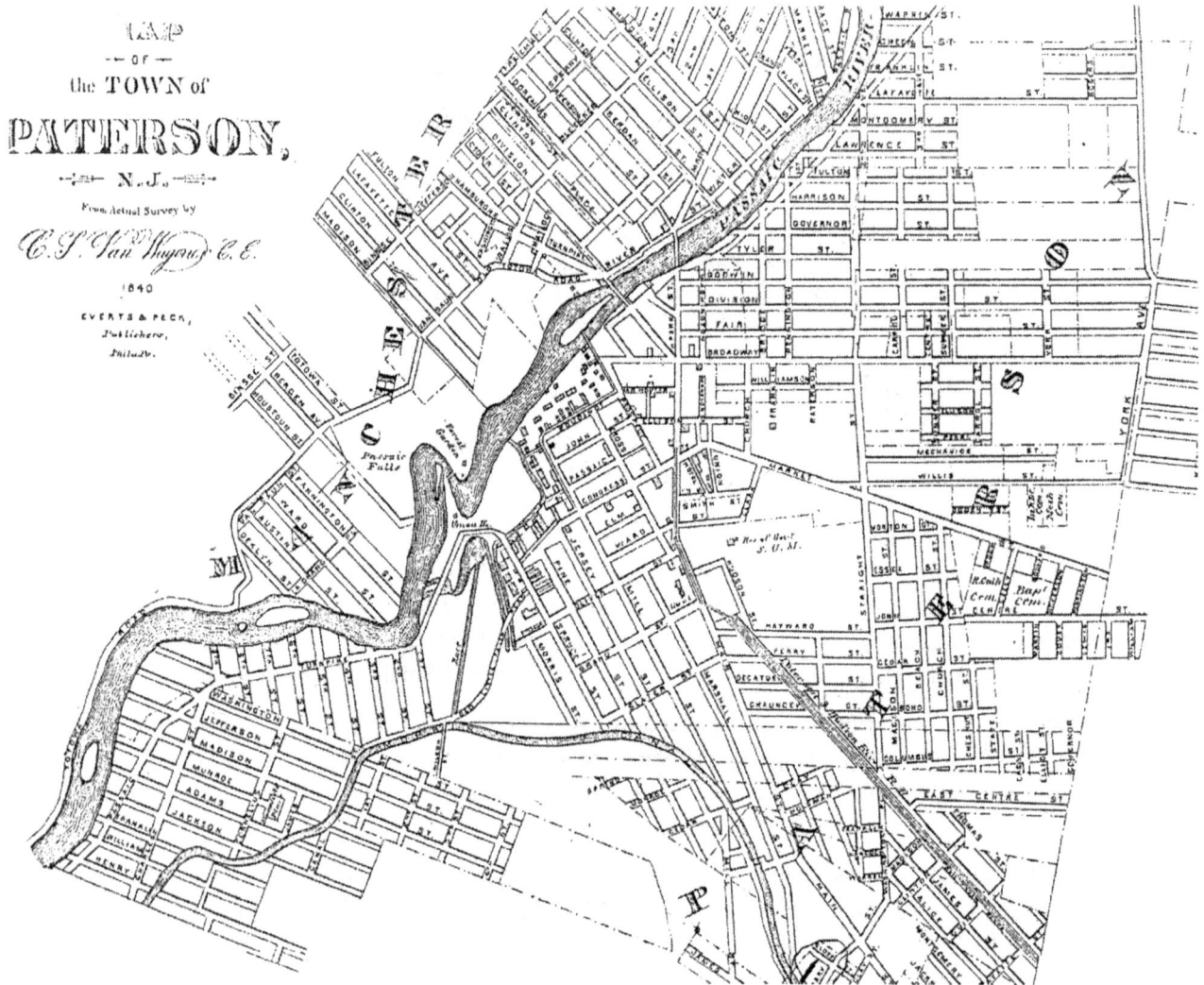

As the mother of direct ancestor Sarah Ann Allison, born in 1823, she is of great interest, but her name has never been verified. There is a strong family tradition that it was Jane. Inconclusive evidence for this is found in records of the Cross St. Methodist Church, in Paterson. In 1849 Jane Ellison was "excluded for neglect," (probably lack of attendance). Another possibility is that her name was Keziah. That name appears on a mortgage that was granted by William and others to his father, John, in Monroe in 1820.

William Allison was in the War of 1812 in the 2nd Co, 2nd Regiment Orange County Militia. He was a private in Ward's Regiment, Captain Livingston's company in 1814. While he may have been called for guard duty around Manhattan, or to repair the old fortifications at West Point, there was no combat in the Orange County region during that conflict.

The 1820 Census for Monroe shows William and his second wife with four sons and one daughter. He is living next to or together with his older brother Anthony and his family. A matching of names on the census and old maps places this site about a mile from his father's farm on Lot # 19 and near the lower Quaker Meeting House, in Monroe, now Woodbury, New York. This location is separate from his father John and brother John.

64

The 1825 New York State Census for Monroe shows William as a farmer on a small three acre lot, with one cow and two hogs in still a different part of town. His family had grown to five sons and two daughters.

Life on a small farm in the 1820s was incredibly hard, especially for his young wife. She cared for seven children, spun and wove for clothes and blankets, tanned hides for shoe leather, churned butter, made candles from beef tallow and tended a garden. William may have worked as a farm laborer, a woodcutter or in a nearby tannery to sustain the family on the small plot.

These arduous living conditions caused some of the Allisons to begin leaving Orange County, New York where four generations of the family had lived since 1719. Anthony, William's brother, with his wife Mary with four children under 10 years of age, migrated to Paterson, New Jersey, between 1820 and 1825. A number of lawsuits against Anthony at that time indicate that he may have left the area to escape payment of debts. William and his family followed him in 1826. Both had large families to support and little land or resources. They traveled south, about thirty miles, along what is now Route 87, the New York Thruway to Paterson. At that time, the City was a flourishing textile center that offered jobs opportunity for a better life.

After the Revolutionary War, America was without a manufacturing base. As a colony it had been forbidden to make products that would compete with British exports The founding fathers saw an immediate need to make the new nation self sufficient. In 1791, Alexander Hamilton saw the opportunity to harness the energy of Paterson's great falls and the city became our nation's first manufacturing center.

William may have been employed in the textile mills. Anthony, a blacksmith, likely found great demand for his skills in the bustling city. By the mid 1830s, Paterson had a population of over 10,000. The spinning of cotton, flax and wool employed 2500. A large proportion of the workers were children. In 1833, the Gazetteer of the State of New Jersey, a publication that gave detailed images of many places in the state, described the city: "The advantages that Paterson possesses for a manufacturing town are obvious. An abundant and steady supply of water; pleasant and fruitful country, supplying its markets fully with excellent meats and vegetables, its proximity to New York, where it obtains the raw material, and sells manufactured goods; and with which it is connected by the sloop navigation of the Passaic River, by the Morris Canal, by a turnpike road, and by a railroad, render it one of the most desirable site in the Union."

In Rev Samuel Fisher's Census of Paterson in 1827 and 1829, the Anthony and William Allison families were living on Mill Street. The 1830 Federal Census shows a William and Anthony Ellison in Aquackanonock which included Paterson at that time. Fisher's last census, in 1832, shows William on Ward Street and Anthony on Mill Street. These places were all close to the textile mills.

William's children, Eliza, Isaac and direct ancestor Sarah Ann are shown in the Cross Street Methodist Sunday school records, starting in 1827. A William Allison appears in the records of this church in1833, but this may have been his son. A Jane Ellison is shown joining the church in 1847. If this is William's wife, this is the same year that her grandchild, James Mayers, first son of her daughter Sarah Ann, was baptized there. James, age two or three, died about 1849. Jane was "excluded for neglect" from the church the same year, probably for not attending. This Cross Street church, and its offshoot on Prospect Street, were places of worship for the family for the next century.

In 1838, William Allison was named as one of the heirs eligible to receive script for an unclaimed bounty land grant owed to his father John Allison for Revolutionary War service. His sister Sarah Brooks applied for the grant. In the 1840 census William is shown with his wife and two children, probably Sarah and Isaac still living at home. There is no death record for him in the New Jersey archives, which began in 1848. This indicates that he died between 1840 and 1848.

William and his wife are not found in the "all names" 1850 census. This indicates both had died by that time. Their youngest daughter Sarah Ann, a "female 15-20," may be living with her older sister Eliza Anderson in the mill area, on Congress St. in 1840. Here, she may have met her husband James Mayers.

In an effort to trace William and Anthony Allison, of Monroe New York, in Paterson, it was necessary to sort out other Ellison/Allison families in the city. These families are not related. Dr. William Ellison, a prominent Paterson physician, was born in Ireland and died in 1828. Ellison Street was named in his honor. He left no children. Another William Allison, a peddler, who was also born in Ireland, lived in Paterson for many years until his death, in 1870. He had many children and grandchildren. Their names litter all types of records during that time. A Jane Henny, "wife of William Ellison" is shown living at131 Mill Street in an 1869 obituary, but she does not appear to be Jane the wife of William Allison, from Monroe New York.

Anthony Allison and his wife Mary continued to live in Paterson for many years. In the 1850 census, they lived with their daughter, Catherine. In that year he was age 70 and Mary was age 59. Anthony died before 1860 and Mary died in 1865, as their names do not appear in the census data for those years. Children of Anthony and Mary Allison:

Catherine	born 1814 NY; died 1856; married Ephriam Ward; died 1856.
Mary	born 1814 NY; died 15 June 1856; married Stephen Cooper 1887.
Isaac	born 1821; died after 1860; married Mary Jane Clark 17 September 1844, born 1825 NY; died 21 September 1865. Paterson residences: 74 Oliver St. in 1859, 81 Mill St. in 1860.
John	born 1811 or 1817 NY; married Mahala _____, born 1818 NY.

William and his wife were probably interred in Sandy Hill Cemetery in the Methodist section. It was Paterson's only cemetery at that time. Records of their burials have not been found, but others show that their sons, John, Isaac and son-in-law James Mayers had plots there. In1914, this Cemetery was closed and all burials, if claimed, were exhumed. Five sets of remains were removed to the Mayers plot in Cedar Lawn Cemetery in 1917. Possibly William and his wife were among them.

They were people of great strength, and courage who choose to leave the poverty of a small farm to improve the quality of their lives in an industrial city. William and his family were the first ancestors to live in New Jersey. Their descendants, through their daughter, Sarah Ann Mayers, still live in that state after almost two centuries.

NOTES & SOURCES

Drew University Archives.

National Archives.

Federal Census.

New York State Census, 1825.

New Jersey State Census, 1865.

Fisher's Census of Paterson, NJ, 1824-1832.

Rev. Daniel Niles Freeland, *Chronicles of Monroe in Olden Times* (New York De Vinne Press), 1898 New Jersey Gazetteer for 1834.

Section II: Mayers Family History in England

From 1670, by Individual Ancestor

The name Mayers did not evolve into its present form until 1778. The most common early version is Meare, a spelling that is close to its probable derivations, the French Maire, a town official or Mire, a doctor. Versions of the name appear over the centuries as MEARE, MEYERS, MAYRS, MEARS and, finally, MAYERS. Names derived from French are common in England since most people assumed surnames for the first time when the Normans conquered the country in 1066. Variations appeared in early times when most people were illiterate and scribes or clergy spelled a name the way it sounded to them.

The ancestry of the Mayers Family in England can be traced through parish registers, census data, wills and other records to provide a direct line back to about 1670 in Macclesfield, and nearby towns in the county of Cheshire.

Tools, weapons and burial mounds show that Cheshire was inhabited by Bronze and Iron Age people. Roman roads crisscross the area and Celtic place names are common. Macclesfield was founded by Anglo-Saxon people before the eleventh century. Their lives centered on growing corn and animal husbandry and changing very little over the centuries until the industrial revolution in the mid- 1700s. Cheshire had ample ploughable land, pasture and woodland for timber. In Macclesfield, the Bollin River flowing through the town, provided water, and meadows along it could be cut for hay.

In the reign of Edward the Confessor, 1042-1066, the area was well established. After the defeat of English King Harold by the French Normans under William the Conqueror at Hastings in 1066, Macclesfield was devastated by the invaders and remained a thinly populated forest area for the next 200 years. The town is listed in the Domesday Book. This account of people and property was ordered by William the Conqueror in 1086 to find out how much each landholder had in land and livestock and to determine its value and therefore how much tax could be collected. It provides a remarkable record of medieval life in England. The word doomsday comes from the old English word dom, meaning accounting.

The social and business center of the town has always been the market place, located on high ground, where it could easily be defended. It still stands in the shadow of St. Michaels Church, first built there in 1278. A chapel in the church was built in 1422 to receive the body of the knight, Sir Piers Legh, who fought at Agincourt and died later in the same campaign.

Macclesfield yeomen were famous for their skill and accuracy with the longbow, the first weapon that could penetrate armor. Their skill turned the Battle of Agincourt into an English victory in 1415. They fought at the battles of Bosworth Field and Flodden Field, in 1513, and many other pivotal conflicts in English history.

The long bow was invented in the Macclesfield area along the Welsh border. It transformed military tactics during the Hundred Years War (1337-1453). Macclesfield men were among the 500 longbow men that fought with Edward III against the French. The longbow ranged in height up to six and a half feet and could accurately kill at 150 yards and pierce armor plate.

Macclesfield became a textile center by the eighteenth century. When James Mayers migrated to America in 1839 half of the silk mills in England were in the town. The Mayers family was employed in this industry in England for four generations, from 1758 to 1832.

The earliest direct line ancestor that can be identified with certainty in Cheshire is Hugonus Mears who was born about 1670. During the period from 1574 to 1690 about 350 entries for the Mayers name, or its many variations, are found in Macclesfield and surrounding towns. Since parish records for Cheshire start in the mid 16ᵗʰ century, it may be possible to extend this line back even earlier, with further research in the future.

In 1978, I retained the services of Mr. William Eyre. He was recommended by the British Association of Genealogists as the best-qualified researcher in the Cheshire, Macclesfield area. Residing in Stockport, ten miles north of Macclesfield, he spent hundreds of hours researching the Mayers family roots.

His primary sources of information were the records of Prestbury Parish. These include St. Michaels, the mother church of the Mayers family, where James Mayers, the progenitor of the family in America, was baptized. It was founded in 1278 and its registers of marriages, baptisms and deaths, many in Latin, date back to 1572. The family also appears in the records of Christ Church in Macclesfield, built in 1775. Mr. Eyre's search also included census data and wills.

Mayers family history goes back to 1574 in the Staffordshire area and 1589 in Macclesfield. I have been unable to connect the numerous entries of people with variations of the name earlier than these dates. The following interesting entries might provide clues as to the parentage of Hugonis or Hough Mears/Meyers, our earliest direct line ancestor that can be identified at this time.

1660, August 26, Hugh filuis (son) Matthei and Elizab Mere, baptism, Stoke on Trent Parish Registers.

1673, August 3, Hugo filuis Johannis and Elizabethae Mear, baptism, Burslem Parish Registers

A badly damaged will was found in Pott Shrigley, a small village four miles northeast of Macclesfield, provides another clue of early Mayers ancestry. The will of William Meare proven October 11, 1673 mentions a brother Hugh, father of three daughters and references, Bagnall and Stoke- on-Trent. The many entries in Staffordshire indicate that the Mayers migrated from there to Macclesfield a few miles north. However, the Mayers name is also in Macclesfield records in the 1500s. We are certain that all generations that followed Hugonis lived in Macclesfield.

HUGO/HUGONIS/HOUGH MEYERS OR MEARE 1.

Hugo / Hugonis / Hough Meyers or Meare, born about 1670, Macclesfield, Prestbury Parish or Staffordshire; died unknown; married Mary _____; died 6 November 1759. One known child:

> 2. i   GULIELMUS (WILLIAM), baptized 8 July 1694, St. Michaels, Macclesfield.

Hugo Meare is the earliest of the direct line of Mayers ancestors that can be identified at this time. We know very little about him. The Prestbury Parish records show that his wife Mary died November 6, 1759. He possibly had a brother, or uncle, William of Pott Shrigley. He may have had have been born in Macclesfield or migrated there from Staffordshire, about forty miles south.

The Parish Registers of St. Michaels, Macclesfield's cathedral also show that Gulielmus (William) son of Hugonis Meyers was baptized on July 8, 1694. Based on the assumption that Hugo, the father, was in his early twenties that year indicates that he was born about 1670, when this child was baptized.

Medieval Macclesfield was an agricultural community with pastures for grazing sheep and cattle along the River Bollin. Feudalism had disintegrated and nearby forestland was being turned into grassland. During Hugo's lifetime the population was increasing and new cottage industries such as hating, soap boiling, spinning and weaving of woolen cloth were beginning. Silk buttons were starting to be made which would evolve into silk weaving. It was the town's greatest industry for the next 200 years. Epidemics of plague decimated the population during this period. Death records in the parish registers show that life was short for many people.

Wages were low for the average agricultural worker, about nine pence per day. This was slightly less than a soldiers pay. Women stayed at home, growing food, milking cows and caring for children. Infant mortality was high due to disease, malnutrition and poor midwifery. Children went to work at an early age. Couples waited until they could afford to be married which was usually in their mid twenties.

St. Michaels sat on high ground and overlooked an active marketplace. In the center of the market was an ancient stone Celtic cross, around which all business of the town was transacted. Markets were held weekly and an annual fair in Macclesfield, associated with the Feast of St. Barnabas, took place there each June. Fairs had a holiday atmosphere and were the only chance in the year for farmers from the surrounding countryside to get into town. Hard drinking and entertainment by dancers, acrobats, jugglers and musicians added to the festivities. Profits from these markets and fairs contributed to the prosperity of the town.

Hugo lived during the reigns of Charles II, who was restored to the throne after the death of Oliver Cromwell. This period in English history was marred by constant warfare with both the Dutch and French, but battles and action was far from the bucolic country of Macclesfield in Cheshire and the distant warfare had little impact on its inhabitants.

No evidence has been found of the death of Hugo or his wife. Before 1700, common people were usually buried in unmarked graves on the south side of the church, in a shroud. A reusable "parish coffin" was used at the service and interments were on top of others to save space.

WILLIAM MAYRS/MEARS 2. I AND MARGARET SHELMERDINE

Williams Mayrs / Mears 2. i, baptized 8 July 1694 St. Michaels, Macclesfield, Cheshire; died 26 September 1775, burials probably at St. Michaels; married Margaret Shelmerdine 8 June 1714 St. Michaels. Nine children, all baptized at St. Michaels:

i	Rebecca Mears, baptized 1 December 1723; daughter.
ii	Betty (illeg), baptized 3 November 1747; died 1 January 1748.
iii	Anna Mears, baptized 6 June 1726; died 27 August 1727.
iv	Anne Mayrs, baptized 20 April 1729; son Thomas (illegitimate) died 20 January 1751.
3. v	WILLIAM, baptized 6 June 1731; married MARY LITTLEWOOD 23 September.
vi	Sarah Mayrs, baptized 6 September 1733.
vii	Martha Mayres, baptized 8 September 1734; died 12 June 1746.
viii	Ralph Mayers, baptized 19 July 1737.
ix	Margaret Mayers, died 29 September 1737.

During William's lifetime, the records at St. Michaels began changing from Latin to English. With his children, the Mayers surname evolves into its present form. Macclesfield continued to be an agricultural community during these years, and William like his father Hugonis, was a farmer or shepherd. Records in his generation show that many children died in the Mayers and other families in the town.

William was age 51 in 1745 when he witnessed the most memorable event in the history of Macclesfield. Prince Charles Edward Stuart, "Bonnie Prince Charlie", the Scottish pretender to the throne of England, invaded England. His army left Scotland and marched south to attack London. After spending a few days in Manchester, he arrived in Macclesfield on the first of December with 6000 infantry troops and 500 cavalry.

The Prince hoped to pick up supporters along the way but the people of the town were loyal to the king. Many citizens fled, taking their valuables and other property with them. The army was billeted in homes in the town. The soldiers and behaved well, but provisions were commandeered and all public monies taken.

The Prince continued on to London but did not take the English capitol city due to lack of the support that he anticipated from English citizens. In retreating, the army passed back through Macclesfield, plundering and robbing anything of value. The rebels left town on December 9, 1745. They continued back to Scotland where they were brutally defeated at the Battle of Culloden. After that, Prince Charlie fled to France.

WILLIAM MEARE 3. V AND MARY LITTLEWOOD
THE LAST FARMERS

William Meare 3. v, baptized 6 June 1731 St. Michaels; died unknown; married Mary Littlewood 23 September 1751 (Prestbury Parish Register). Three children, all baptized St. Michaels, Macclesfield:

4. i   THOMAS, baptized 4 February 1753; married Elizabeth Hough 21 February 1778.
   ii   Mary, baptized 11 November 1755; died 21 February 1778.
   iii   Rebecca, baptized 27 August 1758; died 21 June 1778.

William and Mary were children in 1745 when Bonnie Prince Charlie sacked Macclesfield. Like their forefathers, they spent their lives engaged in farming, or animal husbandry. At this time the silk industry began. Silk thread was being made on hand-driven machines for buttons and sewing. Many townspeople were employed making silk buttons in their homes. The button industry was organized by Macclesfield merchants who bought the materials wholesale and distributed them to families. Women and children made buttons by hand with a needle in their homes. The buttons were hawked by peddlers throughout England and sold in markets. Macclesfield buttons were exported to Holland and America. The weaving of silk cloth would not begin for several years.

An 18th Century map of the town shows a maze of tiny fields, most under three acres, but total farm land was about the same as was recorded in 1086. About this time, farming the land within the town was gradually being discontinued and the number of cottages increased. The industrial revolution had not yet arrived and many people still worked the land within the town boundaries.

William lived during the reign of George III (1760-1820), a tumultuous time in England. The Seven Year's war, known to us as the French and Indian War, ended in 1763 and the country emerged as the world's greatest colonial power. England thrived under peaceful conditions until the War in the American colonies began, in 1775. Napoleon seized power in France in 1803 and hostilities with that country lasted until 1814.

Except for tapping resources and manpower these conflicts did not disturb the peaceful countryside of Cheshire, Perhaps Macclesfield men transported to the rebellious colonies in America in the 1770s were the Redcoats that exchanged musket fire with Corporal John Allison at Fort St. Johns, Fort Montgomery, or Yorktown.

THOMAS MAYERS 4. I AND ELIZABETH HOUGH
THE FAMILY'S FIRST SILK WORKERS

Thomas Mayers 4. i, baptized 4 February 1753 St. Michaels Macclesfield; died unknown; married Elizabeth Hough 19 April 1778 Prestbury Parish Church. Eight children:

i   Mary, baptized 30 January 1779 Christ Church Macclesfield; spinster; died 17 March 1825, St. Michaels.

ii   David, baptized 6 October 1781 St. Michaels; silkman, piscer; married Ann _____, Living Bank Top, 1841 Bank St. 1851. Children all baptized St. Michaels: Sarah, born 20 May 20, 1804; died 30 April 1815; Thomas, baptized 18 May 1806; Jessie, baptized 25 June 1808; David, baptized 27 June 1810; Samuel, baptized 22 August 1813.

iii   Rebecca, baptized 20 March 1782, St. Michaels; died 11 April 1827.

iv   Betty, born 1787; silk piscer; in 1851 living on Bank St, age 66.

5. v   THOMAS, born 1788; married BETTY BROWN.

vi   William, baptized 5 May 1793 at Christ Church.

vii   Joshua, baptized, 26 April 1795 at Christ Church.

viii Daniel, baptized 2 September 1798 at Christ Church.

Thomas and his family witnessed the beginning of the industrial revolution in England. It would forever transform the agrarian society and change the lives of the Mayers who had always lived off the land. With this generation they became industrial workers. Thomas was shown as a silk worker at the time of his marriage to Elizabeth Hough, in 1778. The people of Macclesfield had been engaged in silk manufacture since the early 1600s. Work began on a small scale in cottages using hand driven machinery.

The art of producing silk thread and cloth was brought to England by the French Huguenots who were expelled from their homeland for religious reasons in 1685-88. These refugees from religious prosecution settled in Spitalfields, London. They began making silk yarn in Macclesfield in1744. The town had ample water for dyeing the fabric and powering machinery and it was located near to markets. During the lives of Thomas and Elizabeth half of the silk mills in England were in Cheshire. Before 1800, production in the town was limited to the twisting or "throwing" of raw silk into yarn. They were "silk workers," not weavers who made cloth in London. Actual weaving began in the town in 1790. Their grandson, James Mayers, was probably the first weaver in the family.

With the use of steam and waterpower from the River Bollin, large mills were built in Macclesfield. By 1801 the population reached 9,000. Conditions became crowded the air polluted etc and the town lost its quaint, market village character.

Thomas and his family were likely employed in one of the new mills, although they may have worked at home in a typical garret house (a house with an attic). These three storied, row houses were designed for silk working families. The top floor used for weaving loom sand had long windows to allow as much light in as possible. Families lived below where women and children worked the spinning looms and performed other operations to support the weaving. Outside stairs permitted other workers access without passing through the living accommodations on the lower floors. Many of these dwellings can be seen today in Macclesfield.

View of 108 Steps, Macclesfield, as portrayed in the woven silk picture,
which was produced by James Arnold, Tie Specialties, Ltd.

Macclesfield from The Common. An engraving of about 1815 showing Roe's windmill and the early
industrialization of the town. Christ Church and Sunday School are visible on the horizon and the cupola of
Roe's Button Mill can also be seen in the middle ground to the right of the large chimney.

THOMAS MAYERS 5. AND BETTY BROWN
A SILK WORKING FAMILY IN THE EARLY 1800s

Thomas Mayers 5., born about 1778 Macclesfield, Cheshire; died after 1851; married Betty Brown 6 September 1807; died 1853, Prestbury Parish Church Records. Ten children, all baptized at St. Michaels, Macclesfield:

	i	William, born 1807; baptized 29 January 1809.
	ii	Thomas, born 1811; only evidence of him is from brother William's letter to father Thomas in Macc. 1 February 1847 re visit to Thomas in East Bethlehem, Washington Co., Pa.
	iii	David, baptized 3 January 1813.
	iv	Elizabeth, baptized 19 February 1815; picer/winder living with parents on Davies Street in 1841.
	v	Martha, baptized 16 February 1817.
	vi	Sarah, baptized 6 June 1819; died 25 May 1820.
6.	vii	JAMES, born 1820; baptized 3 October 1823; died 1887 Paterson, NJ; married SARAH ANN ALLISON.
	viii	Rebecca, baptized 13 May 1821; died 11 May 1827.
	ix	Mary Ann, born 1827; piscer/winder Davies St. 1841, Buxton Rd. 1851; daughter Mary, age 12 in 1851.
	x	Daniel, born 1828; silk winder, living with parents on Davies St, 1841.

Thomas and Betty lived in Sutton. This small village is a suburb of Macclesfield, on the opposite bank of the Bollin River. It was a short walk over a bridge from their home on Davies Street to Mill Lane and the silk factories. Thomas and Betty also lived at Common Gate, Dumber Macclesfield and 9 West Street, London Road Sutton. Thomas is shown in church records, at the baptisms of his children, as a silkman. The census of 1851 lists him as a carter, (one who transported materials).

It appears that all members of the Mayers family were employed in the silk industry and are described by occupation in the 1851 census. A piscer was a spinning mill worker who joined up broken threads by twisting. A winder transferred yarn from one spool to another. While they may have worked at home, the nature of the specialized tasks indicates they were employed in a mill. It is likely that the family was employed at the Ryle Mill. This silk "throwing mill" was owned by the brothers, William and Rueben Ryle. John Ryle, a younger brother, was superintendent there. He migrated to America with Thomas Mayers son James in 1839.

In 1978, C. B. Martin, Librarian at the Wilmslow Library, about 10 miles from Macclesfield, reported, "the houses on Davies Street were demolished some years ago and the area is now occupied by council flats." Before the area was leveled, a photo was taken showing a weaver's garret house. It could have been the Mayers home. Older maps show the location of Davies Street off Buxton Road between Commercial Road and Fence Avenue. Mr. Martin also said that it was very near to Buxton Road and could have been a corner house, listed first on Davies Street and later on Buxton Road, the address of the Mayers family in the census of 1851.

Houses on Davies Street, Sutton, Macclesfield, Cheshire, England.

In 2008, Sharon Mayers of Michigan found my 1999 online entry on a Mayers message board. She contacted me with her data on the entire Mayers line back to Hugonis in Macclesfield. Her information matched my findings exactly. We then determined that her source was an earlier version of this book, which she discovered at the Family History Center (LDS) in Salt Lake City. What was astonishing was that her husband, Colin, traces his ancestry to William, baptized 1809, the son of Thomas and Betty Brown. For the first time, we learned that James Mayers, the silkman who migrated to Paterson, New Jersey, had two brothers who also came to America.

Line Drawing from Alfred Barlow's History of Weaving published 1878. Details of the garret include the trap door access, typical small paned windows and canaries. Whilst male members of the family undertook the majority of the weaving, the women and children undertook other tasks such as winding the pirns.

Amazingly, between 1845 and 1870, William wrote several letters from America to his father Thomas and son William in Macclesfield. The letters survived and were carried to this country by William's great-grandson, Clifford Mayers, in 1929, and then passed down in the family.

William left a wife and two children in England in 1845 and traveled to Indiana where he soon acquired an 80-acre farm. He provided an interesting picture of life on the frontier and vivid description of the Native Americans in the area. In 1847, he visited Thomas another brother living in Washington County, Pennsylvania. After his wife died in England, William remarried Elizabeth Thompson about 1845. He took his second wife's last name at that time. While is possible that his first wife may have still been alive, this often happened when the wife's father did not have a male heir and had a substantial estate.

Apparently James, in Paterson, was not was not in contact with either of his brothers who were in this country. In 1869, William, in a letter to his son inquires about his brothers James and Thomas. "I will be glad if you will inform me where my brother James is and whether Thomas is still living." William is last found in the 1870 census in Wilmington, Auburn, Indiana.

The lives of Thomas and Elizabeth spanned much of the reign of Queen Victoria. This was a time of great prosperity and expansion for Great Britain. Thomas lived past 1851 and Elizabeth lived until 1853. I could not find their

Tombstones in the churchyard of St. Michaels. Most of the old cemetery that surrounded the church has been paved over and few markers remain. This was the family that James Mayers and his brothers left to come to America.

The Sunday School movement in Macclesfield was founded by John Whitaker in 1796. In 1813, money was raised by voluntary donations for a purpose built non-denominational Sunday School of Roe Street. The building, which cost £5,600, held 2,500 children, the majority of whom worked in the mills six days a week. Macclesfield Sunday School became the center for religious education and social life in town. In addition to providing religious instruction and formal education, if offered a program of social events both in the evening and at weekends.

NOTES & SOURCES

Ayre, William, Genealogist, Smithyfield, Whaley lane, Whaley Bridge, Stockport, Cheshire. England. Letters and data to Robert A. Mayers, 1978-1979, describing the study tracing the Mayers ancestry in Cheshire, England. R.A. Mayers collection, Watchung, NJ.

Census Returns of England and Wales, 1851, Kew Surrey, England.

Clayton, D. J. A History of the Church, St. Michaels, Macclesfield, 1990.

Davies Stella C., *A History of Macclesfield*, E. J. Morten, Macclesfield, 1976.

Dolan, J.R. *English Ancestral Names*, Clarkson N. Potter Inc, 1972.

The Domesday Survey (1086) A translation of the entry relating to Maaclesfield is contained in: Beamont, W. A literal Translation of the Portion of the Domesday Book relating to Cheshire and Lancashire, 1880.

Tate, J., The Domesday Survey of Chester, Chetham Society, Vol. 75.

Home, Robert, *Macclesfield As It Was*, Hendon Publishing Co., Ltd. Hendon Mill, Nelson, Lancashire, 1978.

Imperial Gazetteer of England and Wales, 1872, 230.

Macclesfield *The Official Guide*, J. Burrow & Co. Ltd. London (1970s), Macclesfield Express, December 18, 1980, *A Family Tree Hanging by a Silken Thread*. Article, describes efforts of Robert A. Mayers in tracing the ancestry of the Mayers family in Macclesfield and Paterson.

Macclesfield Historic Trail, Pamphlet, Macclesfied Borough Council, Carne, R. M., April, 1980.

The Macclesfield Charters, Written in Latin, in the custody of the Town Clerk, Macclesfield; 1261-HenryIII, 1334-Edward III, 1465-Edward IV, 1564- Elizabeth I, 1606-James I, 1678,-CharlesII, 1684- Charles II.

Parish Registers, St. Michaels, Christ Church, Macclesfield, Prestbury Parish.

St. Michaels Church-Macclesfield.com.

JAMES MAYERS 6. VII AND SARAH ANN ALLISON

James Mayers 6. vii, born March 1820; baptized 3 October 1823 St. Michaels Church, Macclesfield, England; died 1 May 1887; married Sarah Ann 1841 Paterson, New Jersey; born 1823 Monroe, New York; died 31 July 1869, int. 3 August 1869. Eight children, all born Paterson, New Jersey:

	i	Eliza, born 1843; unmarried; died 27 November 1922.
	ii	George, born 1845; died 23 March 1859, killed in factory accident, age 14.
	iii	James, born 6 August 1846; baptized 15 May 1847; died as an infant.
	iv	Enoch or Isaac, baptized 1849; died as an infant.
	v	William, born 1854; died 6 December 1893; silk dyer; married (1) Mary Blakley 24 December 1872, born 1854. 2 children. Sarah, born 1876; died 1932; unmarried; James, married Sadie Clark. (2) Bridget, born 1864 Ireland. Four Children. William, born 1886 NY; Katherine, born 1889; Mary, born 1891; John, born 1893.
7.	vi	JOHN, born 22 May 1858; died 30 March 1932; silk weaver; married MARGARET BERTRAM 1881, born 1859 Glasgow, Scotland; died 1940. Nine children.
	vii	Sarah Ann, born 4 July 1858; died 24 June 1922; married Alexander Arnot, born 1859; marble carver; died 1917. Three children: Lydia, born 1883; unmarried; teacher, normal school in 1920; Georgia, born 1886; unmarried; teacher in grade school in 1920; Edna, born 1887; died as an infant.
	viii	Georgiana, born 1860; died 1898; married J. R. A. Power, born 1825; liquor merchant; died 1911. One child, died at birth with mother.

Sarah Ann Allison migrated with her family from a small farm in Monroe, New York to Paterson, New Jersey, in 1826, at age three. She is the ancestral link of the Mayers family to the Allisons, one of America's first great families. Through the Allison family, the Mayers can trace their roots back to medieval Yorkshire, to America in 1630, to Haverstraw, New York, in 1719, to Monroe, New York, in about 1800 and finally to Paterson, New Jersey, in 1826.

The year and location of her birth in New York was found in the Paterson census data of 1850 and 1860 and on the mortality schedule for 1870. The cemetery records for the Mayers plot at Cedar Lawn Cemetery in Paterson list her age as 46. In the 1920 census, her daughter, Eliza, listed her mother's birthplace as New York as did her son John in 1930. Her middle name, Ann, appears on the 1855 mortgage when she and her husband James Mayers purchased a home at No. five Mill Street in Paterson.

Sarah Ann was the daughter of William Allison, a farmer from Monroe, New York. William is shown in census data in both Monroe and Paterson with a daughter of Sarah's age. Her mother's name is unknown. Her grandfather, John Allison, was a Revolutionary War veteran. Her surname appears both as Allison and Ellison as it does with other generations.

An 1827 Sunday school record from the Cross Street Methodist Episcopal Church in Paterson, at the Drew University Archives, shows Sarah Ellison. She appears again, eight pages later as Sally Ellison with her sister Eliza and her cousin Catherine in a group of about 150 children.

Her family lived on Mill Street in Paterson, in 1827, and on Oliver Street, in 1832. No other details of her youth are known. It is likely that her parents died before 1840. The census in that year shows a girl, age fifteen to twenty, probably Sarah, living, on Congress Street, with her married sister, Eliza Anderson. It is likely that she obtained a rudimentary education at the Methodist Sabbath School. Most children, at that time, attended no public schools and worked in the textile mills where a large proportion of the workers were children. Her home locations were all near Paterson's mill area. As a young girl she may have worked in one of the many textile mills, a short walk from home where she may have met the young English silk worker James Mayers.

Sarah Ann Allison and James Mayers were married in about 1841. He was born in 1820 to a family employed in the silk industry in Macclesfield, Cheshire, England. This town lies about thirty-five miles southeast of Manchester, in the heart of the textile industry of England. It was the leading silk producing city in England. His father was a silk carter and all eight of his siblings worked in the mills of the city. It was not uncommon for children to start work at age five as "bobbin boys," handling the reels on which silk thread was wound. Most children obtained a basic education at a Sabbath school that children attended each Sunday, for ten hours, on their one day off.

At age nineteen, James migrated to America. He sailed on the ship Marion from Liverpool. After a fifty day winter voyage and arrived in New York on April 19, 1839. (See below - The Voyage of the Marion.) A friend, John Ryle, age twenty-one, son of a family of prominent silk mill owners in Macclesfield came with him. Both of them probably worked together in the silk mill owned by the Ryle family in that city. The youths are shown as silk weavers on the ship's passenger list. This interesting document lists the names, occupations and country of origin for all 71 passengers. James Mayers and John Ryle remained close friends and business associates for the rest of their lives. The two young men aspired to be entrepreneurs in their new land and upon their arrival, immediately began to implement their plans.

When the Marion landed at South Street, James Mayers headed directly to Paterson, New Jersey, where there would be a demand for his skills in the textile industry. While silk cloth was not being made yet in America, cotton and other types of fabrics were being produced in the booming city. At first, John Ryle joined a small experimental silk startup operation founded by Samuel Whitmarsh in Northampton, Massachusetts. When this business failed he returned to New York City to open a store on Maiden Lane where he sold silk goods imported from his family's mill in Macclesfield. This street ran along the north side of the former World Trade Center.

Later, in 1839, Ryle followed his friend to Paterson to evaluate the possibility of manufacturing silk in the abandoned Colt Gun Mill. They began production the next year. James Mayers set up and managed the dyeing operations. This enterprise was the first successful manufacturer of silk in America. The efforts of these industrial pioneers spawned one of the country's greatest industries of the nineteenth century. Over the next sixty years, three thousand more silk workers and their families followed them from Macclesfield to Paterson.

In his first years in Paterson, James Mayers may have been living in a boarding house on John Street, now Ellison Street, in the mill area. There, he may have first worked in a dyeing operation run by Emanuel Leazer on that street. Sarah was lived a few doors away at No.12 John St. with her sister, Eliza Anderson, and her brother, George Allison, and his new bride Phoebe Ann Lane. Sarah's home, church activities and possible employment probably brought her in frequent contact with her young neighbor, James Mayers.

We can estimate that they first met about 1840 when she was 17 and he was 20. Based on the birth date of their first child, they married about 1841 in Sarah's church, the Cross Street, First Methodist. Few marriage records were kept during that period as that church was being served by rotating itinerant ministers. Records do exist for the following year. In 1842, Reverend Daniel Kidder married James Mayers' friend John Ryle to Sarah Morffit.

During the 1840s, the young couple continued to live on John Street a few hundred yards away from the Gun Mill. James continued to work perfecting the silk dyeing process and managing the dye operations for John Ryle's new firm, the Pioneer Silk Company.

The lives of James and Sarah followed the typical pattern of 19th century families. They married young and children soon followed in rapid succession. Families were large and infant mortality was high. These early years of their marriage were filled with both joy and sadness.

After the arrival of their first two children, Eliza in1843 and George in 1845, the next two babies, James and Enoch or Isaac did not survive. Both of these deaths may have occurred in 1849 when James purchased cemetery plot # 69 in the Methodist section of Sandy Hill Cemetery. In 1849 Sarah is listed as a member of the Prospect Street Methodist Church, an offshoot of the Cross Street Church. It was in that year three of their children Eliza, George and Enoch (Isaac), were baptized there.

Sarah Ann Allison Mayers, 1823-1869   James Mayers, 1820-1887

THE NATURALIZATION OF JAMES MAYERS

James Mayers became a citizen of the United States on November 5, 1844, after swearing to "entirely renounce and abjure all allegiance and fidelity to Victoria, Queen of the United Kingdom of Great Britain and Ireland."

This event occurred about five years and seven months after his arrival in America on April 19, 1839. The legal requirement, being five years residency in the country, shows that he did not wait long to adopt the United States as his home.

Serving as his witness was, naturally, his old friend, John Ryle. Since a witness must himself be a citizen, Ryle must have become a citizen a few months earlier.

The following original document can be seen at the Passaic County Court House, Paterson, New Jersey, reference page 338, Naturalization Records, Passaic County, 1837-1895.

PASSAIC COMMON PLEAS.

October **TERM, A. D. 18**44

PASSAIC COUNTY, *ss.* *John Ryle*

a Citizen of the
United States, being duly *on his oath* according to law, doth depose and say, that
James Mayers

an alien, a native of
England with whom this deponent is well acquainted, hath
resided within the limits, and under the jurisdiction of the United States, three years next preceding his arriving to the age of twenty-one years; that, including the said three years of his
minority, he has resided within the United States five years at least, and within the State of
New-Jersey one year at least, and has not been at any time during the said five years out of
the Territory of the United States; that, during the last three years thereof it has been, to the
best of this deponent's knowledge and belief, the bona fide intention of the said
James Mayers to become a Citizen of the United States, and
that during all that time the said *James Mayers*
has behaved himself as a man of good moral character, attached to the principles of the Constitution of the United States, and well disposed to the good order and happiness of the
same.

Sworn and subscribed in open Court,
this *5* day of *Nov 1844*
~~A. D. 18~~ *John Keenen Clk*

John Ryle

PASSAIC COUNTY, *ss.*

James Mayers being duly sworn,
according to law, on his *oath* doth declare and say, that he will support
the Constitution of the United States—and that he doth absolutely and entirely renounce and
abjure all allegiance and fidelity to every foreign Prince, Potentate, State or Sovereignty
whatever, and particularly to *Victoria Queen of the United Kingdom*
of Great Britain & Ireland of whom

he was heretofore a subject.

Sworn and subscribed in open Court,
this *5* day of *November*
A. D. 18*44*
John Keenen Clk

James Mayers

The 1850 Federal Census, the first census that lists names and data for all members of families, is a genealogists dream and lists the Mayers family:

James Mayers	Age 28	Dyer	Born England
Sarah	27		New York
Eliza	7		New Jersey
George	5		New Jersey
Phebe A. Allison	30		Pennsylvania
Sarah M. Allison	9		New Jersey
Hannah Richardson	16		England

James and Sarah are shown with their two surviving children. The record verifies that Sarah was born in New York. Phebe Ann Lane married George Allison Sarah's brother on March 4, 1840. Sarah M. Allison was their daughter. George must have died before 1842, at about age twenty-three, and his widow and child continued living with the Mayers family. Hannah Richardson may have been an au pair, boarder, or even a relative from Macclesfield. We find evidence of her wedding in 1856, at age 22, to a "huckster." Cowan was probably a merchant who worked at open air market only a block away. The wedding took place at the city jail!

In 1855, James and Sarah bought a house at five Mill Street, where they lived for the remainder of their lives. The mortgage shows that the home was purchased from John Ryle for $1,200. The house was across the street, about one hundred yards, from the Gun Mill. It was razed in 1974 when a swath was cut through Paterson's historic district to clear for a highway. It was never built and many historic sites in Silk City were lost.

Mortgage at home at No. Five Mill Street, Paterson, NJ, John Ryle to James and Sarah Mayers, 1855

Fortunately, in 1933, James B. Mayers, a grandson of James and Sarah, and an architect, drew a picture of the house with a floor plan. (See below-Archeology at No. 5 Mill Street). John Ryle lived a few doors away at No. Twelve Mill Street. His house still stands. It was preserved when the area was declared a national landmark in the 1970s.

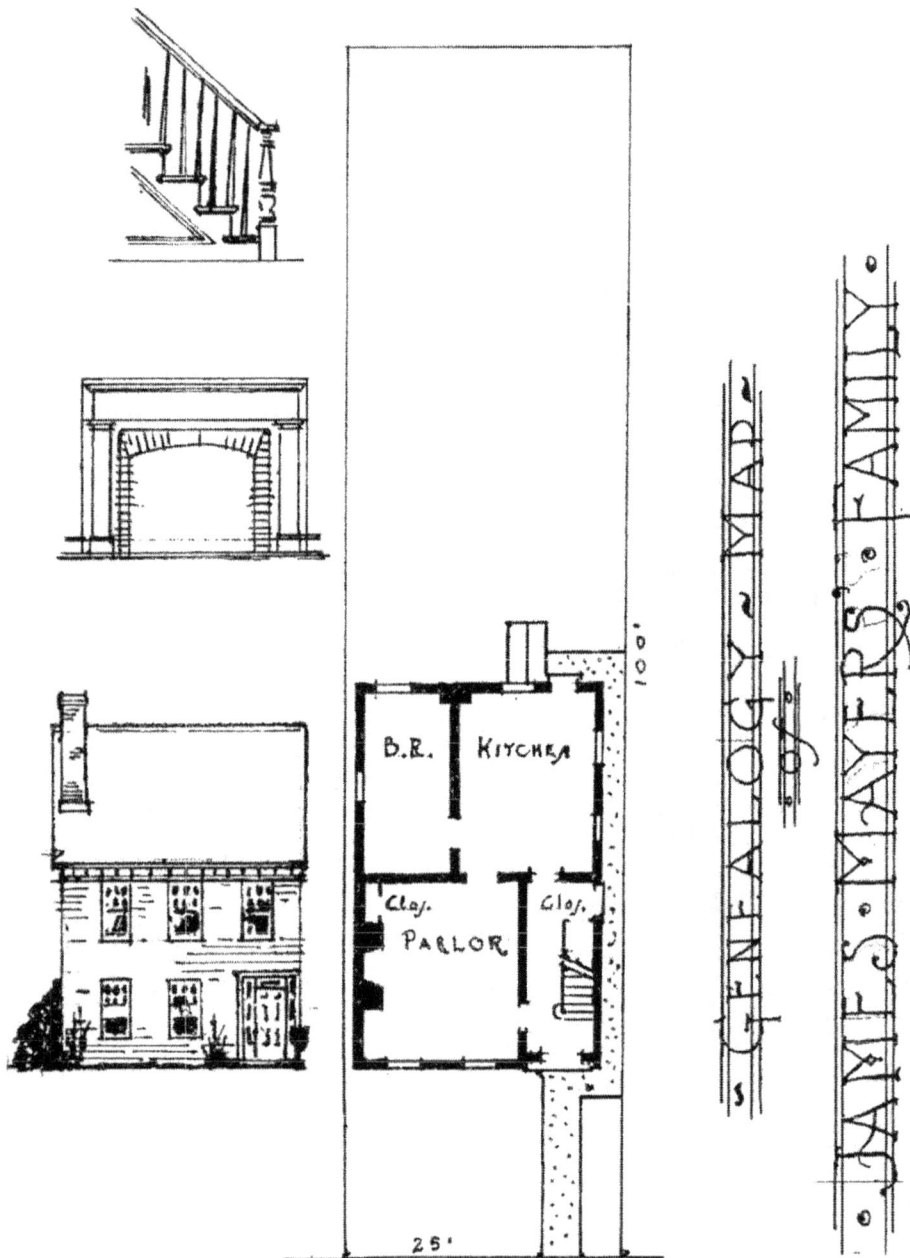

GENEALOGY MAP of JAMES MAYERS FAMILY

James B. Mayers · 12 · 2 · 33 ·

B.R.   KITCHEN

Clos.   PARLOR   Clos.

100'

25'

5 MILL ST.
PATERSON, N. J.
ORIGINAL HOME of
The MAYERS FAMILY.

Time has not been kind to the historic center of industrial Paterson. Some of the original raceways that channeled water from the Passaic River to power machinery are still intact. They were designed by Pierre L'Enfant, who also designed the layout for the City of Washington, D.C. The old Colt Gun Mill, where James spent so many of his working days stands in ruins after a fire. It was used as a textile dyeing operation until 1980.

In 1859, George, age 14, the oldest son of James and Sarah, was tragically killed while helping his father in the dye house at the Gun Mill. His clothing caught around the shaft of a machine and he was killed instantly. A complete account of the heartbreaking event appears in the Paterson Daily Guardian of March 25, 1859. Inexplicably, the boy was living with his uncle John Allison a few blocks away, at 133 Mill Street at the time.

Daily Guardian

ON, MARCH 23, 1859.

a in North-eastern New Jersey.
ction comprising Hudson, Bergen,
together with part of Essex and
nties, if we mistake not, is destined
annual progress, during the five
ing. Many important bills con
h them have recently passed the
; while the spirit of improvement
e gone abroad, is not likely to stop
ompletion of works already in pro
ontemplation. We propose to re
counties separately, and so begin

HUDSON.

ition of Bergen tunnel will make
one of the most important in this
e New Jersey Railroad, the N. J.
Morris and Essex, the N. Y. &
he Northern road all, having their
Jersey City, will make it only
a business centre to its older
ross the Hudson. In addition to
mercial facilities, and those to be
the Long Dock, the entire line
y City down to Constable Point
aimed at no very distant day, giv
y over five miles of water front.
stated by Senator Cobb, that these
taining 4000 acres, would now
e State Treasury, $200 an acre or
or the whole. Such an estimate
sitive that they will be re-claimed
no very distant day.

railroad charters have been ob
parties who design turning
it. One of these extends from
to Bergen Point, with a branch
shores of Newark Bay. Horse
lso be built from Hudson City to
and from Hoboken to West Hobo
nately these places are designed to
ated, giving with the increase cer
ke place, a population of one
housand souls, in less than ten

BERGEN COUNTY

long the line of the Pallisades, see
essity of superior communications
ery quietly to work, during the
and built the railroad, from the
est of Hoboken to Piermont. Its
rly in the season will attract popu
laces along the line, from English
ood upwards, as well as Hacken
hich place a branch will by and by
ted) and some parts of Rockland
We do not regard the prospects of
ize as very brilliant for some time;
rable location will enable it to be
t a minimum outlay, while the les
are practical railroad men, will per
duct the business. That it will
raw a dense population to that
ounty is beyond dispute; and this
ll eventually render the investment
on. Already speculation is rife
oute. In some neighborhoods we
00 an acre being demanded for
three years ago would scarcely
$75 or even $50. It is to be
ds up that way are not going
strikes us, however, that they
ing prices too soon. To make a
d thing out of it, their better poli
would be to hold out inducements
s on extremely moderate terms.
a settlement has been fairly com
will be time enough to double or
prices asked for real estate. It is
to dam the current too soon, un-

contrary, there is probably work for all to do. The only fear is that, like almost every enterprize of the sort, the business may be pushed beyond the point of safety, causing Insurance Companies to explode, as Banking corporations have in too many instances already done. We shall be glad to see the rates of Insurance reduced, believing them still too high in Paterson, after the expenditure of so much money every year on Water and *Fire Associations*. Were Agents to unite and institute the strictest possible search into the *origin* of fires, it is our firm belief that these would become so scarce that property might be profitably insured at from one-half to one per cent per annum—a point which we hope to see reached, and with entire safety too, ere the lapse of many years.

THE N. Y. STATE PRISON at Auburn was the scene of a dreadful affair last Saturday.—A disorderly convict having been ordered additional punishment, made resistence to the officers and a general revolt took place among those employed in the same shop. They armed themselves with hammers, files, bars, and such implements, when the guard were ordered to fire upon the rebels. The first attempt appears to have been unsuccessful, the weapons not being in proper order. This encouraged the prisoners, who began to assail their keepers until a discharge was made, when two of the party fell mortally wounded A third (colored) received a ball in the thigh. The excitement was promptly allayed.

EXPLOSION.—In Broom street, N. Y., yesterday a building occupied by Jacob Perth, a gunsmith, was blown up, caused by a spark falling upon a quantity of powder in a can lying contiguous. The doors and windows were blown out and the house otherwise shattered. Jacob was also pitched into the rear; but he appears to have been more frightened than hurt. No other person was injured.

WINTER WHEAT.—A gentleman from Northern Illinois informs us that the crop of wheat sown last Fall in that part of the country was nearly all killed by the severe frost in January, occurring at a time when the blade was unprotected by snow. Everything therefore depends upon the Spring crop. If the same disasters should occur as did last season, the prospects for next year would be far from cheering.

GEN. HENNINGSEN, the Fillibuster Chief, was to leave Washington to day for Savannah to collect emigrants for Arizona. The emigrants of the Arizona Association will rendezvous at Powder Horn, Texas, in July, and at El Paso in the beginning of September. Three hundred men are engaged to come down the Mississippi from the West to join the Expedition, and men are also assembling in New-York, Ohio, Kentucky and Alabama.

THE PIERMONT STRIKE.—On Tuesday the pier laborers in the employ of the Erie Railroad Company, numbering from one hundred to two hundred and fifty men, struck for their back pay, and an advance on their wages to one dollar per day. They have only been receiving ninety cents per day. These men thought that longer forbearance had ceased to be a virtue, and gave notice that, unless two months' wages were advanced, and they were allowed one dollar per day from the 1st of March, they would cease work; or if the company preferred paying them up entirely they would quietly quit and seek work elsewhere. The company accordingly paid them all up, but refused the increase of pay requested. Accordingly, on Tuesday night, the freight, instead of being landed at Piermont, was sent on to Newburg, together with the clerks and checkers on the pier.

THE HARDEN POISONING CASE.—The fall of this young man in Warren County is a mysterious affair. He entered the ministry about two years ago on trial, and has not been received into full connection. His age is only 22 years, and he married a very estimable girl about 6 months ago. His parents reside near Blairtown, Warren County, near the Paulins Kiln, his father being a respectable farmer in that neighborhood. What fell spirit could have induced a man so young in years, so lately married, to the perpetration of so foul a crime, under all the circumstances is hard to divine. It is thought some other circumstances came in to the aid of his evidently unregenerated heart, to induce him into so awful a crime as the poisoning of his young wife. It is said that a young woman with whom he enjoyed some intimacy before his marriage with his wife, was at the house on a visit, and that the plan was concocted between them. The woman, it is said, purchased the poison, and at the proposition of Harden it was taken in a dose of salts, he at the same also taking a dose, but not compounded with the poison. Who made the mixture is not stated, but it is said, and probably with truth, that it was the combined act of both. Harden's story is, that his wife, in consequence of a difficulty between her mother and himself, destroyed herself. Whatever may be the true history of this unfortunate affair, it has its lessons upon all.

DREADFUL DEATH FROM HYDROPHOBIA.—Some six weeks ago Joseph Wright was bitten by his own dog, that afterward, biting several persons and a number of animals, and giving decided symptoms of rabidness, was put to death. Wright thought little of the circumstance at the time, supposing the animal vicious rather than mad, and nothing occurred to cause alarm until last Wednesday, when he experienced a great deal of pain in the arm upon which the dog had fastened his teeth. The pain increased until he deemed it advisable to send for a physician, who gave him a lotion, but intimated to no one the danger of his patient. Wright's suffering increased, the pain extending to almost every part of his body, until Sunday, when he became raving mad, and his disease was declared to be hydrophobia. He raved at times, and tore his hair and teeth, and foamed at the mouth, and screamed like a demon, presenting a sight terrible to behold. It was necessary to bind him to the bed to prevent him from committing violence upon himself, and often in his exquisite misery, he prayed to be killed at once and relieved of his agony. The sight of water, or the mention of the term, threw him into spasms, and he fell trembling and groaning upon the floor.—Those who witnessed the poor man's madness say they never knew before how supremely wretched man may be—it was awful to contemplate, and would have startled and horrified the dullest and most impassioned nature. At last death came, in mercy, and touched him with the hand of eternal stillness. Nature was exhausted, and he expired about 11 o'clock night before last.

Wright was a young man, a moulder by profession, and had been married but one year. He leaves a wife with an infant child.—*Cincinnati Enquirer.*

The body of a gentleman—indigenous—was washed ashore a short time since from the Mississippi. In his pockets were found: "One duelling-pistol; one bowie-knife, one speech of Jefferson Davis; one speech of Senator Toombs; one copy of *The Mississippian*, edited by Barksdale; three copies of the President's Lecompton Message; a photographic representation of an alligator devouring an eagle—supposed to be the province of Mississippi in the act of exterminating the 'star and stripes.'"

We learn that the old Friends' Meeting House, at Westfield, Burlington county, was burned on Sunday, about two P. M. Nothing was saved, the edifice being completely burned out, leaving nothing but the bare walls. No cause is assigned for the fire, except probable defectiveness in the arrangement of the stove pipes. The congregation had left the Meeting House about two hours before the fire broke out. The edifice was erected about the year 1800.

A poor young man once fell in love with an heiress, and the passion being returned, it only wanted the parents' consent to make

Local and State Items.

Fatal Accident—Boy Killed.

George Meyers, aged about 13 years, son of James Meyers, was killed instantly in the Dye House connected with the Silk Mill of John Ryle, in this city, a few minutes before 12 o'clock to day. It appears the boy was employed with his father in the Dye House, and was alone in the room at the time of the accident. There is a horizontal iron shaft across the end of the room, about three feet from the floor and about ten inches from the wall. His clothing must have caught around the shaft. A man employed in the adjoining room heard the boy scream, looked in the door, and then ran to stop the mill, when the boy was found to be dead. His arm and back were broken.

Coroner C. C. Blauvelt viewed the body, and decided that no inquest was necessary.

LATER.—The boy was fifteen years old and resided in the upper part of Mill street, near Mr. C. Braun's place. The boy was found under an end window, a cloth was in his hand and wound round the shaft, and it is supposed that he was playing with a dusting rag and had it wound about his hand leaning over the shaft and looking out of the window, at the same time perhaps whipping about the cloth in his hand in playful activity.

The man at the dye-tub a few feet distant, heard a sharp cry of "quick," and this was all the deceased was heard to utter, as his head was struck against the wall by the force of the shaft which was revolving at the rate of eighty revolutions per minute. His body was jammed in behind the shaft, and it was only by uncoupling the latter that the body was extricated. It was then placed on a door, when it remained until taken to the residence of the parents.

When the dyer heard the cry of "quick," he stepped to the door and saw that the boy was fast. He first ran to the boy but could not extricate him, although the shaft had already stopped. The wheel was then stopped and with much difficulty the deceased was taken out.

It seems almost impossible that any accident could occur in the place where the poor boy met his death. The end of the rag must have gotten fast about the shaft, and being unable to loose it from his hand, ere he could utter more than a single word, his head went with an awful force against the stone wall, and he was dead.

THE PROPOSED ROAD TO PREAKNESS, to which reference was made the other evening, would strike that valley near the middle and cross the Totowa mountain through the Van Houten property, reaching the city line on the lands of Ira Ryerson, and connecting with a street which will terminate at the new bridge above the Falls. Mr. Ryerson offered to donate [illegible] as much land as might be necessary for this thoroughfare, provided the city would commence working it as soon as the new road was ready. The proposition was not accepted, on the ground that to bridge the Oldham brook and fill up the swamp adjoining it would require a heavy outlay—the Mayor supposed nearly $1000. It was believed as the measure was got up with a view of benefiting private property, that such an outlay would be unjustifiable at present. We suspect, however—so wicked are newspapers—that the failure of the scheme to bleed the rich settlers in the Totowa valley, by taxing them for gas and water, had at least as much to do in the matter as a disposition to serve the public. As mere lookers on we were led to suppose that the whole thing had been cut and dried before the meeting of Council.—

of himself was
pect street, yest
jail to get sober
quackanook.

PARLIAMENT.
requisite in the
our Common C
liminatory Law
jons. Mayor S
several the othe
like propriety.
bur, who voted
to present a m
against publishi
dum, and the
wards the close
lishing was befo
fore a motion
cided that this
motion was bef
has read the r
ceedings knows
time for both H
motion is pendi
therefore be im
of our Executi
here it is differe
ple, scarcely kn
the time, unle
Knowles meant
also little know
prised to see so
port some of th
cisions.

A PATERSON
John Cox, well
ers as a worth
was killed abou
sion of a steam
About the beg
having no emp
wife and four c
vided for, and
he continued fo
made an engag
engine in the v
miles S. W. fro
work there for
neer, when the
was taken by a
tiring up Mr.
ual in the appa
tioned the matt
instant the boi
ing to pieces,
roof a distance
was entirely lif
ing been broke
sons last even
upper part of M
much liked by
and industrious
England.

Just such a
J. P. Ramsey,
Council has
New York city
Broadway.
Council is matt
dear performan
destruction upo
intention of th
Paterson in bet
But why do
rowdies. Poor
his foray upon
demon attack
chivalry of Do

JAMES DUN
business promi
put up a neat
at the corner of

The Death of George Mayers, son of James and Sarah Mayers, 1859

That same year, James Mayers, age 39, started his own silk dying business with the encouragement of his friend John Ryle. Ryle also invited another Englishman, William C. Browne to come to Paterson to join the new venture. The firm of Browne and Mayers was located at 311-329 Straight Street. It first employed ten people. James directed the manufacturing and technical operations while Browne handled the sales. The business peaked during the Civil War with contracts for dyeing army uniforms. One was for dyeing of 5,000 blue woolen army jackets for the Union troops. In 1863 Browne was accidently killed on the tracks of the Erie Railroad.

For a short time after Brown's death, James partnered with Albert King back at the Gun Mill. In 1872 he joined with John Scott to start a business that over the years, grew to $300,000 in sales and to 200 employees. The firm wove and dyed silk and was located on the site of Grant Locomotive Works. The business continued until 1881, when Scott on a business call in New York City, was assaulted, robbed and fatally injured on Greenwich Street, while he was on his way to the ferry. James finished his working days back with his old friend John Ryle, managing the dye operations at the Gun Mill.

Great Falls Historic Area, Paterson, New Jersey

While his active career prospered and his family grew another great tragedy struck the Mayers family. Sarah Ann died on July 3, 1869 at age 46. James bought the 16 by 18 foot plot No. 193 at Cedar Lawn Cemetery, for her burial. Eighteen descendants, from three generations now rest with them in that small plot of hallowed ground. The records at the cemetery show that she died in Connecticut. I found this to be in error after a thorough search of records in that state.

James never remarried. After Sarah's death, Eliza, their eldest daughter assumed the responsibilities of the home and cared for the younger children. She never married and remained at No. 5 Mill Street caring for her aging father.

The 1870 Census for the Sixth Ward of Paterson shows the family at that time.

James Mayers	Age 50	silk dyer	born England
Eliza	26	keeps house	New Jersey
Sarah	19	Works in silk mill	New Jersey
William	17	Apprentice in machine shop	New Jersey
John	12	Attends school	New Jersey
Georgiana	10	Attends school	New Jersey

Will of James Mayers

In the name of God. Amen. I James Mayers of Number Five (5) Mill Street Paterson New Jersey, Being of disposing mind, memory and understanding, do make and publish this my last will and testament in manner following, that is to say:

First. It is my will and I hereby direct that all my just debts, and funeral and testamentary expenses be paid by my Executrix hereinafter named, as soon as conveniently can be after my death.

Second. All the rest and residue of my estate, both real and personal of which I may die seized or possessed, or in any way entitled to, I give, devise and bequeath unto my daughter Eliza Mayers, absolutely.

Third. I nominate, constitute and appoint my said daughter Eliza Mayers to be the sole executrix of this my last will and testament and hereby revoke all former wills by me, at any time made.

In witness whereof I have hereunto set my hand and seal this twentieth day of June, Eighteen hundred and eighty five.

Signed, sealed, published & declared by the Testator James Mayers, as and for his last will and testament in the presence of us who at his request and in his presence and in the presence of each other have subscribed our names hereto as attesting witnesses.

James Mayers (L.S.)

Peter Ryle #25 Church St Paterson N. J.
John H Reynolds 346 Broadway Paterson N. J.

Passaic County, ss. Peter Ryle one of the witnesses in the annexed writing purporting to be the last Will and Testament of James Mayers the Testator therein named, deceased, being duly sworn, doth depose and say that he saw the said Testator sign, and seal the said annexed writing, and heard him publish and declare the same as and for his last Will and testament; that at the time of the doing thereof the said Testator was of sound disposing mind, memory and understanding, as far as this deponent knows, and as he verily believes that John H Reynolds the other subscribing witness thereto was present at the same time with this deponent, and together with him subscribed his name thereto as a

Will of James Mayers, 1885

In 1882, James, age 62 is described by Huesser in The History of Silk Dyeing as being retired, advanced in age and suffering from chronic rheumatism. This condition likely resulted from a lifetime as a dyer. This occupation that required constant exposure to dampness from the water used to rinse the fabrics. James Mayers died of cancer on January 2, 1887 at the age of sixty-seven. He rests beside Sarah and many of his family and descendants at Cedar Lawn Cemetery in Paterson.

He left his entire estate to Eliza. My father who remembered his mother, Margaret Bertram passed on a personal recollection of him to me. She described her Father-in law as above all a gentleman, very kind and sympathetic to her challenges of raising her young family. Portraits of James and Sarah disintegrated over the years, but fortunately photographs of them survive.

James remained close to the Ryle family to the end of his days. Peter Ryle, the son of his lifelong friend John Ryle, was a witness to his will. John Ryle's death followed that of James Mayers by only ten months.

The progeny of James Mayers and Sarah Ann Allison includes seven generations of descendants living in many parts of the county today. The marriage of James, the young Englishman who played a key role in founding one of America's greatest 19th century industries, and Sarah, the little farm child who saw so much sadness in later life as a mother, began the Allison- Mayers- family ancestry.

Thompson & Ryle Houses, Mill Street, being prepared for relocation, 1979

EXCERPTED FROM THE HISTORY OF THE SILK DYEING INDUSTRY IN THE UNITED STATES BY ALBERT H. HEUSSER, SILK DYERS ASSN. OF AMERICA, 1923, 175-185

WHILE New England may, upon good grounds, claim priority in the matter of Silk Dyeing in the United States, much experimental and constructive work was accomplished in Paterson, New Jersey, a community designed by its founders to be a great emporium of manufactures. Few civic plans have so successfully matured as that formulated in November, 1791, by the Society for the Establishment of Useful Manufactures, an organization of gentlemen, mostly citizens of New Jersey, who determined to utilize the beautiful Falls of the Passaic as the source of power for their proposed industrial enterprise.

Alexander Hamilton, the great statesman who advocated the selection of Paterson as the site for the industrial projects of the S. U. M.

To Alexander Hamilton, himself interested in the syndicate, credit has always been given for the selection of the site, which first came to his knowledge during the days when the American army lay encamped in this vicinity in 1780, and he, a young man of twenty-three, was the favored secretary of Washington and a member of his official family. A small settlement of perhaps a dozen houses already nestled at Totowa Bridge, below the basin in the Valley of the Rocks, and here was the tavern, —maintained by the widow of Captain Abraham Godwin, pioneer settler and Revolutionary patriot, —to which the directors of the "S. U. M." resorted for their deliberations. Here, on the 4th of July, 1792, appropriations were made for building factories, machine shops, and shops for the weaving and printing of calico; a complicated system of race-ways was also directed to be constructed for the purpose of bringing the water from above the falls to the water-wheels of the proposed mills. The direction of this engineering operation was entrusted to Major Pierre Charles L'Enfant, a French officer of talent and distinction who had come to America to aid the cause of liberty, and to whom, in the interval, had been awarded the high honor of planning the new Federal City of Washington on the banks of the Potomac.

The Passaic Falls, 1880, after a painting by Julian Rix, who resided in the vicinity of Paterson, and was an intimate associate of the Ryle family.

Upon the new community, by general consent, was bestowed the name of Paterson, in honor of William Paterson, the governor of New Jersey, patriot, soldier, and signer of the Federal Constitution.

Today the visitor to Paterson will find the Passaic Falls somewhat diminished in overflow, but remarkable under any circumstances; while near at hand begins the system of solidly-built sluice-ways (faced with native brown-stone and arranged in three planes, each providing a fall of approximately twenty-two feet), which wind around and beneath many spacious mill buildings of modern construction. In point of interest, however, one ancient factory commands attention above all others, not only because it is the oldest of Paterson's industrial structures, but also because it was here that the science of Silk Dyeing had its beginnings in the acknowledged "Silk City of America." The "Old Gun Mill," so-called, occupies a conspicuous position in the courtyard at the joint termination of Mill and Van Houten Streets, and dates from about 1810. Originally four stories in height, and in size some 90x40 feet, its two upper floors no longer exist, having been razed a few years since because unsafe for the burden of heavy modern machinery. The name "Gun Mill" comes from its association with the Colt family, and the manufacture here of automatic pistols by Samuel Colt, trading as the Patent Arms Company, in 1835. This establishment subsequently removed to Hartford, Connecticut, and the clumsy weapon invented in 1829 has evolved into the famous revolver of today.

In January 1793, Peter Colt, of Hartford, then comptroller of the State of Connecticut, had been appointed general superintendent of the S. U. M., with full powers to administer its affairs, already in a lamentable state because of heavy financial outlays in the construction of the waterways below, and the dams above, the great falls. The first permanent factory building was perfected in 1794, and cotton yarn was spun; in the same year calico shawls and other cotton goods were printed (the bleached and unbleached muslins being purchased in New York), and in 1795-96 cotton fabric was woven in Paterson for the first time.

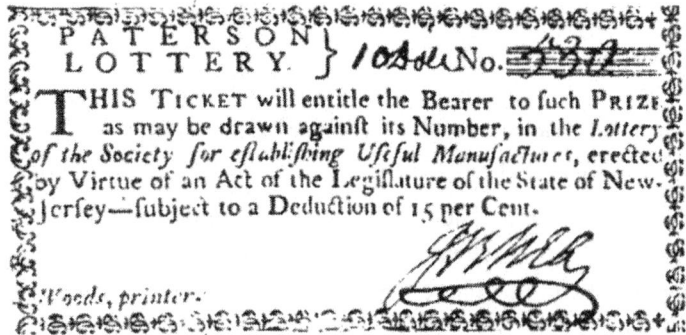

One of the tickets in the "Paterson Lottery," issued by the S.U.M. in 1793-'94 in the attempt to raise funds for the building of factories below the Falls of the Passaic, Paterson, New Jersey (Original in the collection of Albert H. Heusser.)

In 1794, moreover, the Society gave its attention to the culture of the silkworm, and directed the superintendent to plant mulberry trees for this purpose. The present Mulberry Street, in Paterson, is reminiscent of this experimental period in the city's development.

The cotton mill closed down in 1796; the silkworm idea came likewise to naught; in fact all the efforts of the pioneers

The old "Gun Mill" (foot of Van Houten St.), Paterson, New Jersey, as it was in 1910.

had proven to be premature. In 1807 fire destroyed the Society's first mill, but between 1801 and 1814 other mill sites along the race-way were leased, new structures were erected, and in 1814 Roswell L. Colt, a heavy holder of the S. U. M.'s shares, reanimated the operations of the association. It was he, in all probability, who directed the future policy of the Society. Abandoning manufacturing ventures, the organization has for a hundred years and more (thanks to its liberal charter) held real estate and rented sites and power. In keeping with the progress of the age, the "great falls" have recently been still further harnessed for the production of electrical energy, and the modern mills of the Society no longer need the ancient water wheels; many of which, however, are still standing.

The earliest of Paterson's general dyers of whom

record can be found was Richard Yeates. In the "Centinel of Freedom," published at Newark (issue of Nov. 11, 1811), appears the following announcement:

"RICHARD YEATES; DYER FROM ENGLAND.

"The subscriber begs leave to inform the public in General that he has opened a large and commodious Dye House on the premises of Mr. John Parke in Paterson, where he intends carrying on the dyeing of Cottons, Woolens, Silks, and Linens of all colors, and done up equal for neatness to any imported, with the utmost dispatch and on the most reasonable terms. RICHARD YEATES.
"N. B. —Colors warranted to stand washing equal to any imported from England.
"Paterson, Oct. 24, 1811."

It is not to be supposed that Mr. Yeates was a "silk dyer" as the term is now understood, and for this reason we are not warranted in awarding him the honor of being Paterson's pioneer in this exclusive field. He merely dyed silk goods, among other articles, before silk had begun to be manufactured here.

By 1840, Paterson had grown to be a town of 7,000 populations, and possessed 19 cotton mills and one woolen factory, with two dyeing and printing works to accommodate these establishments. Silk had not yet made its entry into the local field. It is interesting to record that now, after a lapse of eighty years and more, Paterson has upward of 850 silk manufacturing establishments, large and small, with 75 silk dye houses, both branches of the industry employing, in the aggregate, 30,500 operatives. The manufacture of cotton goods has ceased almost entirely.

It is estimated that, today, at least 10,000 persons (practically one-third of those employed in the silk industry) are connected with the dyeing and printing establishments. This large percentage may be accounted for by reason of the fact that a great quantity of silk, manufactured elsewhere, comes to Paterson for dyeing.

JOHN RYLE

JOHN RYLE, 1817-1887
The "Father of the Silk Industry" of Paterson. (From Trumbull's *History of Industrial Paterson*," 1882.)

John Ryle is universally referred to as "the father of the silk manufacturing industry in Paterson." To him further credit is due for introducing the art and practice of silk dyeing into the city of his adoption. Upon the fourth floor of the abandoned "Gun Mill," in 1840, as an employee of G. W. Murray, of Northampton, Massachusetts, he began the weaving of silk. Three years later the partnership of Murray and Ryle was formed, and in 1846, Mr. Ryle assumed the sole proprietorship. During these half-dozen years, although the dyeing facilities of New England were at his service, John Ryle little by little acquired the science of doing this work for himself and at his own plant. The Passaic River then, as now, skirted the precincts of his mill-yard, and the situation was ideal for the purposes of a dyeing establishment. Today the locality resembles a veritable village of dye houses, and it would seem as though the members of the "Dyers Guild" had appropriated this old corner of Paterson to their own particular use. In the midst of its newer and more pretentious neighbors stands the old brownstone "Gun Mill"—reduced in height, as has been stated—but unmistakably ancient "and honorable, and withal an industrial landmark which ought to be preserved inviolate.

The career of John Ryle was a singularly successful one, and his long and useful life well deserves a detailed biographical sketch:

Mr. Ryle was born at Bollington, near Macclesfield, England, Oct. 22,1817. He first handled silk as a bobbin boy when he was five years of age, and from that time to the day of his death he was interested in the silk industry. He learned the manipulation of the fibre in all its branches, and at twenty-two years of age was the superintendent in the mill of his two brothers, Reuben and William, in Macclesfield. On March 1st, 1839, he sailed for this country and obtained the position of superintendent in the small silk mill owned by Samuel Whitmarsh, at Northampton, Massachusetts, where he became acquainted with George W. Murray, who had been interested in silk manufacture in England before coming to this country. While in that position Mr. Ryle received an offer from his two brothers in Macclesfield to handle the product of their mill in this country, and for this purpose opened a store on Maiden Lane and William Street, New York City. Mr. Murray, however, induced him to abandon the business of importer, in order to join him in the actual manufacture of silk in this country. Mr. Kyle visited Paterson, where he became acquainted with Christopher Colt, who had experimented at making silk thread for about three months in the old Gun Mill, but had abandoned the project. The result of Mr. Ryle's visit to Paterson was that Mr. Murray purchased Colt's" machinery, as it stood in the fourth story of the pistol factory, for $3,200. He put Mr. Ryle in charge under a contract for three years' employ. That was the foundation of successful silk manufacture in Paterson. Mr. Ryle was among the pioneer manufacturers of spooled sewing silk in this country. It is said that repeated conferences between himself and Elias Howe, the inventor of the Howe sewing machine, made it possible for the latter to overcome one of the chief difficulties he had in perfecting his sewing machine, —a way to feed the silk thread to the needle.

Three years after the purchase of the mill, Mr. Ryle was taken into partnership, and the firm of Murray & Ryle did a nourishing business in the manufacture of sewing silk and twist until the year 1846, when Mr. Ryle, assisted by his brothers in England, was enabled to buy out Mr. Murray's interest. Up to this period Mr. Ryle had not attempted weaving broad goods, but as soon as he became sole owner of the establishment he proceeded to carry out this daring idea. He set a few looms at work and produced several pieces of dress silk of a thousand yards' length. In 1847 he still further expanded his facilities by purchasing the building that contained his machinery. To complete his knowledge of silk manufacture, he went to Europe in 1850 and visited the principal factories of France and Italy.

John Ryle's "Murray Mill," Mill Street, Paterson, New Jersey

In 1854-5 he erected a new mill, which he named the Murray Mill, after his former patron. It was on Mill Street, opposite Ward, 73x200 feet in area, and two stories high. He added other mill properties to this and accumulated a fortune, but lost about $400,000 by a fire in 1869. He immediately erected the mill now known as the Murray Mill, adopting a plan of construction since followed by other silk manufacturers; the buildings of brick, one story high, lighted only from the roof by skylights with a northern exposure, the different rooms separated by solid brick partitions and many of the floors laid with bluestone flagging. It was one of the few establishments where all the processes of silk manufacture, including dyeing, were carried on under one roof. In the early "fifties" Mr. Ryle purchased the romantic heights bordering the Passaic Falls. He conceived the idea' of making this charming spot a public park, free to all comers—a breathing place where the working people of Paterson could come and enjoy themselves. To this end, in the following years, he expended large sums of money in adorning the place with bridges and other structures, and laying out suitable walks and drives. Popularity came with prosperity, and the citizens of Paterson made him their mayor (1869-71). Mr. Ryle died Nov. 6, 1887, while on a visit to Macclesfield, England; his remains were brought to Paterson for interment.

The existing "Murray Mill," a photograph of which is reproduced herewith, is interesting in many respects. Its dye house, which was Mr. Ryle's pride and joy, has, within the last forty years, been occupied by many tenants, the most successful of whom was Edward Riley.

John Ryle made no pretention of being himself a practical dyer, but employed the expedient, to which other industrial pioneers resorted, of engaging skilled artisans who had received their training and experience abroad. In all probability James Mayers, who came from England with Mr. Ryle in 1839, and who had charge of the latter's dyeing department at the "Gun Mill," possessed a thorough knowledge of this branch of the business, and contributed largely to Mr. Ryle's ultimate success.

Paterson's first city directory (1855-'56), published by D. A. Ray (a copy of which was kindly placed at the disposal of the editor by Dr. B. F. Luckey), gives us a very interesting list of the names of the men then engaged in the various branches of the textile industry, and as complete a record of the pioneers as we shall be able to obtain. As a matter of history and of undoubted local interest, we copy the names of all the weavers, although many of them did not, perhaps, handle silk:

The old residence of John Ryle,
Paterson's pioneer silk manufacturer,
still standing at No. 12 Mill Street.

Akin, John, silk dyer, 290 Straight Street.
Barnes, James, color mixer, 9 Sanford's Alley.
Burnett, Ambrose, weaver, 7 High Street.
Buckley, Benjamin, machinist, 37 Clark Street.
Campbett, Winifred, weaver, 49 John Street.
Christie, Andrew, weaver, 31 Godwin Street.
Drew, Ezra, weaver, 9 Benson Street.
Elton, James, spindles, 91 Mill Street.
Firth, Samuel, dyer, 64 Willis Street.
Fisher, Robert, spinner, 27 Broadway.
Greer, John, weaver, 15 Fair Street
Hamil, Robert, silk manufacturer, 22-26 Ward St., and Beaver mill.
Hampshire, Richard, weaver, 96 Broadway.
Hardy, Joseph, spinner, 25 John Street.
Hardy, Robert, weaver, 58 Hamburg Avenue.
Hargraves, John, weaver, 8G Mill Street.
Harper, John, weaver, 9 Prospect Street.
Hinchliff, John, dyer, 133 Jersey Street.
Hiskcth, William, weaver, 38 Hamburg Avenue.
Hughes, Anthony, carder, 30 John Street.
King, Allen, weaver, 54 Marshall Street.
Kirkman, Robert, bleacher, 27 Straight Street.
Kissockt James, silk dyer, 130 Market Street.
Knowles, Allen, weaver, 16C River Street.
Knowles, Caleb, calico printer, 01 Willis Street.
Lockwood, John, weaver, 20 North Main Street.
Malcolm, William S., weaver, 38 Hamburg Avenue.
Marshall, Joseph, weaver, 71 Pine Street
Mawhinney, William Jr., weaver, 26 Cross Street.
Mawhinney, Robert weaver, 21 Passaic Street.
Orr, William, weaver, 24 Fair Street (rear).
Parker, Francis, weaver, 27 Broadway.
Perry, Samuel, weaver, 15 Division Street.
Reed, John, weaver, 68 Congress Street.
Reese, John, spinner, 152 Mill Street.

Ryle, John, silk manufacturer, 12 Mill Street.
Ryle, Peter, silk manufacturer, 3 Boudinet Street.
Singleton, Frances, weaver, 24 Congress Street.
Walker, Richard, dyer, 9 Passaic Street.
Webber, Anthony, weaver, 24 Passaic Street.
Whitehouse, John, weaver, 38 Clinton Street.
Williamson, John, carpet weaver, 102 Mechanic Street.
Wilson, John, weaver, 262 Broadway.

BROWNE & MAYERS

The first firm of custom dyers to the silk trade of Paterson was undoubtedly that of Browne & Mayers. In 1859, John Ryle induced a friend of his, William C. Browne (born at Coventry, England, and subsequently a resident of New York City), to come to Paterson and engage in partnership with his own boss-dyer, Mr. James Mayers; foreseeing that great possibilities were awaiting those who had the confidence and skill necessary to make a beginning in this field. Their establishment was on Mill Street, and from the information at hand, it seems likely that it was in one of the buildings in the old "Gun Mill" yard at the foot of Van Houten Street, and that employment was given to about ten operatives. Mrs. E. Browne Jaeger, a daughter of Mr. Browne, tells us that the partnership was not of long duration, and was dissolved shortly before the Civil War. She says that her father thereupon built the structure still standing at No. 329 Straight Street, and independently engaged in the business of dyeing. Like Mr. Ryle, he was not a practical dyer, but engaged competent men to conduct his shop, himself going to New York almost daily in the pursuit of business. As to the Straight Street premises, Mrs. Jaeger states that the first floor, front, was used as an office; the upper floor as a drying room; the dye-house proper being accommodated by the longer building in the rear. Mrs. Jaeger recalls that, in the early stages of the War of the Rebellion, her father contracted to dye five thousand woolen jackets for the use of the soldiers, having also—for some reason or other—to remove the pockets. She says:

WILLIAM C. BROWNE
(Courtesy of his daughter, Mrs. E. Browne Jaeger, Paterson, New Jersey)

The historic "Gun Mill" precincts, Paterson, New Jersey, illustrating the old and the new. The tank and the modern buildings, some of which are a portion of the Stanford Silk Dyeing Company's plant, contrast strongly with the century old mill in the middle foreground, below the second level of the S.U.M. sluiceway.

"As you may imagine, it took some space to dry those jackets, and the neighboring fences were requisitioned for the purpose, much to the curiosity and amusement of the community. I remember helping to detach those pockets. (Some task! —two from each.) My mother, who never let anything go to waste, made thirty-six quilts of those pockets; she called them "Pocket Quilts," and distributed them among her children and friends as heirlooms. One of these quilts is now stored in our attic, in memory of days gone by."

In 1863, Mr. Browne sold his Straight Street plant to Albert King (Koenig) and soon thereafter purchased a piece of property on River Street, upon which were several small buildings, (the site now occupied by the extensive factory of the Manhattan Shirt Company). In this structure he conducted dyeing operations until his death. It was his intention to engage in the manufacture of silk in connection with his dyeing business, and he had planned to alter and enlarge several of the River Street buildings, but his accidental death on the tracks of the Erie Railroad in 1865 intervened, and Mrs. Browne, his widow, had no

97

alternative but to dispose of his interests. The accompanying portrait of Mr. Browne is reproduced from a crayon picture executed by his son-in-law, the late Mr. Jaeger.

JAMES MAYERS
(courtesy of his granddaughers, the
Misses Lida A. and Georgina K. Arnot,
Paterson, New Jersey)

William C. Browne, at present associated with the Gaede Silk Dyeing Co., is a grandson of his namesake, and—as an expert black dyer—upholds the family reputation.

As to Mr. Mayers, the associate of Mr. Browne, he returned to John Ryle, and continued in charge of the latter's dyeing plant until chronic rheumatism forced his retirement. In 1882, according to Trumbull's "History of Industrial Paterson," Mr. Mayers, although advanced in years, was still living, his house being on Mill Street, opposite the Essex Mill. He, too, is represented in the dyeing activities of the present day, his granddaughter, Miss Sarah Mayers, being associated with the clerical department of the National Silk Dyeing Company.

The late Constant Putoz, who had much information as to the early dyeing establishments of Paterson, has corroborated the fact that John Kyle's dye-house was located in the "Gun Mill" yard: where the dyeing operations were, for the most part, connected with the sewing silks ("machine twist" and "button-hole") which Mr. Hyle then manufactured; he also confirmed the details as to Mr. Mayers' service as the head of that department. Mr. Putoz further stated that, in 1858 or '59—so he had been informed— there was a small silk-dyeing establishment in operation on Hamburg Avenue, conducted by a man named Morelle, who also dyed garments.

Boyd's "New Jersey State Business Directory" for 1860 furnishes partial confirmation of the above statement in that a dye-house at No. 51 Hamburg Avenue is listed therein; but the proprietor's name is given as William Apel. I think we may consider that this is the establishment recalled by Mr. Putoz. Possibly one man succeeded the other, although editorial judgment would give credit to the printed record rather than to personal reminiscence if but one name must be selected as being authentic.

In this issue of Boyd's Directory we also find that Christian Huber, of No. 188 River Street, was engaged in the dyeing business, but it is particularly noted that Browne & Mayers were silk dyers.

ALBERT KING

Albert King, the purchaser of Mr. Browne's modest plant on Straight Street, is repeatedly mentioned in these pages by reason of his connection in later years with the enterprises of the Oneida Community and the Nonotuck Silk Company, but we are indebted to his daughter for most of the intimate biographical detail which follows. As to the early family history, she writes:

"We can trace our ancestry no farther back than 1685. They were French Huguenots; were driven out of France, and settled in Germany. My father was born in Prum, Prussia, June 30, 1826. He was one of thirteen children, and the only one to emigrate to America. He came to Skinnersville, Massachusetts, in 1850, and was head dyer for William Skinner for some years, leaving there to go to Canton, Massachusetts, where he started for himself in the business of dyeing rags and dresses. After a year he was burned out. He then came to Paterson."

Mr. Koenig's business career in Paterson covered a span of ten years (1863-1873). Although born to the Teutonic name of Koenig, he is usually referred to as Albert "King" (which is the English equivalent). His daughter explains that the change came about because William Skinner, unable to pronounce "Koenig," took the liberty of suggesting the change. At any rate, it was as "Albert King" that he, in 1868, renounced his allegiance to Emperor William and became an American citizen, the naturalization papers being recorded in the office of the clerk of the County of Passaic, State of New Jersey. He became affiliated with the Masonic fraternity of Paterson, and took a lively interest in civic affairs.

Two of Paterson's old-time dyers whom the editor interviewed recalled vividly their experiences in Albert King's little dye-shop.

Edward Bodner Sr. (who in 1867 apprenticed himself to learn the dyeing business under Mr. King), stated that the latter agreed to pay him $9.00 per week—with free board, clothing and lodging as an inducement— but minimized the value of the previous experiences of young Bodner in Switzerland, saying that American methods of dyeing were quite different from those in vogue upon the other side, and that he would "have to learn all over again." Mr. Bodner said that the terms of the contract stipulated that he should sleep in the apartments adjoining the plant. Although characterizing his employer as a rather exacting taskmaster, Mr. Bodner—after a lifetime of varied experiences—paid tribute to Mr. King's skill in the dyeing art. He said that one of the largest customers of King at that time was Frederick Baer, silk manufacturer of Paterson, who was operating a plant in the Huntoon Mill, Broadway and Bridge Street.

ALBERT KING, 1826-1885

Albert King's old Dye-house, 329 Straight St., near Essex St., Paterson, New Jersey

Present-day appearance of the rear portico of the premises at 329 Straight Street.

Robert A. Mayers and John Ryle, great grandsons of silk pioneers at Rogers Locomotive works, 1979

Rebuilding of upper raceway, 1979

Robert P. Mayers at Hamilton Statue, 1979

NOTES & SOURCES

Brady, Barry J., Paterson, New Jersey, The Birthplace of the American Industrial Revolution, Archaeology, Vol. 34, 5, Sept/October, 1981.

Cedar Lawn Cemetery Records, Mc Lean Blvd. at Crooks Ave., Paterson, NJ.

Dickerson, Philemon, City of Paterson, Its Past Present and Future Paterson Educational Assn. January 31, 1856.

Federal Census, 1840-1900. Mortality Schedule. 1870. South Ward, Paterson, NJ, 2.

Fisher, Rev. Samuel *Census of Paterson, NJ 1827-32.* Passaic County Historic Society, 1958.

Heusser, Albert, H., *The History of Silk Dyeing in United States*, Silk Dyers Assn. of America, 1923, 175-185.

Margrave, Richard D., Technology Diffusion and the Transfer of Skills: Nineteenth Century Migration To Paterson, University of London, 1985.

Mayers, Robert A., *The Voyage of the Marion*, Cheshire Magazine, 2004, Issue 37.

Methodist Archives, Drew University, Madison, NJ.

Naturalization, Probate Records – Passaic County Courthouse, Paterson, NJ.

NJ Business Directory 1861, Passaic County Historic Society Library, Paterson, NJ.

Ships Passenger Lists, New York, 1839. National Archives.

Trumbull, Levi, R., *A History of Industrial Paterson*, C. M. Herrick, Paterson, 1882.

Northeast Historical Archaeology, Symposium on Paterson, NJ, Spring, 1975.

The Great Falls-S.U.M. Historic District, descriptive booklet, 23 pages, 1971.

The Voyage Of The Marion, Winter, 1839
By Robert A. Mayers

The story of the journey of John Ryle and James Mayers, the founders of the Silk Industry in Paterson NJ,
from Macclesfield, England to Paterson, New Jersey, in 1839.

Two young men, James Mayers and John Ryle, climbed 108 steps alongside a medieval cathedral to reach the higher ground of the ancient Cheshire town of Macclesfield, England. They emerged into a bustling marketplace, the social and business center of the town since the middle- ages. The first Anglo-Saxon settlement was on this site since a steep drop down to the River below provided a natural defense.

The looming presence of St. Michaels Cathedral dominated the market square since 1278. In the center of the market was an ancient Celtic stone cross. Proclamations were made to the peasant population from this spot and early traders set up their stalls around the cross. Here, all business transactions were made in times before the written word. All deals made within the shadow of the cross were considered binding. Tudor timber framed buildings lined the square and housed the town hall, guildhalls and inns. Butchers, fishmongers and merchants boisterously hawking cattle, sheep, wool, iron pots, cloth and corn filled other stalls in front of the buildings. Farmers from surrounding villages brought their produce here by the horse load.

From the high ground, the youths looked down on "Waters Green," the lower town. In earlier times this was known as "The Gutters", a slum area where slaughterhouses, tallow chandlers and other unsavory activities were located. Open drainage flowed past squalid dwellings into the river Bollin. This part of town was savaged, far beyond other sections of the town, by the plague of 1603.

By 1839, evidence of a new age was apparent everywhere in the valley below. The "Green" was now a conglomeration of mills, houses, inns, dye works on the river, graveyards and even a school, but Macclesfield was not typical of the small English country villages of that time. Spawned by the industrial revolution and impacted by events in the outside world over the past 100 years, this bucolic feudal village had transformed into a thriving commercial town. A canal completed just eight years before in 1831 served the mills by providing a conduit for the textiles manufactured in the town which were transported to the large city of Manchester in the north, as well as other major cities and ports.

The home of James Mayers could be seen on the opposite bank of the river in the suburb of Sutton. It was one of a long row of stone garret houses, usually with three stories and long windows to admit light. Weavers could work handlooms on the top floor and live below. Further up the bank, was the mill where it is likely both were employed. It was owned by John Ryle's older brothers. The river flowing past it furnished its power.

Silk was the business of Macclesfield. It was the hub of that industry in England. The young men were silk weavers, as were generations of their families back to the middle 1700s.

These were times of great distress in the silk industry. After the boom years of the 1820s, reduced tariffs were causing competition from a flood of foreign imports, but even worse, the introduction of power looms was causing high unemployment among the handloom weavers. Jobs had declined by sixty percent and many silk workers, reduced to abject poverty were returning to surrounding villages. Workers vented their rage by destroying the new machinery. There were frequent riots and the windows of many mills were smashed.

James and John talked about their future and agreed that it held little promise for them.

As skilled weavers they were better off than most but, with an excess of available workers in their trade, their talents had little value. The opportunity to improve the quality of their lives and to advance their prospects in the world did not appear to exist in this setting. They faced a lifetime of insecurity and the drudgery of fourteen-hour days.

They knew there was a place in the world where their abilities might be valued and where they could improve their chances: a classless land where their skills were still considered high-tech and where they heard that opportunity was limited only by lack of resourcefulness. It was called America. America did not have a silk industry and nobody from Macclesfield had even considered going there earlier.

Even for two optimistic and adventurous young men with little to lose, leaving was a daunting decision. At the same time, with America needing to import all of its silk, bringing their skills here would be the greatest challenge of their lives. James Mayers, age 19, would leave a large family. His father was a silk carter and all eight of his siblings worked in the mills. John Ryle, age 21, had started work as a bobbin boy at the astonishing age of five. Like hundreds of other mill children, both had gained a rudimentary education at a "Sabbath School" which they attended for ten hours each Sunday, their only day off. (The works of Charles Dickens graphically depict life in England at this time.)

Registration Papers for the Ship "Marion," launched Canning, Nova Scotia October 12, 1836, courtesy of the Public Archives of Canada.

Coming from a family of mill owners, John was the better off of the two. It is likely that his brothers were willing contributors to the modest expenses of a voyage. They too envisioned extending their business interests in the new land through these young emissaries.

Despite uncertain prospects for employment and the ominous prospects of an ocean crossing fraught with peril, they decided to embark on a voyage from which few ever returned. Winter crossings of the North Atlantic were best avoided. They would have to book passage from Liverpool to sail as early as possible in the spring.

It was a poignant time as the young men took a final look at their ancestral home and said farewell to their families and friends. This scene was repeated endless times as nine million immigrants left the British Isles through the Port of Liverpool for America during the 1800s.

Tim Boddington, a Cheshire Area historian describes the details of a journey that the two young men would take to reach Liverpool, in 1839. "The first leg of the trip, before the railroad had reached Macclesfield, would be by stagecoach, north to Manchester, a distance of about fifteen miles. The coach left from the Bull Inn, in Macclesfield opposite the Town Hall. (The inn remains open to this day.) They would ride all day through the stark wintry landscape of the Cheshire Peak Country".

"At Manchester, they would board the Manchester-Liverpool Railway, the first public passenger train in the world, for a thirty mile ride. Liverpool Road Station still exists in Manchester, and is part of a very popular technology museum there."

Upon arrival in the port city of Liverpool, tickets for the trip to America were purchased at the ship owner's office, on the waterfront. They would sail on a packet, a vessel that crossed the Atlantic on a regular schedule and carried both freight and passengers on a fixed route. For many years packets were the only means of communication between the two continents.

Amid the forest of masts, they found their ship, the Marion. She was small for a transatlantic crossing, only 112 feet long and 27 feet at her widest. This was the average size for an immigrant packet of this time. Built in St. John, Canada, in 1836,the Marion was a wooden, square-rigged vessel with a "burthen" (carrying capacity) of 427 tons. She was typical of the hundreds of ships in this service until about 1860 when steamships began replacing sail. Liverpool to New York was, by far, the most common route for the packets. At that time there were about twenty making the run.

The Marion carried seventy-one passengers on this trip to New York. Passage was booked for as little as ten dollars per person. Tickets provided for minimum space, typically ten feet, for each passenger and their luggage. A water ration of six pints for drinking, washing, and cooking and one pound of food per day were provided. This usually consisted of bread or biscuit, rice, oatmeal or potatoes. When the time at sea exceeded the predicted length of the trip, these meager rations were reduced. To supplement this bare subsistence diet, people often brought some of their own food which soon spoiled or was consumed a short time into the trip.

Captain William Bonnyman was her master. Time was needed to unload her cargo of lumber from Canada and install accommodations for her new human cargo. As usual, many of the immigrants brought more baggage than allowed and it was not permitted on board. It must have been painful to see dock scavengers eagerly snatch up the beloved possessions carefully selected for the trip.

As the young men ascended the gangway and stepped aboard for the first time they were in the midst of great activity. A roll call was being taken and a doctor inspected the passengers as ship owners could be fined for carrying the sick or disabled. Imigrants were warned that, by law, they were under the same disciplinary rules as the crew and could even be charged with mutiny for disruptive behavior.

The bewildered passengers were herded below. Bunks, four tiers high were assigned and baggage was stowed. To prevent future disagreements, a schedule was set up for turns at the firebox. Cooking could be done on deck, if the weather permitted. Voices with an Irish brogue were heard everywhere and such Gallic sounding names as Mulligan,

Malloy, McKeon and Fitzpatrick were detected above the din. This was the start of the vast wave of Irish migration caused by the potato famine. This exodus would peak over the next decade.

Ship's Passenger List for the "Marion," departure, Liverpool, England, March 1, 1839,
arrival Port of New York, April 19, 1839, courtesy Passenger Arrival Records, National Archives.

A few days after the two arrived, they sailed on the first day of March 1839. Orders shouted from the helm alerted sailors to scamper up the rigging. Lines to the dock were singled up and then quickly cast off in order to catch the morning tide. Most of the first day, the Marion cruised down the Mersey and its estuaries, and then across the Irish Sea. Often, the last land sighted was the coast of Ireland, which the more naive often mistook for an early arrival in America. Before breaking out into the open sea, everyone came on deck to take their last glimpse of land. Few would ever see their homeland, families or friends again.

Captain Bonnyman set the course for New York, sails bellied out as the ship plunged into the first surge of the open North Atlantic. A wave of nausea swept though the passengers. The Captain, a seasoned mariner, would exert every seamanship skill in his repertoire to shorten the trip. Under ideal conditions, the trip had been made in as few as twenty days. But March still brought freezing weather, strong gales and icebergs. This was to be a hard voyage the Marion would be at sea for fifty days.

The winter of 1839 had been very severe. Even before leaving home, the two young men had learned that in a storm in January, just two months before the departure of the Marion, two immigrant packets had gone missing and a third was driven ashore with the loss of all hands. Forty packets were lost over this thirty-year period that marked the height of their use.

During the spring, icebergs broke loose and a longer southerly course was necessary but on this southerly route, the ship often had to slow down in fog and to take temperature readings of the water to see if ice was near. Ice sank many packets in these years and many were last seen heading into the ice fields. Seventy-three years later, in April of 1912, the Titanic would be lost in this same area, at the same time, as the Marion passed through.

A list of all passengers was drawn up at sea as soon as everyone had settled into a daily routine. It provided the names, ages, occupations and country of origin of all seventy-one passengers and would be required immediately on arrival. All were from Great Britain or Ireland. It showed the name of the ship its date of departure from Liverpool, and arrival in New York, its tonnage and the captain's name. So frequent were deaths during these voyages that the printed form had a separate column "Died On Voyage. On this trip, there were no entries here, attesting to the skills of Captain Bonnyman. On most ships names listed in this column were those of small children.

Who were the forty-two men, twenty-three women and six children on this perilous trip? Most were young, forty-two were in their twenties and sixteen teenagers. Only two people were over forty. Hugh Scott and Mary Gannon, both age forty, appear together on the list. Does this suggest an on board romance or would Hugh later send for his family and Mary be greeted by a husband on arrival?

Strangely, there were no married couples aboard. All the women are listed as "spinsters" or "laborers". There are several brother and sister combinations, usually an older sibling in charge of younger children. James Cox, age twenty, was accompanied by his sister Bridget, 20, and three younger brothers. The sisters, Mary and Ann Fitzpatrick, traveled together. Were they orphans or would they later send for their parents as conditions worsened in the old world? Only one single parent, Mary McKeon, age thirty, was aboard with her three-year-old son. Was Mary a widow or did her husband await her in the new world? Many were alone. Would anyone be there to greet them in the new land?

Few among the travelers had any skills or trade. Other than our silk weavers, James Mayers and John Ryle, there was a tanner, a saddler and a baker; all other passengers are identified as "laborers". Yet these young people, all ready to start work, would dig the canals, build the railroads and provide all the muscle and talent that would propel America into a leading world power in just a few decades. Their descendents would provide much of the leadership that would, in less than a century, create the greatest nation on earth.

With so many young, unmarried people meeting for the first time and being confined in close quarters, we can only imagine the many relationships that may have developed. How many love affairs, future marriages and lasting friendships occurred? Or how much disagreement and animosity arose in the cramped quarters? At first, a festive, party atmosphere would prevail, but this was short lived and as private caches of food and beverages dwindled, most settled into the monotonous daily routine.

Passengers were allowed above decks in small groups to wash clothes and to attempt to bathe. There was a chance to cook any unspoiled food they had brought. Most of the trip would be through bad weather with rough seas. Everyone would stay below in their cold, wet bunks, in complete darkness. As weather worsened, sails were shortened and hatchways secured. Pitching and rolling, as heavy seas spilled over the main deck, the ship labored westward for the next seven weeks.

About the time, when everyone despaired of the journey ever ending, a lookout, on the top spar of the mainmast, cried out, "Land Ho". As if in a dream, James and John were able to see a small fringe of land, backed by high hills, on the horizon. This was Sandy Hook, New Jersey, and the Highlands of the Navesink River. This landfall looks the same today and for that matter, as it did in1609 when first sighted by Hendrick Hudson. A lighthouse gradually became visible on the high land. This was the predecessor of the Twin Lights that can be seen today.

As the Marion sailed closer into the approach to New York Bay, she was approached by a fleet of small, fast cutters. These were the boats of the Sandy Hook Pilots who competed for the job of guiding ships into the port. With a pilot aboard, Captain Bonnyman could now step back from the wheel, while a skilled seaman, with local knowledge of the inland waters, conned the ship past shoals. They moved down Ambrose Channel and through the Narrows, now spanned by the Verrazano Bridge. Everyone experienced an uncanny sense of stillness. The pitching, rolling and groaning of the ships timbers, which everyone had grown accustomed to, suddenly stopped, as the ship entered the calm waters of New York Harbor.

There was no Statue of Liberty to lift her lamp beside the golden door to greet the weary, but eager people, who now crowded the main deck. No immigrant-processing center would exist until1855 when Castle Garden opened at the Battery, in1855. There would be no Ellis Island for another fifty- five years.

The young men viewed a city where, other than for a few church steeples, only a few buildings stood over four stories high. The Marion glided a short distance up the East River until she was nudged by a side-wheeler tug to the dockside at South Street. On the nineteenth of April 1839, the ship was motionless for the first time in fifty days. James Mayers, my great-grandfather had arrived in America.

The teeming wharf swarmed with dockhands, hustlers, food carts and ticket sellers. Many would go on to other destinations. The first people to climb aboard were immigration officers. Captain Bonnyman presented the ships passenger list before anyone was allowed to disembark. Little time was spent verifying the information, as the immigration staff was usually overwhelmed with traffic, as many as ten ships arrived in a single day. So, amid chaos and confusion, the Marion's passengers and crew swarmed ashore and bid hasty, but heartfelt, farewells to their friends. Their values and ethnic traditions would blend into the American character, which today, in so many ways, shapes the way we think.

No immigration records have ever been found for James Mayers or John Ryle. Few exist for many of the millions of new Americans who arrived before Ellis Island opened, in 1892. The arrival of the Marion, in New York, is not even noted in the "Shipping and Commercial List for the Port of New York."

In their new land, the two young men married, became citizens and remained friends and business associates for life. History records their achievements in America's emerging industrial economy. Their successes and prosperity would go far beyond the wildest imaginations of the two apprehensive young men who stepped ashore at the South Street Seaport on the nineteenth day of April, 1839.

They started their silk manufacturing operations in the abandoned Colt Gun Mill. John Ryle would soon own the first, and one of the largest, silk mills in Paterson and eventually become Mayor of the City. His efforts in Washington, representing the industry resulted in the passage of a tariff that restricted importing foreign silk, a tremendous stimulus to American manufacturing. He would forever be known as the Father of the American Silk Industry.

James Mayers would direct his friend's dyeing operations at the Gun Mill before he himself, would open the first successful silk dyeing business in America. In Paterson, he married Sarah Allison, whose roots can be traced to fifteenth century Yorkshire and the 1630 Winthrop Puritan Fleet. Today, there are over one hundred descendents of James Mayers and Sarah Allison living in the US. Many are still in New Jersey and have parents and grandparents who lived all their lives in Paterson.

As years passed, many from Macclesfield followed Mayers and Ryle to Paterson where it was possible to rise from weaver to affluent entrepreneur, in a short time. Many fortunes were made here by Macclesfield weavers, Lambert, Strange, Doherty, Wadsworth, Grimshaw, Crewe and Henshall all rose from the loom to become wealthy and prominent men.

By 1910, there were 15,000 Macclesfield people living in Paterson, about a fifth of the town's silk workers. They were a distinct community with social clubs Macclesfield newspapers were available and the Paterson Call published the births, deaths and marriage column from the Macclesfield Courier. In their travels about the city, and business dealings, James and John met so many old friends that it often seemed like they were back atop the 108 steps at the marketplace, in the shadow of St. Michaels. I wonder how many appreciated their role as the pioneers who helped make Paterson the Industrial Cradle of America.

The Marion continued sailing to the United States and Canada on other transatlantic voyages. She carried passengers outbound and lumber on the return trip, but was not under the command of Captain Bonnyman. His fate is unknown. In 1844, her homeport was changed to Cork, a more convenient embarkation point for the flood of Irish emigrants. Shown in Lloyds Register at various times in Quebec, Halifax, New Orleans, Boston and New York, she disappears from the records in 1851.

THE MARION: A THREE MASTED SHIP

Tons: 427. Length: 112 feet. Breadth at midships: 24 4/10 feet. Depth in hold: 18 8/10 feet.

Date launched: October 12, 1836.

Description: Rigged with a standing bowsprit, square stemmed, carvel-built, figurehead-but of woman, built of black birch and pine construction timber.

Builders: Justin Bigelow and Joseph Cox, Canning, Nova Scotia.

Owners:	1836	William Mackay, Merchant of St. John New Brunswick, Canada
	1838	Gibbs & Co. London
	1845	Carroll &Co. Cork, Ireland
	1845	Hargrave & Co. Cork, Ireland
Masters:	1836	Thomas Greece
	1838	J. Arthur
	1839	William Bonnyman
	1845	J. Mills
	1848	J. Maylor

The Marion sailed with James Mayers and John Ryle, silk weavers from Macclesfield, England to America in 1839. She left Liverpool on March 1, 1839, commanded by Captain William Bonnyman, and arrived at the Port of New York on April 19, 1839, a passage of 50 days. There were 71 passengers on board.

Other known voyages of the ship: Liverpool to Quebec-1939, Liverpool to Halifax-1844, Waterford to New Orleans-1845. Cork to North America-1848. Cork to Boston-1849. Cork to new York-1850. Vessel disappears from the record in 1851.

Sources:

Lloyds register of British and Foreign Shipping, 1838-1852.

Public Archives of Canada, Ottawa, Record Group 42, series 1, volume 124, entry 130/1836.

Shipping Register, St. John, New Brunswick, Reel 382.

National Archives, Washington, Passenger Arrival Records, File 168, m237, roll 38, 1.

Merseyside County Museum, Liverpool.

Robert A. Mayers 1980

JOHN MAYERS 7. VI AND MARGARET BERTRAM

John Mayers 7. vi, born 1858 Paterson, NJ; died 27 March 1932; married Margaret Bertram 1881 Paterson, NJ; born 1859 Glasgow, Scotland; died 14 March 1940. Nine children, all born in Paterson, New Jersey (see trees 1-7):

	i	James Bertram (Bert), born 1882; baptized 1 May 1892, of 152 Slater St.; architect; died 1942; married Lillian Tylee, born 1883; died 1960. No children.
8.	ii	John Allison (Al), born 1884; baptized 1 May 1892, of 152 Slater St.; machinist; died 1972; married Susan Van Orden 1905, born 6 March 1880; died 3 December 1968. Two children.
9.	iii	David, born 26 May 1887; died 24 February 1975; married Elizabeth Kupferer 1912, born 1886; died 1955. Three children.
	iv	Grace Winifred, born 3 December 1888; died December 1985; married Frederick Andrew Wood 1919; bookkeeper. No children.
10.	v	May Irene, born 1894; died 3 November 1983; married Joseph Thompson 1918, born 1890 Hillsborough, Ireland; house builder; died 1925. Three children.
11.	vi	Margaret, born 20 September 1895; died 29 January 1969; married Arthur Benson Wickham 1924, born 24 June 1897; accountant; died 22 January 1985. One child.
12.	vii	Perry Bascom, born 9 February 1897, mechanical engineer; died 20 April 1974; married Nora Kelly 1921, born 8 April 1899 Kilasolan, Ireland; died July 4, 1988.
	viii	George, born 1899; died 1901 as a child.
13.	ix	ROBERT EDMUND (Rob), born 23 May 1901; heating contractor; died 24 September 1985; married MINNIE (Wilhelmina) KIEVIT 23 December 1927, born 20 January 1906; died 5 June 1984. Three children.

John Mayers spent his childhood at his father's home at #5 Mill Street, Paterson, New Jersey. After the early death of his mother, Sarah Ann Allison Mayers in 1869 when he was eleven, he was cared for by his older sister, Eliza. The youngest son of James Mayers, a prosperous silk dyer, he continued his schooling into his teens. The Paterson City Directory shows him starting work in 1878, at age 18, as a machinist. He then became a marble cutter and likely worked for his brother-in law, Alexander Arnot. He is later listed as a blacksmith and silk dyer before settling into his lifetime occupation as a silk weaver, in 1884.

In 1881, John married Margaret Bertram. She was born in Glasgow, Scotland, the daughter of Joseph Bertram, who was born in Wales, and Ann Elizabeth Roberts. Margaret came to this country in1871 with her widowed mother Ann. Her mother remarried Joseph Farquhar, a silk weaver, who was born in Northern Ireland in 1846.

The 1895 New Jersey Census and the 1900 Federal Census shows these families, with both mother and daughter, living together at 35 Mary Street, Paterson. In 1901, George the infant son of John and Margaret died. The next year Ann Elizabeth, who lived in the upstairs apartment, fell to her death from the second floor window while hanging clothes. It was a short commute by trolley car to the mill area for John. (I visited the house in the 1970s, but when I returned 20 years later, it had demolished and the site was an empty lot.) In 1902, or 1903, John and Margaret moved, with their eight children, to Spring Street in Paterson.

In those years the streets of Paterson teemed with workers, horse drawn trolleys, carriages and bicycles. All hurried down the streets, to and from the blocks of ponderous three story brick mills with rows of narrow windows. The silk industry started by skilled Englishmen, such as John's father, James Mayers, expanded exponentially after the Civil War. All things came together for Paterson. Manufacturing expertise was supported by energy from the Great Falls, which drove the machinery and provided the pure water for dyeing fabrics. The New York market was close and could be easily reached by railroad, turnpike and ferry.

The 1900 Federal Census

Paterson was called 'Silk City" the glamorous capital of silk manufacturing in America. It produced half of all of this fabric made in the country. Silk had a special alluring quality. Yards of it made the fashionable floor-length dresses of the day. It was the aristocrat of textiles, the queen of fibers and the apparel of royalty. "Ladies" wore silk not cotton.

John Mayers was a ribbon weaver, the most highly skilled occupation in silk manufacturing. He produced fabrics of the highest quality and finest weaves and set up and operated complicated looms. He worked at a number of large silk companies in Paterson including the firm of Dexter Lambert, the largest in the city.

Although union membership was illegal in New Jersey at the time, there were frequent strikes in the mills. The early 1900s was a period of great unrest among the textile workers in Paterson. The agitation was caused by many of the larger manufacturers moving to Pennsylvania where rents were lower and the workforce more docile.

Machinery improvements also made it possible to employ unskilled women and children in Pennsylvania. Also at issue were the abysmal working conditions and demands for an eight-hour day and higher wages. Workers spent ten hours a day, wearing their coats in the winter to keep warm and suffocating in summer when humidifiers maintained a high level of dampness necessary for silk weaving. Dye houses were so filled with steam and acid fumes that nearby objects could not be seen. Young people often died from tuberculosis and lung diseases.

Concern over loom operation was a smoldering problem. With improved machines, one worker could tend three or four looms instead of two. Weavers such as John Mayers resisted this "speed up," which was being introduced in other states.

Fueling the turbulence was the large number of Italian and Polish weavers and dyers, who politically were extreme radicals. Gaetano Bresci, the anarchist who assassinated the King of Italy in 1900, was a Paterson silk worker. Most of these unions had the long-range goal of bringing about a new social order in the world.

The Industrial Workers of the World (IWW) was a militant and revolutionary trade union that had the objective of uniting wage earners all over the world to overthrow the capitalist system. It responded to the turmoil in Paterson by sending inflammatory organizers to the city. Elizabeth Gurley Flynn, Patrick Quinlan, Carlo Tresca and William Haywood and John Reed, were nationally known for being rabble-rousing orators and writers. They had the ability to keep workers united for long periods of time.

The philosophy of the IWW envisioned a society without government or any kind of legal political process. It urged workers to "take possession of the earth and the machinery of production" and to abolish the wage system. It was the first great working class protest movement of the twentieth century. On a recent trip to Russia, I noted the graves of IWW leaders, who were active in Paterson, in prominent places in the Kremlin, close to the tomb of Lenin.

Ribbon Weavers about 1900, operating looms which wove over 40 ribbons at a time. These women are operating two looms.

John Mayers became an activist and a "delegate," an elected representative or shop steward, in the IWW This union was popularly called the "Wobblies," While its views and motives now appear to be unusually extreme, it began in a time when existing unions were ineffective and exploitation, brutality and prejudice, by companies was commonplace. The most potent weapon of the IWW was the long strike. The 1913 silk strike in Paterson was marked by violence on both sides and so much hostility that the strikers' children were evacuated from the city. It was an epic struggle in labor history. The growth of American organized labor, and most protest movements since that time, owe much to the ideas and methods of the "Wobblies".

John Mayers tore down the setup on his loom at the Doherty Silk Mill on January 27, 1913. He joined the protest with 800 other employees who quit work when four members of a workers committee were fired for trying to talk to the company about eliminating the four-loom system. Within a week, 25,000 workers were on strike and 300 silk mills shut down. John was arrested and accused of sabotage along with hundreds of other workers but was not convicted because, while he had stopped production, he did not destroy the loom.

The strike lasted more than seven months but failed due to the lack of funds, hunger among the strikers and brutal strike braking tactics used by the mill owners and Paterson Police. My father, then age twelve, remembered having only porridge to eat for several months. The Doherty Silk Mill, a huge, brick, four-storied building is remarkably well preserved and can be seen today adjacent to the north bound lane of the Garden State Parkway where it passes through Paterson near Exit 159.

Doherty Silk Mill

After the 1913 Strike, John Mayers was "blacklisted" because of his union activism and no mill in Paterson would hire him. In 1914, the Mayers family was forced to move to Newark so John could find work.

By 1930, the elderly couple lived with their youngest son Robert and his wife Minnie, (my father and mother). They lived at 28 Perry Street, Belleville, New Jersey. At age seventy-one, John took a part time job as a gate tender at the Erie Railroad crossing in Belleville, and worked until the day he died.

The earliest memory of my life is that of my grandfather, John Mayers, pushing me in a carriage. I was under two years old at the time. He died of a cerebral hemorrhage on March 30, 1932, at age seventy-three. His wife Margaret spent her last years in Newark, at the home of her daughter, May. She died in 1940 at the age of eighty. Both rest in the Mayers Plot at Cedar Lawn beside James Mayers and Sarah Ann Allison and most of their children.

GRAVE	INTERMENT NO.	DATE	NO IN GRAVE	NAME	REMOVED
	355	5/8/68		Sarah A. Mayers 46yr	
7	7959	5/1/87		James Mayers 66/10/0	
6	8115	15/47/87		Edma Arnot 5mo.	
6	8869	13/9/88		Frances Anderson 8mo.	
6	11824	10/12/93		William Mayers 39yr.	
2	15597	1/23/01		George Mayers 2yr.	
7	25598	7-12-17		Mayers, George	
7	25599	"		Allison, Alexander	
7	25600	"		Allison, Mary	
	30472	11-29-22		Mayers, Eliza 79-0-0 Re	
1	36882	4-1-32		Mayers, John 73-10-7 Reg	
5	42517	3-18-40		Mayers, Margaret 80-7-29 Reg	
8	44335	7-29-42		Mayers, Jas. 59 Ex.	
8	57127	4-25-60		Mayers, Lillian T. 77-2nd	
12	63252	2-1-69		Wickham, Margaret 73 Ex	
11	66883	4-24-74		Mayers, Perry B. 77	
4	73198	6-8-84		Mayers, Minnie D. 78	
12	73576	1/26/85		Wickham, Arthur B. 87 2nd	
3	73935	8-29-85		Mayers, Robert Edmund 84	
2	75722	7-7-88		Mayers, Nora 90	

Burials, Mayers Family plot
Cedar Lawn Cemetery, Paterson, New Jersey

Mayers Family plot, Cedar Lawn Cemetery, Paterson, New Jersey.

NOTES & SOURCES

Brockett, L.P. *The Silk Industry in America*. New York: The Silk Association in America, 1876.

Carey, George, *The Vessel The deed and The Idea: Anarchists in Paterson 1895-1908*, Undated manuscript. Collection, The American Labor Museum.

Carey, George, *La Questione Social, an Anarchist Newspaper in Paterson, New Jersey*, Undated manuscript. Collection, The American Labor Museum.

Federal Census, Paterson, Passaic County, NJ, 1860-1910, Newark, Belleville, Essex County, NJ, 1920-1930.

Flynn, Elizabeth Gurley, *The Rebel Girl*. International Publishers, New York, 1973.

Golin, Steve, Defeat becomes Disaster: The Paterson Strike of 1913 and the Decline of the IWW. *Labor History*, Spring, 1983.

Gutman, Herbert G., Work, Culture and Society in Industrializing America, Vintage Books, NY, 1966.

Golin, Steve, Bimson's Mistake: Or, How the Paterson Police Helped to Spread the 1913 Strike. *New Jersey History*. Vol. 100, No. 1-2, Spring-Summer, 1982.

Herbst, John A. and Keene, Catherine, *Life and Times In Silk City*, American Labor Museum, Botto House, Haledon, NJ, 1984.

Kornbluh, Joyce l., *Rebel Voices, an IWW Anthology*. Charles H. Kerr, Chicago, 1988.

Norwood, Christopher, *About Paterson-The Making and Unmaking of an American City*, Harper Colophon Books/ Harper and Rowe, New York, 1975.

Paterson, Social and Industrial History, Paterson Dept. of Community Development, 1980.

Silk City, Studies on the Paterson Silk Industry, Philip B. Scranton, Editor, N. J. Historical Society, Newark, 1985.

Zieger, Robert H., Robin Hood in the Silk City, The IWW and the Paterson Silk Strike of 1913. N.J.H.S. Proceedings, 1966, Vol. 84 182-195.

Wallerstein, Jane, *Voices from the Paterson Silk mills*, Arcadia Publishing, Charlestown, S. C., 2000.

Wyckoff, William Cornelius, *The Silk Goods Of America*, D. Van Nostrand, 1879.

Mayers Family Trees as of 2010

Children of John Mayers and Margaret Bertram

For those of us in the 17th generation, descending from Robert Ellisse, John Mayers and his wife Margaret Bertram are our Grandparents and pass down the ancestry of the Mayers-Allison bloodline. Their children were our mothers and fathers. A tree has been prepared for each of them. Most of our cousins of the 17th generation are still here to honor the memories of their parents, with the exception of Alice daughter of May, David Jr. Betty, daughter of John and Susan and Perry Jr.

> TREE 1. John Allison Mayers (Al) 8. ii 1884-1972.
> TREE 2. David Mayers 9. iii 1887-1983.
> TREE 3. May Mayers Thompson 10. v 1894-1983.
> TREE 4. Margaret Grace Mayers Wickham 11. vi 1895-1969.
> TREE 5. Perry Bascom Mayers 12. vii 1897-1974.
> TREE 6. Robert Edmund Mayers 13. ix 1901- 1985.

All names in the trees spelled with CAPITAL LETTERS are direct Mayers-Allison descendants and carry the bloodlines of these families that begin in medieval England.

In marriages, without children, which ended in divorce, the spouses have been omitted. Marriages ending in divorce are designed "m.e.d." where it was shown in the data received from family members.

The data is a snapshot of the family as of May 2005. It will change frequently in the future. I encourage each family to designate a person who has the interest to update their branch for future generations. The trees now include 102 living direct descendants residing in many states spanning the country. I can continue to be a central point for updates which I will send out in the future to those interested.

Special appreciation is owed to cousins providing information on the many changes since the last update over twenty-five years ago. Reporting for their branches were: Mildred (Mitzi) Mayers Caruso, George Catino III, Betty Mayers Drogan, Mary Lou Mayers Rowe, Catherine (Kappie) Teed Mayers, Jane Mayers Rowland and Alan Arthur Wickham.

Mayers Family Photo, Summer 1914
Rear, Left to Right: Robert Edmund Mayers (1901-1985), Susan Vanorden Mayers (1880-1968),
John Allison Mayers (1884-1972), David Mayers (1887-1975), Margaret Mayers Wickham (1895-1969).
Front, Left to Right: Anna Margaret Mayers (1906-1918, d. influenza epidemic),
Margaret Bertram Mayers (1859-1940), Elizabeth Kupferer Mayers (1886-1955),
David Mayers Jr. (1913-2004), May Mayers Thompson (1894-1983)

About 1939, Dave Mayers Farm, Hope, Warren Co., New Jersey
Left to right: Perry Bascom Mayers, David Mayers, Arthur Wickham,
John Allison Mayers (Al), Robert Edmund Mayers (Rob), James Bertram Mayers (Bert)

Mayers cousins, picnic at Mary Lou's, Essex Fells, New Jersey, 1997.
Left to right, back row: David Mayers Jr., Betty Mayers Drogan, Perry B. Mayers Jr.
Front Row: Mary Lou Mayers Rowe, Jane Mayers Rowland, Mitzie Mayers Caruso,
Eileen Mayers Brophy, Peggy Mayers Higgins, Robert A. Mayers, Dorothy Mayers Ehlinger.

TREE 1:
DESCENDANTS OF JOHN ALLISON MAYERS AND SUSAN ANNA VAN ORDEN

JOHN ALLISON MAYERS 8. ii, born 6 February 1884; baptized* 1 May 1892 Paterson, NJ; machinist; died 27 September 1972; married Susan Anna Van Orden, born 6 March 1880 Paterson, NJ; resided Elmwood Park, NJ; died 3 December. Two children.

ANNA MARGARET, born 1906; died 1918, influenza epidemic.

ELIZABETH JANE, born 18 November 1919; died 18 November 2006; married Casimir Joseph Drogan, born 16 January 1916; postman; resided Elmwood Park, NJ.

*"Allie" and "Bertie" (John Allison and James Bertram Mayers) baptized 1 May 1892; parents were John and Maggie Mayers. Records of Cross Street Methodist Church, Paterson, NJ.

2010

TREE2:
DESCENDANTS OF DAVID MAYERS AND ELIZABETH KUPFERER

DAVID MAYERS 9. iii, born 26 May 1887 Paterson, NJ; died 24 February 1975; stationary engineer; married Elizabeth Kupferer 1912, born 1886; died 1955; resided Essex Fells, NJ. Three children.

DAVID JR., born 2 May 1913; died 20 January 2004; President Alumax Corp.; married Catherine Cooley Teed 1935, born 22 November 1915 Roseland, NJ; resided San Mateo, CA. Four children.

1. DAVID III, born 5 March 1936 West Orange, NJ, Economics Prof. UCLA; married Marisel Garcia 15 December 1979, born 6 May 1953 Cuba; resided Riverside, CA. One child.

    i MELLISSA ALYN, born 19 November 1985 Culver City, CA; student Santa Barbara, CA.

2. WILLIAM HENRY, born 17 November 1943 Berwyn, IL, chemical co. executive; married Diane Rae Schuster 16 June 1967, born 12 June 1946 Riverside, CA; resided San Rafael, CA. Two children (twins).

    i ERIC TEED, born 1 July 1972 San Mateo, CA; theater mgmt., Portland,OR.

    ii STEPHEN ROSS, born 1 July 1972; teacher, San Francisco, CA.

3. JUDITH ANNE, born 23 July 1945 Oradell, NJ; retired in Santa Barbara, CA; married _____ Light November 2005.

4. THOMAS TEED, born 31 May 1950 Spokane, WA; construction operating engineer, Rancher; resided Hemet, CA.

JANE MAYERS, born 18 June 1916 Irvington, NJ; math professor; married Richards Atwell Rowland 16 January 1943, born 20 December 1910; died 29 April 1985; geologist; resided Belaire, TX. Two children.

1. JANE ELIZABETH, born 1 December 1943 Glen Ridge, NJ; married Timothy Logan, born 21 December 1943; engineer. Three children.

    i KELLY GAIL, born 4 May 1967 Houston, TX; married Hector Arvizo 18 May 1991, born 15 July 1968 Bakersfield, CA; resided Richmond, TX. Two children.

        a. JOSHUA, born 30 September 1994 Houston, TX.

        b. BRIANNA, born 18 April 1997 Houston, TX.

    ii KATHLEEN GILLIAN, born August 1973 Houston, TX.

    iii KRISTINA ALLISON, born 26 October 1978 Houston, TX; married Clint Wood 4 January 2003, born 16 September 1973.

2. JOHN RICHARDS, born 5 February 1946 Baltimore, MD; owner, Page Boiler Works/CPA; resided Dallas, TX; died 2006; married Nancy Griffin, born 10 November 1946; m.ed. Two children.

    i KERRI ANN, born 10 August 1967 Houston, TX; married Adam Haynes 5 May 1995, born 23 August 1965 Dallas, TX; resided Dallas, TX. Two children.

        a. JACKSON ROWLAND, born 9 August 1999 Austin, TX.

b.   MARSHAL GRIFFIN, born 1 October 2001 Austin TX.

ii   JOHN RICHARDS JR., born 29 May 1970 Houston, TX.; married Melinda Jane Kehr 22 January 1983, born 15 August 1957 Tulsa, OK. Two children.

a.   ADAM KEITH CHUMLEY, born 8 August 1975 Tulsa, OK, son of Melinda

b.   ANDREA JANE, born 15 November 1984 Houston, TX.

MARY LOUISE, born 10 July 1924 Essex Fells, NJ; resided Essex Fells, NJ; married Alan Blake Rowe 1 September 1962, born 18 January 1909 Colchester, VT; banker; died 10 August 1995.

TREE 3:
DESCENDANTS OF MAY MAYERS AND JOSEPH LOCKHART THOMPSON

MAY MAYERS 10. v, born 20 February 1894 Paterson, NJ; died 3 November 1983 Bloomfield, NJ; married JOSEPH LOCKHART THOMPSON 1918, born 24 September 1890 Hillsborough, Ireland; house builder; died 24 July 1925; resided Paterson, NJ. Three children.

1. HOWARD, born 1923 Belleville, NJ; died 1925 in infancy.

2. WARREN, born 2 February 1925 Newark, NJ; died in infancy.

3. ALICE EILEEN, born 28 February 1921 Paterson, NJ; died 3 April 2001; resided Bloomfield, NJ; Married (1) Donald Malanga, born 1918; died about 1985; m.e.d.; (2) George Catino Jr. 19 June 1948, born 2 March 1921 Newark, NJ; died 17 December 1992; real estate broker. Six children, first two by first husband, rest by second.

    i   DONALD CATINO, born 11 November 1938 Newark, NJ; medical doctor; son of Alice, previous marriage; resided New London, NH; married (1) Jill South McEntree 8 October 1966, born 27 December 1940 Cavite, Philippines, (2) Pamela Ann Ball, born 23 September 1953 Grayling, MI. Four children, three by first wife, mother of fourth unknown.

        a.   JENNIFER LYNN, born 14 April 1969 Boston, MA; resided Mexico.

        b.   DONALD LINDSLEY, born 7 August 1970 New London, NH; married Jessica Sue Johnson 22 May 1999, born 9 March 1971 Hyannis, MA; resided Exeter, NH. Two children.

            I.   MYA SUE, born 10 February 2004 Boston, MA.

            II.   BRIGGS CHAMBERLAIN, born 11 July 2006 Portsmouth, NH.

        c.   LAURIE ANN, born 14 September 1973 New London, NH; married Robert Anthony Durkin 20 September 1997, born 13 February 1969 Portland, OR. Four children.

            I.   JILL SOUTH, born 8 April 1999 Boston, MA.

            II.   TIMOTHY ROBERT, born 15 August 2001 Boston, MA.

            III.   JOHN MICHAEL, born 22 September 2003 Boston, MA.

            IV.   MAXWELL JAMES, born 4 September 2005 Boston, MA.

        d.   ANTHONY PATRICK YATES, born 2 June 1989 Concord, NH.

    ii   JUDITH MAY CATINO, born 13 December 1941 Newark, NJ; educator; resided Bloomfield, NJ; married (1) John Borden Tupper Jr., born 29 August 1937; m.e.d., (2) Nicholas Robert Madonia 31 January 1982, born 18 June 1941; C.P.A.; resided Passaic, NJ. Three children, first two by first husband, third by second.

        a.   KAREN ELIZABETH, born 21 February 1964 Belleville, NJ; married Bryan Phillip Thryselius 16 January 1986, born 2 August 1963; m.e.d. One child.

            I.   KRISTIN ELIZABETH, born 2 June 1986 Geneva, IL; married David Anthony Kapp 3 August 1996, born 27 February 1968; resided Carol Stream, IL.

b.   JOHN BORDEN TUPPER III, born 27 December 1969 Willoughby, OH; educator.

c.   NICHOLAS JOSEPH, born 12 October 1982 Montclair, NJ.

iii   GEORGE CATINO III, born 2 May 1953 Newark, NJ; family historian; resided Pompano Beach, FL.

iv   JEAN ELLEN CATINO, born 9 April 1956 Newark, NJ; married George Richard Shirk 5 August 1994, born 3 June 1952 Oelwein, IA; magazine publisher; resided Mammoth Lakes, CA.

v   ELLEN BETH CATINO, born 11 December 1957 Belleville, NJ; resided N.Y.C.; married Felix Juan Cabrera 1 May 1992, born 21 August 1949 Havana, Cuba.

vi   JOHN JOSEPH CATINO, born 15 September 1961 Belleville, NJ; resided West Newbury MA; married Maureen Alyce Bertolami 8 April 2000, born 25 November 1966 Cambridge, MA.

a.   JOHN JOSEPH Jr., born 18 July 2004 Beverly, MA.

2010

TREE 4:
MARGARET GRACE MAYERS AND ARTHUR BENSON WICKHAM

Arthur B. Wickham was born in Jersey City, New Jersey, to Smith M. Wickham and Elizabeth Kiellen on June 24, 1899. This Wickham family was from Ridgebury in western Orange County, New York, and was involved in dairy distribution and farming. The family is descended from Noyes Wickham, born in 1740 in Southold, Long Island. He migrated to Orange County after the Revolution. Ira J. Wickham and his son Smith moved to Jersey City together before 1900 but the rest of the Wickhams stayed in Orange County. The Wickham family history has been described by Evelyn Hale (1975), and by A.A. Wickham and James W. Petty (1996).

Arthur B. Wickham served in World War I, in France with the Army Engineers. About 1917, his mother Elizabeth Kiellen and a sister Mildred died in the great influenza epidemic of that time.

About 1924 Arthur B. Wickham met Margaret G. Mayers while working at the National Carbon Company in Jersey City. They were married in 1924 and soon moved to 268 De Witt Avenue in Belleville. Arthur B. Wickham worked for the American and Foreign Power Company at #2 Rector Street in Manhattan for over 25 years. He joined the Belleville Masonic Lodge in 1921 and was a member for 60 years. Arthur B. and Margaret Wickham were members of the Fewsmith Presbyterian Church in Belleville.

The couple had one son, Alan Arthur, who was born on September 4, 1935. Alan married June Noel Pitkanen and they have two daughters, Jennifer Lynn Nielson and Rachel Margaret Richmond. They have four grandchildren, Valerie Noel, Stephanie, Sarah Modine and Luke Alan. June Wickham died in 1997. Alan married Rita Clare Gayle in 1999.

Following Arthur Wickham's retirement in 1957, he and Margaret were able to retire to Tom's River, New Jersey, and frequently traveled to Florida and the West from there. Margaret died on January 25, 1969 and Arthur B. on January 20, 1985. They both rest in the Mayers Plot in Cedar Lawn Cemetery in Paterson, New Jersey.

Alan A. Wickham 2005

DESCENDANTS OF **MARGARET GRACE MAYERS** AND **ARTHUR BENSON WICKHAM**

MARGARET GRACE MAYERS 11. vi, born 20 September 1895 Paterson, NJ; died 29 January 1969; married Arthur Benson Wickham 1924, born 24 June 1897; accountant; died 20/22 January 1985; resided Belleville, NJ. One child.

1.   ALAN ARTHUR, born 4 September 1935 Belleville, NJ; chemist; married (1) June Noel Pitkanen 21 December 1963, born 24 December 1931 Silver Bow County, MT; resided Salt Lake City, UT; died 10 December 1997; (2) Rita Clare Gayle 6 April 1999 Chichester, Sussex, UK, born 1 March 1946, Lake Charles, LA; resided Port Townsend, WA. Two children by first wife.

      i   JENNIFER LYNN, born 23 October 1965 San Francisco, CA; married Kent Lee Nielson 23 April 1983, born 26 February 1963; m.e.d. Two children, twins.

          a.   STEPHANIE HOPE, born 11 October 1983; married Robert Christopher Baird 2009, born 5 May 1983 Salt Lake City, UT.

          b.   VALERIE NOEL, born 11 October 1983; married Tom Cadmartin 26 November 2008, born 7 March 1951 North Beach, CA; resided San Francisco.

      ii   RACHEL MARGARET, born 22 October 1968 Salt Lake City, UT; married April 1995, Mike Richmond Jr.; resided Ashland OR. Two children.

          a.   SARAH MODINE, born 14 August 1996, Sand Point, ID.

          b.   LUKE ALAN, born 10 January 2000, Ashland, OR.

TREE 5:
PERRY BASCOM MAYERS AND NORA AGNES KELLY

Perry Bascom Mayers, born 9 February 1897 Paterson, NJ; died 20 April 1974; married Nora Agnes Kelly 8 February 1921 Brookline, MA, born 8 April 1898 Lower Kilasolan, County Galway, Ireland (near Athlone, Caltra, Mt Bellow); died 4 July 1988. Five children, first three born Boston MA, fourth and fifth in Belleville, NJ.

Margaret Ann, born 11 July 1922. Five children, all boys.
Eileen Elizabeth, born 1 January 1924. Four children and one adopted.
Dorothy Bertram, born 28 September 1926. Four children.
Mildred (Mitzi) Grace, born 22 July 1934. One child.
Perry Bascom Jr., born 7 November 1936; died November 7, 2008. Three children.

Perry Bascom Mayers, named after a minister in Paterson, New Jersey, was the seventh of nine children. He descended from a family of silk weavers and after graduating from grammar school went to work in the silk mills. He walked to and from work to save the fare. While still very young, he joined the Navy. There was little money or employment available at this point in his life and the Navy and a life at sea offered him security. One of his voyages took him to the British Isles. On the way back, on the SS St. Louis, he met young Nora Kelly, a passenger. He was smitten by her, and she, by him. After arrival in New York, they agreed to correspond. She then departed for Boston with her sister Dehlia. Shortly afterward, World War I began. He did not see her again for four years. When the war ended he made a trip to Boston. There was a mutual declaration of love and they made plans to marry. She worshiped him like a Greek God and that lasted for a lifetime.

Perry B. Mayers was a great humanitarian. He gathered clothes, cigarettes and little treats and then went to Penn Station in Newark, New Jersey, and distributed them to the poor and homeless. He and Nora also gathered clothing, bed linens, curtains, etc., which were sent to a family in Ireland that had eight boys. They helped them for many years.

Perry became a Stationary Engineer through his knowledge of ship boilers, home- study and on the job training. He worked in the Isolation Hospital (Soho) in Belleville, New Jersey, until his retirement. One of the Engineers who attended his funeral said, "Perry taught me everything from A to Z" and tutored me until I passed all the necessary exams to become a Stationary Engineer.

Perry was a great gardener, growing every imaginable vegetable. He also grew dahlias that measured thirteen inches in diameter. Another retirement activity was raising parakeets, some of which he taught to talk. He also made "hooked rugs" and everyone in the family, and the extended family, was given one. He loved classical music and reading, sometimes into the wee hours of the morning. He read the entire set of the Harvard Classics and much more.

Nora Kelly Mayers was a fraternal twin to a sister Kitty who remained in Ireland. In her youth she was afforded whatever education was available for farm children. While this was not a great amount of formal training, she fared well in life. She had the courage to come to America with two dollars in her pocket to unite with her sister Dehlia. She did domestic work, which was available to immigrants. She had the good fortune to meet, and eventually marry, that tall handsome sailor from New Jersey. She loved opera and poetry.

The Records at Ellis Island show that Nora's parents were John Kelly and Margaret Graftery. The record (Ship's manifest, line 20, frame 0432, 68) shows that Nora Kelly, age 19 arrived here on October 9, 1916. Her passage was paid for by her sister. Her final destination was to Boston, Massachusetts, to her sister, Julia Kelly, who lived at 93 Gray St. She was 5' 2''tall with dark hair and eyes.

The family, as with everyone at that time, unfortunately got caught up in the "depression of the late twenties and early thirties. They thought that moving to New Jersey would be to their economic advantage, so they moved to Belleville, where Perry's brother, Rob, and sister Margaret, lived. Things were just as difficult in New Jersey, but they weren't alone- there was family. During World War II, Perry returned to sea and served as an Engineering officer in the Merchant Marine. He was on many dangerous convoys, including the run to Murmansk, Russia where many ships were sunk by German subs. Nora went to work in a defense factory in town where products for the war effort were made.

Nora was psychic in many ways. She predicted President Kennedy's assassination, and begged Perry to call someone to warn him. He thought that if he did the "men in white coats" would come and take them away. Nora was a good cook. She could roast a turkey like no one else. Back in those days we had family Sunday dinners, which always included Aunt May Thompson, who lived next door on Dawson Street.

Perry and Nora had a good life. They loved each other and therein lies the secret. They were able to do quite a bit of traveling in their retirement years, which included several trips to Ireland to visit family. Perry passed away April 20, 1974 at age 77 and Nora on July 4, 1988, at 90. They are interred in the Mayers family Plot at Cedar Lawn Cemetery in Paterson, New Jersey.

Mildred (Mitzie) Mayers Caruso, May, 2005

TREE 5:
DESCENDANTS OF PERRY BASCOM MAYERS AND NORA AGNES KELLY

PERRY BASCOM MAYERS 12. vii, born 9 February 1897 Paterson, NJ; died 20 April 1974; stationary engineer; married NORA AGNES KELLY, born 8 April 1899 Kilasolan, Galway, Ireland; died 4 July 1988; resided Belleville, NJ. Five children: Margaret, Eileen, Dorothy, Mildred and Perry Jr.

1. MARGARET ANN, born 11 July 1922 Boston, MA; married (1) Robert O'Brien; (2) John Joseph Higgins, born 5 November 1918; resided Manasquan, NJ. Five children, first by first husband, rest by second.

    i   BRUCE PERRY O'BRIEN, born 23 January 1944; died April 17, 1993.

    ii   JOHN JOSEPH JR., born 12 February 1950; resided Neptune. Two children, twins.

    iii   JEFFREY WAYNE, born 12 February 1950; resided Amityville, Long Island, NY; restaurant business, real estate; married Stacy McMinn, born April 1967 Rockville Center.

    iv   JAMES BERTRAM, born 8 February 1960; married Lorrie Glashan 22 October 1982, born 2 June 1959; resided Brielle, NJ. Two children.

    a.   JESSICA, born 21 August 1983; resided Ohio.

    b.   RORY JAMES, born 28 December 1985; resided Brielle, NJ.

    v   STEPHAN PAUL, born 5 February 1962; chef; resided Florida.

2. EILEEN ELIZABETH, born 1 January 1924 Boston, MA; married William Christopher Brophy 31 December 1954, born 24 December 1916; died 12 December 1998; resided Spring Lake, NJ. Five children.

    i   WILLIAM JOSEPH, born 30 December 1944 Keller, TX; son of William from previous marriage which ended by death of wife; married (1) Kathleen Kinney; (2) Paula D. Moody April 1991, born 16 October 1953 Odessa TX. Two children by first wife.

    a.   JENNIFER LYNN, born July 1972; married (1) Matt. Knori; resided Stillwater, OK; m.e.d.; (2) Kindall Young 2006. Two children by first husband.

    I.   LAUREN MARY, born November 1992.

    II.   GAGE MATHEW, born May 1998.

    b.   CAROLYN HEATHER, born March 1975; married Duane Mikulencek, resided New Orleans, LA. Three children.

    I.   JUDE, born 14 February 2003.

    II.   _____, born 6 February 2006.

    III.   Henry, born 6 February 2006.

    c.   Pamela Bachtell, daughter of Paula D. Moody.

    ii   EILEEN CAROLYN, born 16 April 1957; resided Wall, NJ; teacher; married Phillip Scaduto 25 April 1981, born 5 June 1957; m.e.d. Four children.

  a.   JACLYN JENNIFER, born 14 April 1982; married Stephen Achille, born 22 July 1982; construction estimator; resided Lincroft, NJ. One child.

  I.   MATHEW RYAN, born 25 September 2008.

  b.   JESSICA LYNN, born 20 October 1983 Little Silver, NJ.

  c.   JOHN PERRY, born 29 October 1985; died 30 October 1985, born prematurely.

  d.   LAUREN MICHELLE, born 31 July 1987; student; resided Wall, NJ.

iii   JOHN CHRISTOPHER, born 17 May 1958; resided Mt. Pleasant, SC; married (1) Mary Lynn Mihm 2 July 1994, born 6 January 1971; m.e.d.; (2) Susan Techner 6 October 2001. Two children, first prior to marriage, second by first wife.

  a.   MORGAN, born 20 June 1989 NJ, son of Brigit Knutstad; resided Stevens Institute, NJ.

  b.   CASSANDRA RACHEL, born 22 September 1995, Bartlesville, OK.

iv   KATHLEEN CLAIRE, born 30 November 1959 Point Pleasant, NJ; nurse; married (1) William McKelvey; m.e.d.; (2) Damon De Grassie 2006, born 7 December 1957 Paterson, NJ; HVAC teacher. Three children, two from first husband, third by John Braco.

  a.   KAITLIN EILEEN, born 25 November 1984; resided Point Pleasant, NJ.

  b.   WILLIAM CHARLES, born 10 February 1988; resided Point Pleasant, NJ.

  c.   JOSHUA JOSEPH BROPHY, born 29 March 1995.

v   DOROTHY ANN, born 8 November 1962 Lake Como, NJ; married Todd Dwyer 22 July 1988, born 11 May 1960; resided Lake Como, NJ. Two children.

  a.   TYLER AUSTIN, born 5 October 1993; student; resided Lake Como, NJ.

  b.   CALAN JOSEPH, born 23 March 1996; student; resided Lake Como, NJ.

3.   DOROTHY BERTRAM, born 28 September 1926 Boston, MA; married Norman Joseph Ehlinger 18 September 1946, born 15 October 1924; resided Stuart, FL. Four children.

i   SHARON BETH, born 25 September 1948 Madison WI; attorney; resided Grand Rapids, MI; married Jack Imhoff 1970, born 1948; m.e.d. Two children.

  a.   KIMBERLY ANN, born 24 September 1970 MI; nurse; married Heath Campbell 1998; resided Wyoming, MI. Three children.

  I.   ANDREW RYAN, born 1987 Grand Rapids.

  II.   ALEXANDER, born 1999 Grand Rapids.

  III.   ABIGAIL GRACE, born 2002 Grand Rapids.

  b.   JASON MICHAEL, born 21 January 1973 Michigan; attorney; resided South Carolina; married Jennifer _____. Two children, twins.

  I.   AIDAN CHRISTOPHER, born 14 June 2003 Greenville SC.

  II.   COLLIN MICHAEL, born 14 June 2003 Greenville SC.

ii   MICHAEL FRANKLIN, born 5 April 1953 Kirksville, MO; restaurateur; resided Florida.

iii   NORMAN JOSEPH JR., born 14 December 1955 Orville, OH; doctor; resided Missouri; married Laura Ann Brooks. Two children.

    a.   JESSICA LEIGH, born 8 July 1984 Chesterfield, MO; pre-med college student.

    b.   JOHN JACOB, born 2 July 1988 Chesterfield MO; student.

iv   JOHN CRAIG, born 28 December 1960; entrepreneur/real estate; married Joann Katz, born December 1961 MI; teacher; resided Michigan. Two children.

    a.   AUSTIN TYLER, born 26 February 1991 Marietta, GA.

    b.   RACHAEL MCKENZIE, born 26 February 1994 Marietta, GA.

4.   MILDRED GRACE, born 22 July 1934 Belleville, NJ; teacher, Pt. Pleasant, NJ School System; married Julius John Frederick Caruso, born 24 June 1928 Newark, NJ; died 3 May 1993; sales exec.; resided Point Pleasant Beach, NJ. One child.

i   KELLY ANN, born 29 October 1960 Pt. Pleasant, NJ; computer programmer/analyst; resided Ringoes, NJ; married Glenn Pietrucha; m.e.d. Two Children, twins.

    a.   ALEXANDRA CARUSO, born 22 August 1999 N.Y.C.

    b.   ETHAN CARUSO, born 22 August 1999 N.Y.C.

5.   PERRY BASCOM JR., born 7 November 1936; electrical contractor; died 7 November 2008; resided Belleville, NJ; married (1) _____ (2) Eleanor McGibbon O'Neill, born 11 January 1945 Paisley, Scotland; resided Belleville, NJ. Three children, two by first wife, one by second.

i   PERRY THOMAS, born 2 November 1961 Belleville, NJ; police chief, Montclair, NJ; married Denise Marie Prudente 25 April 1987 Jersey City, NJ. Two children.

    a.   ANTHONY THOMAS, born 15 August 1989.

    b.   ALLISON PERRI, born 29 March 1993.

ii   DIANE, born 11 February 1963 Belleville, NJ; married John Santos 25 April 1992; resided Point Pleasant, NJ. Two children.

    a.   THOMAS PATRICK, born 28 March 1993.

    b.   MICHAEL JOSEPH, born 7 July 1998.

iii   SCOTT, born 26 February 1974 Belleville, NJ; electrician; married Carolyn Hannenberg October 2003; teacher; resided Belleville, NJ.

ROBERT EDMUND MAYERS 13. IX, AND MINNIE KIEVIT

ROBERT EDMUND MAYERS 13. ix, born 23 May 1901 Paterson, NJ; died 24 August 1985; married Minnie (Wilhelmina) Delia 23 December 1927 Passaic, NJ, born 20 January 1906 Passaic, NJ; died 5 June 1984. Three children, all raised in Belleville.

21. 1925

SWAM FROM BATTERY TO CONEY ISLAND

Edward Spies (left) and Robert Mayer, Newarkers, who spent four hours and fifteen minutes yesterday battling the waves in New York Harbor.

With the turn of the tide at 12 15 o'clock yesterday afternoon two members of Newark Lodge of Elks jumped into New York Bay at the Battery to swim to Coney Island. At 4:30 they reached their objective, having covered the distance, between fourteen and fifteen miles, in four hours and fifteen minutes.

The swimmers were Edward Spies of 243 Mulberry street and Robert Mayer of Belleville. Mayer alone felt any ill effects of the swim. For almost half the trip water got into his eyes making them smart and causing him no little bother.

When the swimmers first started off everything was in their favor.

The tide swept them out and the bay was smooth. Off Gravesend Bay, however, they ran into a stiff southeast wind, which whipped up large waves.

Every hour the men were fed hot soup or malted milk through small tubes from the deck of the Sea Spray, the boat which accompanied them, commanded by Philip L. Fitzpatrick, vice commodore of the Passaic River Yacht Club.

Before taking to the water the men greased their bodies with tallow to keep from getting overchilled. For most of the trip the two used the breast stroke, but ocassionally changed to a crawl.

Newark may soon be represented in the list of swimmers who have successfully battled the stiff currents of the English Channel.

Eddie Spies, 243 Mulberry Street, who in company with Bob Mayers of Belleville created a new record for the Battery to Coney Island swim, is planning an attempt to conquer the fighting waters.

Spies and Mayers, A. A. U. card holders, recently hung up the time of four hours and fifteen minutes for the stretch between the Battery and Coney Island through a choppy sea that swept them three miles off their original course.

"They thought we were goners," declared Spies in recounting the story. "The waves, high as houses, swamped our motorboat convoy and

boats by means of a rubber hose. Food is generally taken, as by Gertrude Ederle, from small bottles. This new stunt proved successful and will probably come into great favor with swim contestants.

Robert E. Mayers (Rob), my father, was the youngest of nine children. His working class family endured long periods of poverty during strikes and other times when his father, a silk weaver, was unemployed. At an early age he learned to swim in the Morris Canal, which passed through Paterson, above his home on the present path of US Route 80. He enjoyed this sport all of his life and later became a serious, competitive, distance swimmer.

Rob attended grade school and went to sea at an early age, on a voyage to New Orleans. While painting the side of the ship, a scaffold collapsed, throwing him and other sailors into the water. Panic ensued, most couldn't swim, but all were rescued. Then to the amazement of the entire crew, young Rob dove back into the water to retrieve his hat. He was very close to his older brother Perry. When the lads were growing up they enjoyed playing pranks. These included stringing a nearly invisible thread across an alleyway at a height where it would skim off the derby hats of men who were passing by. They hid a pet white rat in their father's bed "to surprise him". Their father could not get a job in Paterson after the strike of 1913 because he was "blacklisted for his union activism." The family moved to Newark the following year. In Newark, Rob worked delivering groceries from the old center market to homes in the Military Park area.

At that time, the best opportunity for a young person of his means was to learn a trade. He became a licensed union steamfitter in 1920 and worked at this occupation into the early 1930s. At the same time he continued his swimming and water polo. These activities centered at the large pool at Olympic Park an amusement park in Irvington, New Jersey In 1925, he and his friend,

Ed Spies, swam from Battery Park to Coney Island. Battling the waves of New York Harbor, they covered a distance of fourteen miles, in four hours and fifteen minutes. To my knowledge, their record has never been broken. This event was planned as preparation for an attempt to swim the English Channel. They were unable to do this due to a lack of financial backing. Rob played the piano and enjoyed classical music all his life.

Rob met Minnie Kievit at Olympic Park. She had planned to go to another amusement park with a friend but had missed the bus. Minnie attended grade school and went to work in a textile mill at about age thirteen. Her parents, Adrian Kievit and Clara Devogel came from second generation Holland Dutch families, from Passaic, New Jersey. Adrian's father had come to America with his family in 1851, from Ouddorph, Holland. They owned a brownstone quarry in Passaic.

Rob and Minnie were married in 1927 at the Trinity Methodist Church on Autumn St. in Passaic. He brought his bride to his home at 28 Perry Street, Belleville where they lived for the next thirty-five years. His brother, Perry, and sisters, Margaret and May, also lived in Belleville with their families and there was much interaction among the families. Their first child was born Robert Adrian (Bob) was born in 1930. About 1932, Rob opened his own heating and plumbing business. The 1930s were the difficult years of the "Great Depression" and it was a struggle to find work and pay the mortgage. In 1936, after having a rare year of prosperity, the family was able to take a cruise to Bermuda. Minnie became a Republican District Leader and served on the Republican County Committee during this time.

With the onset of World War II, it became impossible to get materials to continue in his own business and Rob became a marine pipe fitter. He worked at the Federal Shipyards in Kearny, New Jersey, where new destroyers for the US Navy were being built at a frantic pace. Coincidentally, ten years later I served in the Navy on one of these ships. Later, he worked at Todd Shipyards in Hoboken repairing battle-damaged ships. Minnie also went to work to help the war effort and was employed by the Railway Express Co. in Newark. It was hard work, on the night shift, on the cargo platform. In 1942, tragedy hit the family when their second child, Peter, age four, was killed by a truck in front of their home. He rests with his grandparents Adrian and Clara Kievit at Ridgelawn Cemetery in Delawanna, New Jersey.

When the war ended, Rob went back into his own plumbing and heating business, which prospered. After a few years, which included completing several jobs for the Belleville Board of Education, he took a full time position with the Board supervising the installation and maintenance of heating and plumbing equipment at Belleville's ten schools. Rob was

Robert Edmund Mayers (Rob) about 1938

133

an active member of Masonic Lodge #108 in Belleville and Minnie was in the Eastern Star Chapter.

In 1956 when I returned from the Navy, we built a summer home on Vernon Ave, Shark River Hills, Neptune, New Jersey, where the family had vacationed for many years. Rob and Minnie retired to this home with their daughter Joyce in the 1960s. In 1977, their golden wedding was celebrated and attended by many friends and family. The event was held at the Officers Club at the Earl Navy Base and hosted by Minnie's sister Anna May and her husband Admiral "Dina" Short. At "the shore" they enjoyed their later years and were active in senior citizens groups. Minnie's two sisters Dorothy and Kathryn (Cass) lived close by and my family, which included their three grandchildren, joined them on weekends during the summer months.

Minnie died suddenly at home in 1984 and the next year Rob passed away the next year after a short illness. They rest with their ancestors and many other family members in the Mayers plot at Cedar Lawn Cemetery in Paterson, New Jersey.

Minnie Kievit Mayers
1906-1984

ROBERT ADRIAN MAYERS AND NORMA DOLORES LEHMANN

Robert (Bob) was born in Passaic General Hospital near the home of his mother's family the Kievits. He grew up in the home of his parents at 28 Perry St. Belleville. During the 1930s, despite the great depression, the neighborhood was teeming with happy children of all ages. Good times and holidays were spent with cousins in Belleville and on weekly visits to Clifton and Passaic to see grandparents, aunts, uncles and cousins on the Kievit side of the family.

Bob attended School #3 and was an active cub scout. In 1939 at the age of nine, he won a "soapbox derby" race, competing against fifteen other small homemade racing cars. Summers were spent down "the shore" at Shark River Hills and family gatherings at Uncle Dave's farm in Warren Co. As a teenager Bob was active in the Order of DeMolay and became the Master Councilor, the top office in his chapter, in 1948. He became a Master Mason in 1951. He attended Belleville High School and worked as a laborer, during summers for the Board of Education in order to pay for his college tuition.

Norma was born at the home of her parents in Irvington, New Jersey. Her mother, Pelagia, was age forty-five at the time of her birth, and her father Paul was age sixty. Both tailors, they emigrated from Berlin, Germany in 1908. They lived in a German neighborhood and that was the language spoken at home and by their friends, neighbors and local merchants. Frances, Norma's only sibling was twenty-four years older. She was an accomplished piano instructor and was widowed most of her life. Norma was her primary caretaker for many years, until she died, at the age of ninety-five, in 2004.

In 1936, the Lehmann family bought a home at 90 Overlook Ave. in Belleville. Paul made custom tailored men suits in the basement of the home and a large quantity of homemade wine each year. Pelagia did all the hand sewing on the suits. When Norma started School # 5 she did not speak English. She soon learned the language and remained at the top of her class through high school. After graduating from Belleville High she worked at the Prudential Insurance Co., in Newark, as an executive secretary. Pelagia, her mother became ill and was confined to her bed for most of Norma's teenage years. These were difficult times for a young girl going to school, or working full time while still caring for her aging parents. Pelagia died at age 65 when Norma was age 20.

Bob and Norma met in High school, in 1946, when she was age fourteen and an entering freshman. Bob was sixteen and in his junior year. They were introduced by Norma's friend who Bob had been dating. After high school Bob entered Rutgers University and Norma continued to work for the Prudential. Pelagia passed away in 1952 at the age of sixty-five when Norma was only age twenty

Bob was graduated from Rutgers with a B.A. in Political Science, in 1953, and joined the Navy the same year. After attending Officer Candidate School, in Newport R.I. he was commissioned an Ensign in 1953 and assigned to sea duty on a destroyer. He served on the USS Hunt DD 674, as Gunnery Officer. The ship made an around the world cruise in 1954 and operated in the western Pacific for most of that year. Bob was promoted to lieutenant (jg) in 1954 and assigned to the 3rd Battalion 6th Marines as Naval Gunfire Liaison Officer, later that year. This military service was during the Korean Conflict.

Bob and Norma were married on July 23, 1955 at the Grace Episcopal Church, in Nutley, New Jersey, by Rev. Welles Bliss. A reception followed at the Hotel Robert Treat in Newark. Bob was still in the Navy. Norma's father, Paul, passed away, at age eighty three, five months after the wedding on Christmas Day.

Bob left the Navy in 1956 and joined the Personnel Dept of the Weston Electric Co., in Newark. The couple lived at the home of her late parents at 90 Overlook Ave., Belleville. Norma resigned from Prudential when they were expecting their first child, Robert Paul, who was born in 1957. This same year Bob joined the Westinghouse Corporation, in Metuchen, New Jersey, as Personnel Administrator.

Their second son, Ron, was born only fifteen months after his brother Bob, and daughter Dawn arrived in 1962. With three small children in the house, Norma was an exceptionally busy young mother. Bob joined the Thomas and Betts Co. in Elizabeth as Personnel Manager in 1958. Ron, age four, became gravely ill in 1963. He was rushed to the hospital for an emergency operation and his life hung in the balance. He soon recovered and grew to be a robust and athletic man.

In 1962, the family built their dream house on 226 Ridge Road in Watchung, New Jersey. It was built on almost three acres, high on a hill with a panoramic view of the valley below. When they first moved to this "wilderness," the street was nothing more than a dirt road that ended at their house. The road was soon extended and many young families joined them in new homes. Many of these neighbors became lifelong friends. In the early days there was an active social scene on Ridge Road and adjoining streets, with parties almost every week. The Mayers children had many playmates and attended Watchung grade schools and Watchung, Regional High. Summers were spent in town at the Brook Hill Swim and Tennis Club, and weekends and vacations were spent at the family summer home, in Shark River Hills.

When the children were young, Norma was a Brownie leader for Dawn, and an assistant den mother for Ron who was in the Cub Scouts. Bob was an assistant scoutmaster for his sons. When the children grew older, Norma became a member of the Watchung Rescue Squad and served as treasurer. The family attended Grace Episcopal Church, in Plainfield.

At Thomas & Betts, Bob was promoted to Vice President, directing the company's overseas manufacturing operations. He represented the firm in the community on the Board of Directors of the Union County Chamber of Commerce and as Chairman of the United Fund. He received the "Young Man of the Year" award for the County in 1962. After

Robert A. and Norma D. Mayers, July 23, 1955

fourteen years he left T&B and continued in the human resources field as Director of Industrial Relations at both the Amerace Corp and North American Philips. In 1975, he joined the Airco Corporation an as Vice President of Human Resources and was responsible for all personnel and labor relations activities at 123 locations nation wide. When Airco was acquired and reorganized ten years later, he left the company to begin a new career in Human Resources Consulting. He joined Manchester Partners International where he became Executive Vice -President and Partner, with direct responsibility for the firm's offices in New Jersey, New York and Connecticut. He retired from Manchester in 2002 at age seventy-two.

During their years together, the Mayers family has been avid travelers. They visited Caribbean Islands and in 1971 flew to California and drove back, crisscrossing the county to stop at many national parks and cities. After the children left home for college and their own careers, Bob and Norma continued to see much of the world on annual vacations. Their trips included China, Australia, the Middle East, Scandinavia, Russia and South America and most of Europe. Major holidays are celebrated together with the children and five grandchildren. Christmas Day is hosted by Norma at home in Watchung.

In 2001, they built a shore home next door to son Bob and family at 46 South Bay Ave in Highlands, New Jersey. The waterfront homes are on the Shrewsbury River. Summers are spent between Watchung and the shore where the family enjoys boating, fishing, the beach and frequent get-togethers. Winters include a vacation each year to Dawn and Bill's winter home in Naples, Florida and a cruise or other trip.

They frequently drive to the Delaware area to visit Dawn and Ron and their families. In 2005, they celebrated their 50th Wedding Anniversary by inviting their children and grandchildren on a cruise to England on the new ship, Queen Mary II. A gala golden wedding celebration for over hundred family members, friends and neighbors was held at the shore homes of the family on September 10, 2005

Bob is an active author. *The War Man,* a biography of his Revolutionary War ancestor Corporal John Allison, was completed in 2009 and published by Westholme Publishing. He is an enthusiastic genealogist and historian. His research on the Mayers and Allison Families, conducted over many years, are the subject of this book. Bob is a member of ten historical societies and is a frequent speaker and contributor to historical publications. He belongs to the Watchung Writer's Group and is Chairman of the Advisory Board for the Piscataway Group Home.

Norma manages the family's finances and improvement projects at their two homes. Born of European tailors, she became a skilled seamstress and acquired her mother's cooking skills. To stay fit, Norma jogs and attends aerobic dancing and Bob swims.

As a result, they have been blessed with excellent health.

TREE 6:
DESCENDANTS OF ROBERT EDMUND MAYERS AND MINNIE DELIA KIEVIT

ROBERT EDMUND MAYERS, born 23 May 1901 Paterson, NJ; died 24 August 1985; heating contractor; married Minnie (Wilhelmina) Delia Kievit 23 December 1927, born 29 January 1906 Passaic, NJ; died 5 June 1984; resided Belleville, NJ. Three children.

1. ROBERT ADRIAN, born 7 April 1930; corporate officer/consultant, human resources; married Norma Dolores Lehmann 23 July 1955, born 5 April 1932 Irvington, NJ; resided Watchung and Highlands, NJ. Three children.

   i ROBERT PAUL, born 9 February 1957 Belleville, NJ; manufacturing engineer; married Christina Cowell 27 June 1987; attorney; resided Highlands, NJ. One child.

      a. ROBERT KEVIN, born 2 April 1994 Highlands, NJ.

   ii RONALD JAMES, born 4 June 1958 Belleville, NJ; mechanical engineer; married Catherine Fleitzer, born 8 June 1957; m.e.d.; resided Boothwyne, PA. One Child.

      a. MARK JAMES, born 22 June 1992, Newark, DE; resided Elsmere DE.

   iii DAWN MARIE, born 8 January 1962 Belleville, NJ; married William Howard Schieffer 23 April 1983, born 21 October 1961 Elsmere, DE; Naples FL Partner, accounting sourcing firm; resided Hockessin, DE. Three children.

      a. CHRISTOPHER WILLIAM, born 22 September 1983; project manager; resided Arlington, VA.

      b. ALLISON MARIE, born 28 August 1987; student, University of Alabama.

      c. ANDREW ROBERT, born 27 April 1990; student, University of Alabama.

2. PETER ALLISON, born 1939 Belleville, NJ; died 1942.

3. JOYCE ANN, born 3 April 1945 Belleville, NJ; resided Piscataway, NJ.

Transatlantic Anniversary Cruise, Queen Mary 2, New York to Southampton, July 17-23, 2005

Rear: William H. Schieffer, Ronald J. Mayers, Andrew R. Schieffer
Row 2: Allison M. Schieffer, Dawn M. Mayers Schieffer, Mark J. Mayers
Row 2: Christopher W. Schieffer, Robert P. Mayers, Christina Cowell Mayers
Front: Robert A. Mayers, Robert K. Mayers, Norma D. Mayers

APPENDIX A:
PATERSON, NEW JERSEY CHURCH RECORDS – MAYERS AND ALLISON FAMILIES

A search of all Paterson churches shows that our Allison family was Methodist Episcopal. The earliest evidence of this is found in 1827, when a Sunday school record shows Sarah, or Sally, and her sister, Eliza, in the Cross Street Church. After the marriage of Sarah Allison and James Mayers, about 1841, the Mayers family remained Methodists for the next eighty years, until the death of their daughter Eliza in 1922. The 1827 date is important since it confirms that the Allison family migrated from Monroe, New York, to Paterson about that year.

There were two Methodist Churches in Paterson in the 19th century. These were the Cross Street, First Methodist and its offshoot, the Prospect Street, 2nd Methodist. Both were a short walk from the Allison and Mayers homes near the mill area. The Cross Street Church, founded in 1820, was demolished in1903. Actually, its first building was on Prospect St., but, with the great expansion of it congregation, it moved to larger quarters, on Cross St. in 1837. Cross St. was later renamed Cianci St. and St. Michaels Roman Catholic Church, built in 1903, now stands on the former site of the old First Methodist.

The Prospect Street Church was started in 1845 in the old building that the Cross Street Church moved out of in 1837. Our family alternated their membership over the years between these two churches.

The central repository for New Jersey Methodist Church records is at the Drew University Methodist Archives Center in Madison, New Jersey. All of the data about our ancestors that has been collected took several visits to this extensive collection. These archives include original documents of church membership, baptisms, marriages and deaths. Paterson Methodist records were contained in eight cartons-all of which were examined for evidence of the Mayers and Allison/Ellison families. Alan Wickham assisted in this on site search.

All entries found for the families over a sixty-year period are in this timeline:

1820: First Methodist Church was built on Prospect St. between Ellison and Van Hounten Streets. It did not have a full time minister but was served by "circuit riders". "A room next to the pastor's house served as a school." Written records were begun in1821. (Note; Ellison St. was named after William Ellison, the town doctor. He was born in Ireland, died in 1828, and is not connected to our family.

1827: Sunday School, where basic academic subjects were probably taught all day, started with 150 "scholars." Sarah or Sally (two entries made on different days), Eliza and Catherine-Ellison children, are enrolled. This original document is fragile and difficult to read without magnification. It is for the years 1825-1828 and is entitled, Class Record 1825, State of Wisham(?). This is very significant data, which proves that our Sarah or Sally (Mayers) was in Paterson at age three or four. Eliza was probably Sarah's sister born 1811, died 1873, married Alexander Anderson. Catherine was Sarah's cousin born 1814, died 1856 married Ephriam Ward. She was the daughter of Anthony Allison. Another child _____ Ellison is also listed. The initial appears to be an "I". This may be Sarah's cousin Issac, born 1821 died 1856 married Mary Jane Clark.

1831: Eliza Ellison was in Day's Class March 31, 1831. Dropped December. 5, 1831. She married Alexander Anderson March 3, 1831 at the Waldwick, New Jersey Methodist Church, where she probably joined in that year.

1833: William "Alliissn" Ridgeway's Class. This could be the Father, or brother, of Sarah.

1836-1837: New church built at N. W. corner of Cross and Elm Streets. This larger building needed for growing population in neighborhood of Mill and Market Streets where textile industry was rapidly growing.

1838: Membership includes 360 children in "main school" and 70 to 80 in "infant School."

1841: Great "revival" and growth of church to almost double its membership under Rev. Daniel P. Kidder, a famous Methodist missionary.

1842: John Ryle married Sarah Moffett. I saw this wedding certificate at the home of his great-grandson John Ryle in 1978. James Mayers and Sarah Allison must have been married around this time or, possibly, in 1841. This date has been estimated, based on the year of birth of their first child Eliza in 1843. An extensive search over the years, in Paterson and other New Jersey towns, still has not produced their marriage document. A certificate may have been issued directly to them and lost or the wedding might have been performed by an itinerant minister who kept his own records and took them away with him. The search for this vital record should continue for it may show the names of witnesses and other key information that could add to verifying the parentage of Sarah.

1844: PROSPECT STREET CHURCH (Second Methodist) started by members of the Cross St. Church (First Methodist). New church met in the original First Church building of 1820. Allison/Mayers members transferred to Prospect Street and all records relating to them appear here, until 1860.

1845: Mary Allison was a member of Class #4 and continues to 1852. In 1854, Mary lived at 74 Oliver St. She died September 21, 1865. She appears to be Mary Jane Clark, the wife of Sarah's cousin Isaac.

1847: James Mayers was baptized May 15, 1847. This child was the second son of Sarah Allison and James Mayers. He was born August 6, 1847, but does not appear in the 1850 Census. Since there are two older children in the family who were not baptized at this time, his baptism was, most likely, done since the ten month old was not expected to survive.

1847: Jane Ellison was in Frederick Gilmore's Class. This tantalizing bit of information is one of the only clues of the possible mother of Sarah. Family oral tradition indicates that a Jane was in the family since Sarah has been referred to by this name. Could Jane have become an active member to prepare for the upcoming baptisms and deaths of her grandchildren? Sometime in 1849, possibly after these events, she became inactive. She too may have died before 1850 since she has not been found in that census.

1849: Eliza, George an Enoch (Isaac) baptized January 1, 1849, by Rev. S. J.? Monroe. While the name Enoch appears in a later typed copy, an examination of the original at Drew, while very difficult to read, looks more like Isaac. This child does not appear in the 1850 Census, so he must have died later that year.

1849: Sarah Mayers was in Class #1. She may have become active in the church after the baptism of her three children earlier that year.

1849: James Mayers bought plot # 69 in the Methodist section of Sandy Hill Cemetery on January 6, 1849. This was apparently for his infant sons James and Enoch (Isaac).

1849: Eliza Anderson is "admitted" (accepted). This is Sarah's sister shown earlier as Eliza Ellison. She attended Sunday school with Sarah, in 1827. She married Alexander Anderson. The couple must have been living in Paterson at the time.

1849: Jane Ellison was "excluded for neglect" (probably for lack of attendance).

1850: Children of John Ellison baptized, February 3, 1850 by Rev. James Ayers. They were Anthony, Emilene, Henrietta and Samuel. John was born 1811/17 in New York. This John is the son of Anthony Ellison, Sarah's uncle.

1851: Sarah Mayers was in Class # 1.

1851: The Second Methodist Church opened a new brick building on Prospect Street. It was the largest Church in Paterson at that time.

1853: William Ellison married Sarah Cornvine, March 4, 1853- Relationship unknown.

1853: Sarah "Maires" of Mill Street was a member.

1860: Sarah and Eliza Mayers are members. This was Sarah with her seventeen-year-old daughter.

1860: Sarah and Eliza Mayers transfer back to the First Methodist on Cross Street.

1860: John Allison "probationer" is dropped. John may be the grandson of Sarah's uncle Anthony.

1867: Sarah "Mayres" is not a member; Eliza Mayers is "removed without certificate".

1869: Sarah E. Ellison, age 20, married Andrew Clark, age 24, boilermaker. This Sarah is the daughter of Isaac, a cousin of Sarah Mayers.

1869: Sarah Allison Mayers died at age forty-six, on July 31, 1869. She was buried at Cedar Lawn Cemetery on August 3, 1869. No church record or obituary for this event has been found.

1871: Eliza Mayers, daughter of James and Sarah, was a member and "lived on Grand Street near railroad."

1875: Sarah Ann Mayers married Alexander Arnot, age 26, marble carver, February 5, 1875. This was the daughter of James and Sarah Mayers, born February 5, 1858.

1876: Sarah Ann Mayers was baptized June 22, 1876. This was the daughter of William, son of Sarah and James Mayers and Nancy Blakely. They were married at the First Presbyterian Church, Paterson, on December 24, 1874.

1887: James Mayers died and was buried at Cedar Lawn, on January 5, 1887. No church record has been found for this event.

1892: "Bertie" (James Bertram Mayers born 1882) and "Allie" (John Allison Mayers born 1884) baptized May 1, 1892: Parents are John and Maggie Mayers, my grandparents.

1893: David and Grace Mayers, baptized June 18, 1893. Parents are John and Maggie Mayers.

1893: Georgiana Mayers, daughter of James and Sarah, age 33, married John R. A. Powers age 64 on August 16 1893. She was youngest daughter of James and Sarah Mayers.

1903: First Methodist Church on Cross Street closed and merged with the Third Methodist Market Street Church, which was started in 1859. The Cross Street Church was eventually demolished and the name of the street changed from Cross to Cianci.

APPENDIX B:
ARCHEOLOGY AT NUMBER FIVE MILL STREET, PATERSON, NEW JERSEY

THE FORMER SITE OF THE MAYERS HOME, 1847-1974

In October 1978, I attended a lecture on the history of the City of Paterson at the restored Rogers Locomotive Works on Spruce Street. Afterward, I drove down Mill Street past the site of the Mayers ancestral home in the heart of the historical Industrial district.

I was surprised to see archeological excavations in progress on lot number five, the site of the Mayers home, and adjoining land where the John Colt house once stood. Several digs were in progress. These covered about a fifty square yard area on the corner of Mill Street and Van Houten Street, formerly Boudinot Street.

The deeper excavations were about twenty feet and lined with stone drywalls. I heard voices and found two people digging and photographing at the bottom of a shaft. Barry Brady and Felicity Sargeant were part of a team of industrial archeologists working for the city under a federal grant. I showed them the original sketch of the Mayers home drawn by James (Bert) B. Mayers in1933. It is one of the few original house plans of that area to survive. They expressed great interest in the sketch and requested a copy for their archives.

They took me on a tour of the excavated area. The project team had unearthed remnants of brownstone foundations and brick walkways. The deep shafts were privy chambers. These were used as a place to discard all types of trash over a hundred-year period and provided a treasure trove of artifacts. The archeology group used the second floor of the old Franklin Mill, on the corner of Mill Street and Mc Bride Avenue as its headquarters. Barry Brady showed me the many artifacts found on the number five Mill Street lot. Broken china, clay pipes and old bottles had been unearthed.

They explained that the home on Mill and Van Houten had originally been built between 1840 and 1870 by affluent mill owners such as the Colts, Ryles, Thompsons and Mayers whose businesses were literally across the street. After that time, the neighborhood provided housing for mill workers. By the early 1900s the block had deteriorated and became an inner city slum. This explains the reluctance of my father to show me where our ancestor lived.

In 1974, the New Jersey Department of Transportation razed most of the early Paterson home to make way for a highway that would cut a swath through the historic district. The Highway was never completed. The Mayers house probably survived until that year.

Unfortunately, I missed seeing it by only a few years. When I returned a few months later all the remains of the early structures and the clues to learning more about the people who lived there in the past, had disappeared. The property had been obliterated by bulldozer to prepare for a macadam parking lot. Only two structures on lower Mill Street survived. The houses of John Ryle and Thompson were moved to another location along Mill Street in 1979.

In addition to the excavation, the archeologists collected all the deeds and other land records pertaining to the properties. This information, on file at the Passaic County Courthouse in Paterson, traced the land back to the "Society for Useful Manufactures" (S.U.M.) original owners of the city. S.U.M. was founded in 1791 by Alexander Hamilton for the purpose of creating America's first industrial center. Before that the land, known as Acquakanock, had been occupied by a few Dutch settlers who had acquired it from the Lenni Lenape Indians in 1679.

This is the deed history for the site at number five Mill Street:

Grantor	Year		Grantee	Price
S.U. M.	1841		James Speer	$500
James Speer	1845		Michael Griffith	$514
Michael Griffith	1847		James and Hannah Gordon	$500

(A dwelling was probably built on the lot between 1847 and 1850 since the value increased. An 1850 Sidney map shows the house was owned by J. Gordon.)

Grantor	Year		Grantee	Price
James Gordon	1850	Coppersmith	John Ryle	$1,050
John Ryle	1855	Silk Manufacturer	James Mayers	$1,250
James and Eliza Mayers	1892	Silk Manufacturer	John R. A. Power	$2,000
John R. A. Power	1901	Liquors	Tisha Gordon	

The deeds show that number five Mill Street was purchased in 1855, by James Mayers for $1,250 from his friend John Ryle. This sum was made up of $750 in cash and $500 mortgage at 5% for 20 years. It is possible that the John Ryle family lived in this house before moving a few doors away to number 12 Mill Street.

In 1855 James and Sarah Mayers probably needed more living space. In addition to two children of their own, Phebe Allison the thirty-year-old widow and sister-in-law of Sarah, and her daughter Sarah, lived with the family. Also, there was Hannah Richardson, the English teenager, who was an au pair or boarder

The deed record shows that the Mayers home was sold by Eliza Mayers four years after the death of her father James, in 1887. She sold the home to her brother-in-law John R. A. Power, the wealthy Liquor merchant who had married her sister Georgia in 1893. Eliza is shown in that year in the Paterson City Directory as opening a millinery shop at 343 Grand Street and living, in 1895, on Ellison Street.

The site of the Mayers home and the area surrounding it was listed as a Nation Historical Place in 1970. Many organizations and government agencies have worked over the years to enhance and protect the district from neglect. Improvements were held up for several years by the city's decision to allow a developer to construct townhouses, which would have consumed historic site incompatible structures and destroy the raceways. Favorable litigation thwarted the attempt.

The Rogers Locomotive Works has been restored and is now the Paterson Museum, which has exhibits from the city's industrial past. Other mill buildings are still being used for manufacturing or office space. Areas along the raceways have scenic walkways. Bridges have been restored and unwanted tree growth removed. The upper raceway is being completely restored.

A seven-acre plot that is across from the Mayers home site is owned by the City of Paterson and is being considered for development. This site, known as the Allied Textile Printing Site (ATP), is on a beautiful stretch of the Passaic River, directly below the Great Falls. It contains thirty historic mill buildings. These abandoned ruins include portions of the Colt Gun Mill and the Waverly, Todd and Passaic Mills.

In 2009, the 35 acre area was finally designated the Great Falls National Historic Park. With an infusion of federal funds and National Park Service attention, Alexander Hamilton's dream industrial city may once again welcome tourists who will come to see the stunning waterways with its natural beauty of high cliffs, the falls, the river and the historic mill buildings. This National Historic Park status is coupled with a long-term plan for restoration of the surrounding neighborhoods that could lead to the rebirth of Paterson.

The Great Falls S.U.M. Historic District

PATERSON, NEW JERSEY

1. Haines Overlook Park (Visitor Parking) View of Great Falls
2. S.U.M. Administration Building—1934 (Special Events Office)
3. S.U.M. Hydro-Electric Generating Plant—1914
4. S.U.M. Field House—1914 (Tour Office)
5. Bridge across Great Falls to Great Falls Park
6. Passaic Valley Water Commission Pumping and Testing Station—1880
7. S.U.M. Conduit House—1906 (Great Falls Development Corp. Office)
8. Remnant of S.U.M. Steam and Boiler Plant—1876
9. S.U.M. Raceway Gatehouse—1846
10. Upper Raceway—1827-1846 and Upper Raceway Park
11. Old Stony Road—early Indian foot trail
12. Ivanhoe Papermill Wheelhouse—1865 and Ivanhoe Spillway
13. Rogers Locomotive Administration Building—1881
14. Rogers Locomotive Frame Fitting Shop—1881
15. Rogers Locomotive Millwright Shop—1879

16. Barbour Linen and Flax Mill—c. 1879
17. Dolphin Jute Mill Complex—1844-1880
18. Granite Mill (part of Barbour Complex)—1881
19. Rogers Locomotive Workshop Building—1896
20. Rogers Locomotive Erecting Shop—1871
21. Union Works/Rosen Mill—1891
22. Middle Raceway—1792-1802
23. Hamilton Mill—1877-1898
24. Harnil Mill—1857
25. Cooke Locomotive Administration Building—1881
26. Old School #2—1873
27. John Ryle House—1832
28. Daniel Thompson House—1837
29. Franklin Mill—1870-1920
30. Essex Mill—1807-1872 *See Old Yellow Mill foundation in rear
31. Colt Gun Mill—1836
32. Mallory Mill—1870-1890
33. Waverly Mill—1855
34. Lower Raceway—1807
35. Todd Mill —1870
36. Nightingale Mill—c. 1915
37. Phoenix Mill Complex—1815-1870

38. Harmony Mill—1876
39. Industry Mill—1876
40. Edison Illuminating Co.—1896
41. "Nag's Head" Bar—c. 1890 (now Question Mark Bar) Former I.W.W. Headquarters
42. Old Hotel—c. 1845
43. Addy Mill—1852
44. Three Addy Workers Houses—c. 1852
45. Valley of the Rocks
46. Hinchliffe Stadium—c. 1927
47. Launch Site of Holland Submarine—1878
48. Dublin Spring and "Spring's No More" Monument—1931
49. Cooke Locomotive Foundry—c. 1875
50. Elm Street Nineteenth Century Workmen's Homes and Old German Church—1841
51. St. Michael's Church—1929
52. St. Michael's Sisters' Home—c. 1872
53. First Presbyterian Church—1852
54. St. John's Cathedral—1865-1870
55. Passaic Country Courthouse—1903
56. Old Post Office—1899
57. City Hall—1896

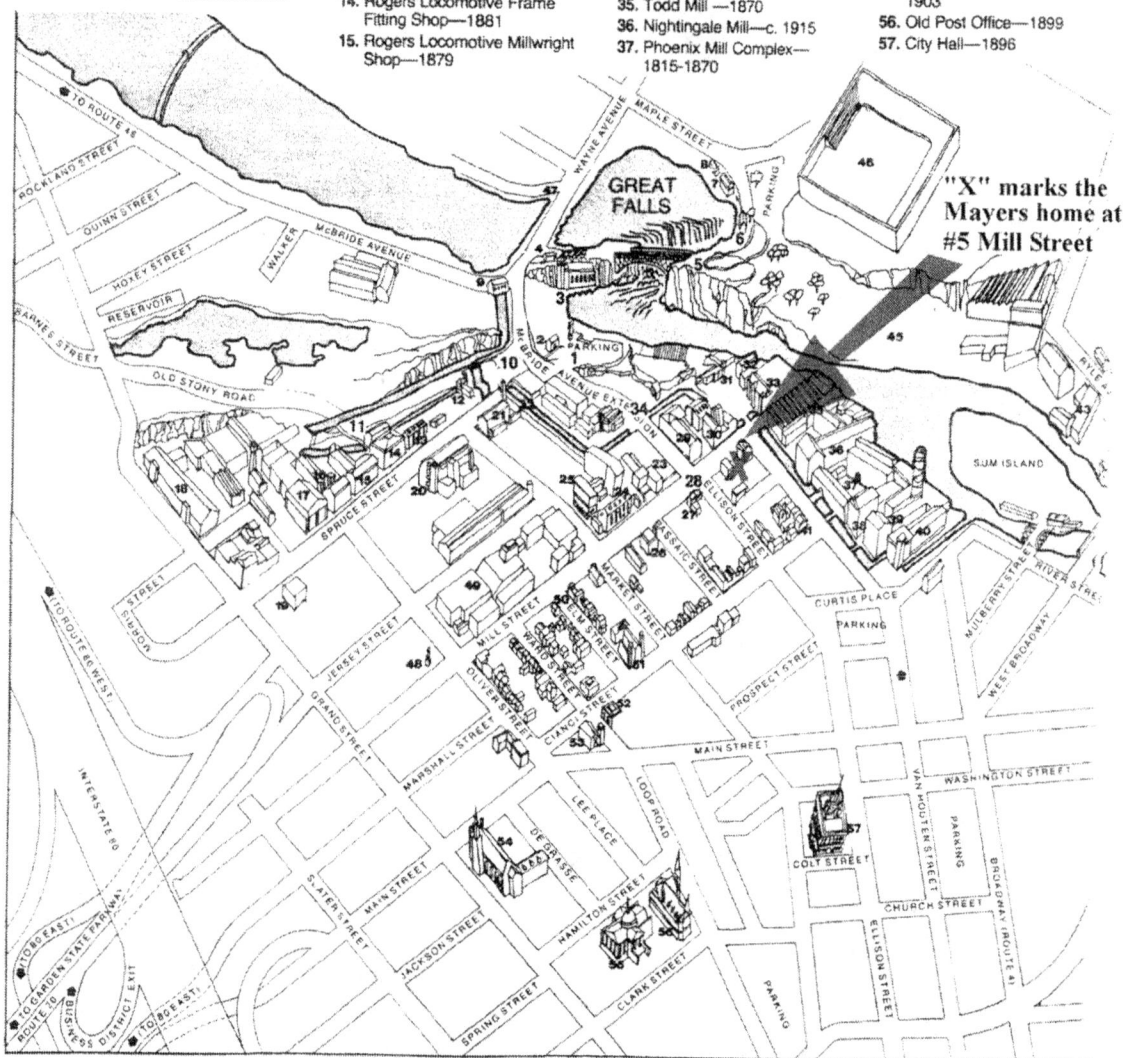

"X" marks the Mayers home at #5 Mill Street

To look at a town without reviewing its past is like reading a sentence out of its context; arid without the following historical notes this book would be like an incomplete jigsaw puzzle.

MACCLESFIELD is of ancient origin. It is mentioned in Domesday Book as having formed part of the demesne of the Saxon Edwin, Earl of Chester, before the Norman Conquest. The invaders laid the district waste and at the time of the Domesday survey, in 1086, the mill of the Earl's manor at Macclesfield was reported to be still standing, but the whole manor was much reduced in value. The four serfs mentioned in the survey, with their families, made a population of about 20 persons. There is reference to pasture for kine and forest land and seven "heys" or enclosures.

The early history of the town is inseparable from that of Macclesfield Forest and Hundred. The Norman Earls of Chester, who were almost royal in their state and power, created here a forest of considerable extent, covering the hills on the eastern border of their territory. In 1237, the Hundred, forest and Manor of Macclesfield were appropriated by the Crown and the forest became a hunting ground of the reigning sovereigns of England and for the Prince of Wales, as Earls of Chester. Edward III was the last king who hunted here.

The chief officer who had the custody of the Forest of Macclesfield was the Master Forester. This office was conferred in 1166 upon Richard de Davenport and remained in the Davenport family for four generations, until 1237. In 1462, King Edward IV granted to Thomas, Lord Stanley, "The office of Master Forester of the Forest of Macclesfield ... together with the office of Steward of the Hundred of Macclesfield to hold to him and to his heirs male ... in as full a manner as his father had it." The Earls of Derby retained the office until the termination of the Hundred.

As time went on, however, forest lands were granted away in parcels and more and more of the district was enclosed and cultivated.

The township of Macclesfield was founded, traditionally in 1220, by Earl Randle, with 120 burgages. Presumably this was Randle III, Earl of Chester, who died in 1233.

In 1261, a charter granted by Prince Edward, the eldest son of Henry III, constituted Macclesfield a free borough with a merchant guild and accorded certain accustomed privileges to the burgesses, at the same time imposing the usual obligation of grinding at the king's mill and baking at his oven. These privileges were confirmed by later charters, the last being that of Charles II in 1684.

In the year 1270 the Manor of Macclesfield was settled upon Princess Eleanor, wife of Prince Edward later King Edward I. In 1278 King Edward and his Queen founded the Parochial Chapel of Macclesfield, which was dedicated to All Saints and All Hallows and, later, at some unknown date in the 18th century, re-dedicated to St. Michael and All Angels. Macclesfield Wakes, one of the oldest fairs in the town, was originally held on November 1st, the feast of All Hallows.

Very little remains today of the original structure of Queen Eleanor's Chapel, but the present church has many interesting features that repay a visit, in particular the Legh and Savage Chapels with their fine altar-tombs and memorials. There was at one time a chantry and Free School attached to the Church, founded and endowed by Sir John Percival, Knight, Lord Mayor of London, who was a Macclesfield man. This was the original foundation of the Macclesfield Grammar School, re-founded by Edward VI as the Free Grammar School of King Edward the Sixth, now the King's School.

The thoroughfare of Mill Street has been used since Saxon times. The part nearest to the Market Place being known as the Wallgate until the end of the 15th century.

OLD MACCLESFIELD

The Market Place must have been the social and business centre of the town even in the far-off days when the first charter was granted to the burgesses. The Market Cross (now preserved in the West Park—to be re-erected in the Market Place) once stood in the centre of the square, and from here the proclamations and public notices were read out to the townsfolk. It was here that the yeomen and archers of the borough must have assembled before marching to the Battle of Bosworth Field, and again to Floddcn Field in 1513. The early Macclesfield bowmen were famous for their skill and accuracy, and their practising ground was a spacious field in the neighborhood of Bowfield Lane (now Victoria Road). This common was enclosed in 1804. The Enclosure Awards are preserved at the Town Hall. To the west of the town, in 1775, Christ Church was built, by Charles Roe, in open fields. By 1825, however, Macclesfield's eight streets had grown to 150, and in 1851 the population numbered 27,472 persons, with an additional 10,000 in the adjoining districts of Sutton and Hurdsfield.

Industrial Macclesfield was awake to the politics or the day. Park Green was the scene of many Chartist meetings during the great rising, and in 1838 the leader of the movement, Feargus O'Connor, addressed a meeting there. It seems that the women of the town were as politically minded as their men folk, for the following resolution was passed: "Resolved that the women of Macclesfield form a procession on Monday, and subscribe for a flag to be presented to Feargus O'Connor, Esq."

In the 19th century new means of transport brought Macclesfield into closer contact with the outside world. The Macclesfield Canal was opened for traffic in 1831. This waterway connects the Trent and Mersey Canal with the Peak Forest Canal near Marple. At the opening ceremony a procession of boats, occupied by the Committee and Directors, and carrying the chief products of the locality—coal, slate, limestone, etc.—passed along the canal. Whilst mentioning canals, it is interesting to note that James Brindley, the famous engineer, once lived in the district of Higher Sutton, and served a seven years' apprenticeship with a millwright.

The first railway station was built near Beech Lane Bridge on the Manchester Road. This was opened in 1845 to connect Macclesfield by railway to Stockport. Thousands assembled to see the first train leave Macclesfield for Manchester, carrying the Mayor and Corporation of the Borough, and the directors of the line. This train conveyed 180 people to Manchester in one hour and brought them safely back in the same time. Once again a procession was formed, headed by a band, and the Mayor proceeded with his party to the Town Hall for "a sumptuous banquet."

After the construction of the Beech Lane tunnel in 1849, a new railway station was built in Hibel Road, formerly Cockshute Lane, and the original station in Beech Lane was demolished. Hibel Road Station became the main station in Macclesfield for the London, Midland and Scottish Railway. The North Staffordshire Railway was completed in the same year to provide the most direct route between Manchester and the Midland Counties via Macclesfield and the Churnet Valley line, but the former Central Station on Waters Green was not built until 1872. This station has now been reconstructed and with the closing of Hibel Road Station is the main station for the town with the electrified line.

Macclcsfield's rapid growth in the 19th century gave rise to grave problems, which required new methods of municipal control. The old charters of the town made no provision for dealing with such questions as sewage disposal, maintenance of roads, lighting, water supply, health, education, parks, libraries and all the other corporate business of a modern town. Municipal government in Macclesfield was reorganized under the Municipal Corporations Act of 1835. With the powers obtained under this and later acts, reforms were instituted and development controlled, so that we have today a town which is up-to-date in its public amenities, busy with industry, and yet which still retains the pleasant aspect of an English market town, closely in touch with the agricultural interests of a prosperous countryside.

On the site now covered by the present Town Hall once stood the ancient Guildhall, the southern side of which faced the Church of St. Michael. Near to the Guildhall was the Royal Bakehouse, or the King's Oven, mentioned in the charter of Prince Edward, where the people were compelled to bake their bread.

Behind the church were the Gutters—apparently a fitting name for what were in medieval days the slums of the town. During the plague in 1603, this district had a high mortality rate, in spite of the most stringent measures by the local authorities to check the spread of the disease. An old manuscript preserved at Capesthorne says: "Watch and ward was kept at every passage from the town, and at the Cross Lanes adjoining the town, to keep in the townspeople. A market in an open space, three-quarters of a mile from the town was held every Monday, when the Justices were present to see that the town and country kept asunder."

The tallow-chandlers had their places of business in the Gutters, which also housed the Shambles, a large covered space devoted to the stalls of the town's butchers who were for a long time forbidden to sell meat in the streets.

Also in the Gutters was the old Grammar School building. The original school is known to have been situated near the top of the "108 steps," the district having been known for many years as "School Brow."

At some period the low-lying Waters Green was connected with the upper part of the town by a series of steps and terraces thus giving Step Hill, the 108 Steps, Bunkers Hill and Brunswick Hill. The latter, together with Brunswick Street, were formerly known as Goose Lane Hill and Goose Lane, and it was down this steep and narrow incline that the ducks and geese were once driven to water in the river which flows along the bottom. Waters Green, which lies below the hill, was named from its continual flooding by the imperfectly banked River Bollin, and has been closely associated with the Wakes Fair and May Fair.

In the 17th century Macclesfield was still a small country town, though not untouched by the civil and religious troubles of the times... During the Civil War, in 1643, the town was besieged by the Parliamentary forces. St. Michael's Church is said to have been considerably damaged during the siege.

The Unitarian Chapel, in King Edward Street, is an interesting reminder of the religious struggles of the 17th century. It is the oldest Dissenting Chapel in the town, being built in 1690, immediately after the passing of the Toleration Act of 1688-9, which granted freedom of worship to Nonconformists. In its austere simplicity this little chapel is a testimony to men and women of this town who were zealous for freedom of thought and speech in former times.

Another old place of worship is the Quakers' Chapel in Mill Street, which shows a stone bearing the date 1705. This was probably the date when the building was erected. The chapel is now used by the Society of Friends and the Town Mission.

In King Edward Street and in Jordangate stand several attractive houses dating from the 18th century. One of the most interesting of these, in Jordangate, is known today as Cumberland House. In 1745, when it was occupied by John Stafford, later Town Clerk of the Borough, the Duke of Cumberland, passing through the town in pursuit of the Pretender's Army, was the guest of Mr. Stafford. The house took its name from this incident.

Ten days earlier the rebels had reached Macclesfield on their way to Derby, and remained for two days in the town. The house at which the Prince took up his quarters was the home of Sir Peter Davenport in King Edward Street. It was afterwards purchased for the Free Grammar School, but is now demolished. Mr. Stafford, in a letter describing the event, wrote:

"An order was given that the Mayor and Aldermen must formally proclaim the Pretender. I escaped being present at so shocking a spectacle, but poor Mr. Mayor and the Aldermen were obliged to be at it. Endeavours were made to give them a peal of bells for fear of insults, but four ringers were all that could be found, and they rang the bells backward, not with design but through confusion."

By 1745, however, the signs of a new age were apparent in Macclesfield. Silk throwsters were already working in the town, and silk button making had been an established local industry for some years. In 1740, Charles Roe set up his business as Silk Button and Twist Manufacturer on Parsonage Green, on the site lately occupied by the Depot Mills. Sixteen years later, in 1756, he introduced machinery into his mill, and so brought the Industrial Revolution to Macclesfield. In the course of the next hundred years, Macclesfield became the acknowledged centre of the silk industry in this country.

The town developed rapidly. When John Wesley preached for the first time in Macclesfield, on Waters Green in 1747, the little town contained only eight streets, and a population of not more than 7,000 persons. Mill Street ran down from the Market Place to a green, as the name Park Green still suggests, and from Park Green to Waters Green were open fields through which the Bollin flowed to meet the Dams Brook in the "Waters." To the east of the Bollin, where the houses of Buxton Road, Black Road and Windmill Street now stand, was a wide expanse of pasture forming part of Macclesfield Common.

INDEX

www.ingramcontent.com/pod-product-compliance
Lightning Source LLC
Chambersburg PA
CBHW080613270326

41928CB00016B/3046